D1222604

Sports of The Times

The Arthur Daley Years

Sports of The Times

The Arthur Daley Years

edited by
James Tuite
with an
Afterword by
Robert Daley

Quadrangle
The New York Times
Book Co.

Picture Credits

Pages 8, 21, 58, 92, 99, 109, 151, 158, 198, 220, 230, 246, 259, 284, 297—*The New York Times.*
Pages 28, 82, 121, 138—Courtesy of the Estate of Arthur Daley.
Page 316—The New York Times/Michael Evans

 For information, address: Quadrangle/The New York Times Book Co., 10 East 53rd Street, New York, New York 10022. Manufactured in the United States of America. Published simultaneously in Canada by Fitzhenry & Whiteside, Ltd., Toronto.

Library of Congress Cataloging in Publication Data

Daley, Arthur.
Sports of the Times.

Originally appeared in the author's column, under the same title, in the New York Times, 1939–1974.
1. Sports—United States—History—Miscellanea.
I. Title.
GV583.D32 1975 796'.0973 74-77949
ISBN 0-8129-0464-8

Contents

Introduction

The Saturday that was January 5 dawned brisk and clear and by midmorning thin puffs of vapor trailed bescarved pedestrians as they shuffled past Saint Patrick's Cathedral on Fifth Avenue in New York. Outside the church, some of the most important people from the world of sports huddled against the chill breeze. Almost lost in the folds of the majestic cathedral, a man stood quietly alone and Steve Cady, a *New York Times* reporter, asked him why he was there.

"I've been reading Arthur Daley since I was thirteen years old, and he's done a lot for me," he said, "so I drove down from New Brunswick, New Jersey to thank him."

Two days earlier, Arthur had collapsed on the street while walking from Grand Central Station to his office. It happened in front of the building that had housed the offices of his favorite football team, the Giants, and the club president, Jack Mara, his closest friend ("On Losing a Friend," page 245). An act of fate, the cliché-makers said. He died minutes later at the hospital and they said, "On his way to write his column—that's the way Arthur would have wanted it." Another cliché.

But life itself is a cliché, and the fact is that with Arthur's sense of the dramatic he would have picked the time and the place just as it happened. He was, as one biographer pointed out, a self-admitted bigamist, the other love in his life having been the former Betty Blake, whom he married in 1928.

When he died, Arthur was only a few months from retirement and the prospect appalled him. After forty-seven years with *The Times*, 20 million words, 11,000 columns, and a Pulitzer Prize, he could barely conceive of a life that did not include a deadline for 800 of his hand-picked words. Long before *The Exorcist* hit the best-seller lists, Arthur was writing about his column as "a monster, an ogre who enslaves the unfortunate creature whose soul it owns," but it was a monster that he loved and cherished.

He roamed the ball fields and racetracks and golf courses across the country and across the world, clipboard in hand, jotting down the important and the trivial. Arthur wrote a book on the history of the Olympic Games and savored pro football, but he left no doubt about his first-choice sport: baseball. He would lean his long, rangy frame back against the swivel chair, clasp hands behind lightly graying hair, and explain that baseball had universal appeal, that it provided the funniest, the most interesting, and the most dramatic people and incidents.

Arthur's love for baseball is reflected in the wealth of columns about the so-called national pastime within these covers. His angular, florid Irish face would be wreathed in smiles as he pounded out some anecdote about his favorite characters—Casey Stengel, Frankie Frisch, or Dizzy Dean. He only tolerated horse racing and never bet, yet his columns out of Louisville on the Kentucky Derby were always sparkling reading.

In my view, Arthur was always at his best and won oak-leaf clusters as a newspaperman in covering heavyweight championship fights. What is important to remember about a boxing match is that there is really no definitive time element: no innings, no quarters, no periods, no chukkers that must be completed. It can end in eleven seconds or it can last an hour or anything in between, so the writer has no idea of what he will have to work with. In the noise and chaos of a typical ringside, Arthur could turn out 800 penny-bright words that captured the color and excitement of the moment with only minutes to deadline. "Arthur," I would chide him, "you write your best when you don't have time to think." He would laugh. He liked that, and he knew it was true.

Arthur was only twenty-three when, fresh out of Fordham, he got the important round-by-round assignment in 1927 at the Jack Dempsey-Gene Tunney fight, noted for the famous "long count" by the referee while Tunney was on the floor. When he covered the 1936 Olympics in Berlin, he was the first *Times* reporter to go abroad on a sports assignment. He followed the Olympics to Rome, Tokyo, Mexico City, and Munich, adding a chapter on each Olympiad to the book that he originally wrote with his predecessor at *The Times,* John Kieran.

There were those who did not admire Arthur as a columnist. Too much baseball, they would say. Or that he was always writing in the past. Or that he wrote only about the good things that people would say and do, and ignore the bad. Most of his critics within the profession were the so-called chipmunks, the new breed of sportswriters who would gather in the press box and chatter away before embarking on their put-down school of journalism designed to awe readers by "telling it like it is."

Arthur shrugged off their barbs and continued to pound away at his typewriter for his millions of readers from New York to Hong Kong and at all the way stations in between served by The New York Times News Service. He had his Pulitzer Prize, won in 1956 for columns written in 1955, and there wasn't a chipmunk, or any other living sportswriter for that matter, with that distinction.

Arthur was the soul of insecurity. He was insecure about the columns for tomorrow, about his expense account, about his travel arrangements, about driving to Florida. But there was a certain charm about his insecurity, especially when he reduced his column production to four days a week and then three days a week to make room for the upstart Bob Lipsyte and the venerable Walter Wellesley Smith. He countered their incursion by dropping more "I's" into his column ("When *I* saw Christy Matthewson pitch") because he knew they couldn't match him on his ground.

Like a cook who is too close to the Baked Alaska to appreciate it, I shared some of the reservations that colleagues had about Arthur's approach. Refusing to write about those he didn't like, for example. He held that the constant knockers eventually destroyed their contacts and sources of information and wound up in ivory towers. He said he could see no point in publicizing a "louse, not when there were plenty of nice, amusing guys around." The point can be argued but it is certainly true that the most dramatic censure of a man is simply to ignore the fact that he exists.

Bill (Don't Call Me Willie) Hartack, the sullen jockey, was among the few people Arthur didn't like and after Hartack won the Kentucky Derby in 1969 ("The Prince and the Peasant," page 280) Arthur was forced to break his rule about being a "hatchet man." Arthur traditionally wrote about the winning jockey after each Derby and on this occasion he delivered a verbal spanking to a deserving victim. Perhaps with this in mind, Bob Maisel of the *Baltimore Sun* wrote in tribute: "I remember being irritated more than once when some young punk who didn't want to talk to the press at that particular moment would be disrespectful to Arthur Daley, or make him cool his heels needlessly. It didn't bother Arthur, though. He took it all in stride, just as he did everything else."

Arthur was described in obituary reports as a "meat and potatoes" man but the description was apt even beyond his eating habits, although it is true that he didn't drink, gave up smoking, and liked the early-to-bed routine. Both the form and substance of his writing were steak compared to the soufflé that others on the beat were whipping up.

In embarking on the job of selecting the best of Arthur's columns, I decided first to weed out the bad from the good and then select the best from the rest. On the first go-around, I found myself stacking all of the columns in the "good" pile. I realized then that Arthur really had not written any bad columns—it's just that some were better than others. He made a believer out of me.

J. T.
March 1974

Sports of The Times

The Arthur Daley Years

Columnists don't just happen. They get to be columnists while, as reporters, they fill in for the regular columnists on vacation. This is an example of the work Arthur did as a stand-in for John Kieran.

1939

After the Battle

December 12

Milwaukee, December 11—The game was over. The once proud New York Giants, heads bowed and spirits crushed by the 27-0 rout at the hands of the Green Bay Packers, walked slowly off the field. All around them delirious fans danced in glee.

The Giants climbed into the bus that was to take them back to their hotel. They sat there in uncomfortable silence, the aching pain inside dwarfing into insignificance the bruises of the outside. Orville Tuttle and Dale Burnett had their faces buried in their arms, two big men unashamedly shedding tears. Jim Lee Howell tried to cheer up his mates. "Fellows," he said, "we're lucky to escape alive."

That sentence came none too soon. There was a splintering crash and a bottle burst through a window of the bus. As if the Packers hadn't done enough damage, it seemed that some crazed fan had decided to complete the job. Fortunately no one was hit or cut, which was about the only bit of luck the Giants had all day.

Not that luck would have helped very much against those rip-roaring Packers. In fact, the more one analyzes the entire matter the more it seems that the New York fortunes changed from good to bad a week ago. When Referee Bill Halloran decided that Bo Russell's placement had gone wide in the final forty-five seconds of the Redskin fray, Washington became the lucky team and the Giants the unlucky one.

No football team in the world could have checked those Packers the way they were rolling yesterday. Even with tank traps, barbed-wire entanglements and antiaircraft guns the Giants could not have brought them down or headed them off.

Green Bay clicked with the irresistible force of the Redskins against the Giants when Cliff Battles ran wild in 1937 and of the same New Yorkers against the same Washingtonians a year later.

The secretiveness of Curly Lambeau in his preparing for the fray could be understood. Curly really had something to show when he turned his Monsters loose. Perhaps behind the locked gates of his practice field he has a fountain of youth at which his veterans drank deeply.

Whatever it was, they found a new spark and a new life. Most of his ancients uncorked the best exhibition of long careers. The Packer line was magnificent, and it was in the line that the battle was won.

Once in a blue moon a forward wall gets a sixth sense such as Green Bay had yesterday. It seemed to know instinctively just when the Giants would snap the ball from center and the charge would come a split second in advance, so artfully timed that off-side penalties were avoided.

The New Yorkers were beaten to the punch on every occasion and their attack made impotent because blockers could not get the proper angle for a block on the wild men from Green Bay. The Packers played with a grim earnestness, silent and forceful. They had too much work to do to waste time in idle conversation.

In this respect this was much different from other games. Usually a few bon mots come forth from every engagement. A week ago, for instance, the huge Turk Edwards was inserted in the Redskin lineup to halt a Giant downfield sortie. The Turk came in, bubbling over with vim, vigor and vitality. As he took his position at tackle he bellowed to Tuffy Leemans, "Run the next play my way."

Tuffy grinned at him. "Anything to oblige," he said with a polite bow. And then galloped right over the Turk for a 20-yard gain.

The Packers were such a great football team yesterday that none of the writers ever will forget them. But what they will remember most about this fray was the press box. That will supply conversational fodder for many a long year.

It really was a lovely press box, too. It was roomy and glass-enclosed. The loudspeaker system was excellent and the announcer a crack workman. But—and this is the largest "but" of them all—it was a mite too high.

They perched it atop the covered stand at the very edge of the roof. Looking down was like peering off a precipice. Ordinarily there would be no objection to that, but at every gust of wind the entire roof trembled.

Whenever one of the heavyweights among the fourth estate shifted his chair there would be an ominous shudder of the entire structure. It was impossible to concentrate on the game. Most of the boys were wondering instead if they had forgotten to pay the last installment on their insurance policies.

As for this correspondent, he has not had such a feeling of relief at planting his feet on solid earth since he stepped off a plane after his first air journey. If the Giants felt lucky to escape alive, the writers felt the same way—doubled and redoubled in spades.

It was Christmas Eve and Ray Kelly, then sports editor of *The Times,* jarred Arthur with the words, "Until further notice, you will do the 'Sports of The Times' column." This was his first official effort.

1942

Helping the Unsung Heroes

December 27

The United Seamen's Service calls them "Our Fighters in Dungarees." They are the men of the American Merchant Marine, those unsung heroes of the war who brave the icy blasts of the Arctic, the sweltering heat of the tropics, blazing infernos of flaming oil, thirst, hunger, bombs, shells, and death.

They are the fearless lads who man our ships, taking precious supplies overseas so that our boys at the front will have the matériel they need. No one inducts them into service. Every man is a volunteer, some of them returning time and time again to another ship after each torpedoing.

The various war charities have been treated generously by sports since Pearl Harbor. Today the United Seamen's Service comes into its own as this worthy cause picks up the entire receipts at the Pro Bowl football game in Philadelphia's Shibe Park.

The cause alone should attract a banner crowd and undoubtedly Joseph B. Eastman would be willing to look the other way if New Yorkers jammed the transportation facilities to Philadelphia. But a "cause" never sold anything in sports. This game, fortunately, can stand solidly on its own feet and its own merits.

For the benefit of a few citizens in the back of the room who have not been paying strict attention to what has been going on, it might be well to mention that the game brings together the champions of the National Football League, the Washington Redskins, and a league All-Star combination including such handy operatives as Sid Luckman, Cecil Isbell, Bill Dudley, Merlyn Condit, and so forth.

The series between the champions and All-Stars has been close and exciting from its very inception. The affair last season was a ringtailed wow as the Chicago Bears, riding the crest of their wave of invincibility, turned back Sammy Baugh & Co. by the tidy little score of 35 to 24.

The Stars have never beaten the champions because it is not easy to whip a hodge-podge assortment of individual performers into a cohesive unit within two weeks. It might be different this time, however. There will be enough vengeful Bears on the premises anxious to make the Redskins bite the dust. The Monsters from the Midway were and are a proud lot. They gloried in their twenty-four-game winning streak and they have not forgotten the rude ending it had when George Preston Marshall's hired hands upset them for the championship a fortnight ago.

Best balanced of the All-Star contingents to date was the last one with Stout Steve Owen of the Giants riding herd. The first one Owen ever handled was in 1938 when he had to operate without any punters. Once, in sheer desperation, he ordered Turk Edwards, the mastodontic Redskin tackle and now assistant Washington coach, to drop behind the line of scrimmage for a kick.

The ball snapped back to the Turk and he studied it carefully. He read the label, counted the stitches, and finally decided that it was a genuine "prolate spheroid" just as the rules prescribed. Not until then did he boot the ball. It was a good kick, too, a neat fifty-yarder.

Completely mystified as to why the Green Bay Packers on the other side of the scrimmage line had not rushed his dawdling punter and blocked the kick a dozen times over, Stout Steve approached Don Hutson afterward and asked him.

"Gosh, Steve," confessed the Alabama Antelope. "When Turk went back there we never thought he'd kick. We figured it had to be some super-duper trick play and we all dropped back to watch it."

Prize kick of the series, however, was in this same fray. The All-Stars were stymied on the Packer 35 and Ward Cuff of the Giants went in to try a 43-yard field goal. Parker Hall of the Cleveland Rams was the holder—after a fashion—and what did he do but place the ball on the ground sideways.

The horrified Cuff merely closed his eyes, swung his right leg firmly and saw the ball slither out of bounds on the 1-foot line. His team-mates shook his hands and pounded him on the back in congratulation. They thought it a masterpiece of placement kicking. To them such accuracy could not have been an accident.

And now another Pro Bowl game approaches. As a spectacle it should be attractive to an extreme. As a cause it can hold its own with all war charities, helping our unsung heroes, "Our Fighters in Dungarees."

1943

From a Sportswriter's Memory Book

March 7

There was a map on the front page of this newspaper a few days ago. It was a map of Berlin with a circle indicating the section of the city which had been pulverized most by an RAF raid. Memories flowed swiftly at the sight of it because this reporter had lived within that circle during the 1936 Olympic Games.

A block from his hotel was the bombed Friedrichstrasse Station. A block or so from *The Times* bureau were the bombed government buildings on the Wilhelmstrasse. Between hotel and bureau was the badly bombed Unter den Linden, which was crossed every day.

The Linden was a gay street during the Olympics. Flags of two-score nations hung lazily and brightly along its broad expanse with the black-hooked cross of the Nazi banner always providing a mental jolt that not even constant seeing could soften.

Those were the days when foreigners could do no wrong. The orders had been given that the non-Germans were to be treated with complete consideration. It reached so laughable an extreme that American sportswriters used to play a daily game at

At the Berlin Olympics the host country suffered a galling defeat in the broadjump as Jesse Owens won over German Lutz Long.

the Reichssportfeld. We had badges, a red wallet and, inside the wallet, our press credentials. A scoring system was worked out whereby par for the course was to enter the stadium without showing anything.

Displaying the badge counted minus one, badge and wallet was minus two, and presenting all three of them was a token of complete failure. It was easy to go for a touchdown. Fast talk in English and never stopping at the command to halt put one inside before the bewildered guardians at the gate knew what had happened. They did not dare block off the way or put a hand on a foreigner. Party orders. At any rate, the game provided a harmless pastime for the Gentlemen of the Press.

They used the same system of gate crashing out at Grunau, where the rowing races were held. The most vivid recollection there was not the University of Washington crew sweeping majestically to a hard-won quarter-of-a-length victory over Italy in the eight-oared final. Two other items stand out with greater clarity.

One was the Japanese crew, which employed the most fantastic stroke any mortal ever devised. A normal crew will use a beat in the low 30s in the middle stages of a race and hit a clean 40 in the final sprint. The midget Nipponese stroked above 50 all the way and looked more like ducks flapping their wings on a pond than an eight-oared crew. Naturally they got nowhere with great rapidity.

The other lasting impression from Grunau came from what could have developed into an international incident. The Americans arrived one day and found that the Germans had appropriated the United States racks in the boathouse. The irate Huskies from the Northwest promptly tossed the German shells outside on the beach. Not a word ever was said about it. Taking the hint, the Reich sweepswingers quietly put their boats elsewhere.

Perhaps Grunau has not been bombed because it would be worthless as an objective. But the Olympische Dorf, the Olympic Village, has been demolished. That was a real good target. It was not intense consideration or loving care of its guests which impelled the Germans to construct solid two-story dwellings in a lovely suburb of Berlin.

Not a bit of it. They never were or could be that altruistic. As soon as the athletes departed, all of the magnificient facilities there were immediately turned over to the German Army to serve as quarters for an officers' training school. Thanks to the RAF, however, the spot has become a smear.

It is odd how fragmentary recollections can be pieced together to form a picture of the whole. At dawn every Sunday morning hundreds of the Hitler Young would pour out of the Friedrichstrasse Station and march off in the rhythmic step which would serve them well when they graduated into the German Army. This hike automatically eliminated any chance of churchgoing and placed the boys under iron-fisted discipline for their most formative years.

Constantly one saw gray-green troops moving about in lorries. They seemed everywhere. There were long lines of soldiers and the black-uniformed SS men forming lanes for mile after mile as Hitler whisked past in his car. Every other soldier or Storm Trooper faced the crowds and the others faced in the opposite direction. With locked arms they held back the populace and, like Janus, could watch two ways at once.

There are memories of Hitler, grim and unsmiling, bobbing and weaving as he watched the runners fleeing along the track. There was one vivid recollection of the saturnine and satanic Josef Paul Goebbels stirring his listeners as his voice rose in crescendo pitch while repeating one word with vibrant and eloquent connotations. That word was "Deutschland"—Germany. There was Hermann Goering, a Nazi with a sense of humor (believe it or not), shaking like a bowl of jelly as 100,000 spectators sang a parody of a popular German song to "Our Hermann."

A fleeting glimpse of oft-bombed Wilhelmshaven lingers among this writer's memories and a half-day stay in shattered Hamburg cannot be forgotten. Neither can the sign on the pier as we docked. It read: "Welcome to Germany." They probably have taken in their welcome mats by now.

Danger, Men at Work!

May 4

They were boisterous, rambunctious and colorful on the field and they were identically the same off it, too. This operative had heard some fantastic stories of the Gas House Gang of Saint Louis on his recent Western trip and sought confirmation the other day from Branch Rickey.

The Deacon of the Dodgers shuddered at the memory of one particular episode and remarked that Frank Frisch, whose job it was to ride herd on this collection of wild men, regularly threw up his hands in despair and said he couldn't do a thing with them. "Deep down in his heart though," added Branch, "Frank enjoyed their antics. That's an impression I always had, anyway."

The most startling performance the Gas House Gang ever unfolded was in a sedate and ultrafashionable Philadelphia hotel where the Cardinals were quartered. The cocktail lounge was jammed by the Main Liners and the elite of the City of Brotherly Love. It was a moment calling for soft lights and sweet music, Philadelphia serenity at its best.

Suddenly some workmen bustled in through the door. They wore overalls and those quaint caps affected by house painters.

None of them looked particularly clean. If any of the startled hotel guests had taken the trouble to look, they might have discovered under the disguises the striking features of Pepper Martin, Dizzy Dean and Rip Collins, the three ringleaders, as well as a couple of supernumaries whose identities have been forgotten.

These workmen arrived on the scene, arguing briskly. They set up a stepladder at one end of the room and began measuring. Dean, a big pad in one hand and a pencil in the other, was the foreman. Martin called out a measurement to Dean only to have Collins loudly disagreeing with him.

Within five minutes these industrious workmen had their end of the room to themselves. Within ten minutes the cocktail lounge was deserted by the remaining customers. In came the protesting manager and recognized the culprits. He ran screaming to Rickey.

Their task in the cocktail lounge completed, Martin, Dean, Collins & Co. departed and bobbed up in the hotel barber shop, which was independently owned. Ignoring barbers and customers alike, they started measuring again.

"Who sent you here?" howled the indignant owner.

"We're getting an estimate for a redecorating job," and Dean laconically and turned his back on him.

"We'll have to move these two barber chairs over to the other side of the room," said Collins sagely.

"You'll do nothing of the kind," spluttered the hapless owner. "I've got a ten-year lease here and the hotel can't touch this shop."

He sent for the manager and the police but the discreet Gas House troupe knew enough to take a hint. Rickey was on their trail, however, fire in his eyes. The talk he gave them must have been one of his most stirring orations. The Deacon blasted them, cajoled them and exacted a promise that henceforth they would be very good little boys. He almost gave them his blessing as the penitent Gas Housers left his room.

But Rickey never realized at the time what temptations and pitfalls lurk along the road of life. As Martin, Dean, Collins &

Co. reached the hotel lobby they discovered to their delight that a huge banquet was in progress in the grand ballroom. It was a youth gathering of some sort, with high government dignitaries on the list of speakers. That was more than the Gas House Gang could resist.

The dais was at the far end of the hall, opposite a stage. Onto the stage stalked this intrepid group of honest workmen. No one paid any attention to them in the beginning but soon every one was turning around to see just who was causing the hubbub behind them. Martin and Collins were shifting scenery and no matter what they did they could not please Foreman Dean.

"That ain't the place to put it," Dizzy shouted. "Put it over there."

A few minutes of this and no one in the hall was paying any attention to the dais. They were watching with fascination the start of a violent argument between Martin and Collins.

"Don't you call me that," roared Collins.

"I will, too," hollered Martin, "and what I said goes double."

Being a man of spirit, Collins could stand no more. He took a swing at Pepper and the hall was in an uproar, every youth on his feet. Martin swung back and it looked like the most violent fist fight ever held. It looked that way, but looks are deceiving. Martin and Collins had worked out a routine of faking a fight, a well-rehearsed routine, which seemed like the genuine article. As a grand finish to the well-staged battle Rip knocked Pepper down just as the harassed and nearly insane manager made one more appearance.

To make a long story short, the villains were unmasked and the dinner resumed in style with Dizzy Dean and Pepper Martin seated on the dais as the guests of honor.

When Dempsey Knocked Out Firpo

September 12

The ancient Romans thought enough of the fleet passage of time to coin a phrase which still lives, "Tempus fugit." And time has been flying with great rapidity ever since. It hardly seems possible that twenty years have passed since Jack Dempsey knocked out Luis Angel Firpo in the greatest fight boxing ever has produced. Yet it is true and the twentieth anniversary of that epic battle will come on Tuesday.

There never was a bout quite like that one for primitive savagery, pulsating excitment, or sheer drama. The script for it is so fantastic that not even an insane scenario writer would have dared envision it. Much too unbelievable even for fiction, it thus became the most vivid page in the history of pugilism.

Within the brief span of three minutes and fifty-seven seconds the fierce-eyed and aptly named Wild Bull of the Pampas had been felled ten times. Within that brief span, too, the then champion of the world had been knocked down twice, the second time going clear out of the ring. As a spectacle this fight was unequaled and 90,000 thrill-sated spectators in the Polo Grounds took with them memories they have or will treasure to their dying day.

The two contestants were a study in contrasts as they sat on their stools before the fight. Firpo was a frowning giant of a man, skin browned and black hair matted. Dempsey, twenty-four pounds lighter, seemed almost a slender boy in comparison, albeit a nervous, high-strung one despite his smiling countenance.

The gong clanged for the first round and a thunderous roar cascaded against Coogan's Bluff, echoing and reechoing in a din which was to grow in intensity as the stark drama of the fight was unfolded. Like an unleashed tiger Dempsey sprang to the attack. His lethal left lashed at the wide-open target of the huge Argentinian. He missed. But Firpo didn't miss with his counter-punch, a looping right-hander from his shoetops. Solidly it crashed against the jaw of the champion and the fight was only five seconds old.

Down went Dempsey for the first time since Fireman Jim Flynn had toppled him six years before. Down he went and up shot the crowd to its collective feet, never to sit down again. The startled Manassa Mauler leaped up before the count was begun, undaunted and unawed.

From a clinch he fired away that terrific left hook. Firpo took it without bending or breaking, whipping in his pile-driver right to Dempsey's jaw in return. Jack was jolted but held his ground. Again the champion's left snaked out to the Wild Bull's jaw. Firpo was rocked to the canvas, but was up in an instant without a count.

The giant unleashed a crushing right only to leave open his own guard. The Dempsey left hit the mark again and Firpo took a count of two. Groggily he reached his feet in time to catch that relentless left once more. One, two, three and he was up, up fighting, too.

The Wild Bull pounded Jack in the ribs with a couple of rights and Dempsey, anxious to get in close, absorbed them as he unleashed a two-fisted attack to the Firpo body. A moment later the Argentinian dropped with an audible thump. As the referee's toll reached seven Firpo appeared gone, but that huge body of his was packed with stamina. Up he came at seven in some inexplicable fashion and thrice more Jack hammered him to the floor in quick succession.

Dempsey was a killer, stalking his prey. Mercilessly he rushed in to finish the job. Then it happened. The battered brute in front of him, fighting on sheer instinct alone, swung that fearsome right. It left him one short second away from becoming the heavyweight champion of the world.

Flush on the jaw of the onrushing Dempsey it landed. Jack catapulted out of the ring head first and feet waving in the air. Friendly newspaper men pushed him back but, as he crawled, dazed, under the bottom strand of the ropes and wearily dragged himself to his feet, he was a beaten fighter. The count had reached nine on him, as narrow an escape as any man ever had.

At that moment, however, that seemed unimportant. Dempsey was so far gone that he could not defend himself, a helpless figure unable to hold up his gloves. However, the erstwhile calm and imperturbable Firpo lost his head. Excitedly he swung that dreaded right time and time again. And he missed his open target on every occasion. Jack staggered into a clinch and he still was holding at the bell.

Feverishly Jack Kearns worked over his stricken gladiator in the too-brief one-minute rest period. It could do no good, everyone felt. The invincible Jack Dempsey was about to be dethroned. However, they reckoned without the great fighting heart of a great fighting man.

As the second round began, Firpo seemed bewildered by his touch of prosperity. Slowly he came out to the center of the ring, there to find that he had a raging tiger on his hands again. Dempsey pounded away at the body at close quarters and whipped out his left hook. Down went the Wild Bull for a count of two. More infighting and the giant slid slowly down for a count of four.

The next time the champion made no mistakes. No sooner had his left hook found its mark than he followed up with a terrific right cross to his sinking opponent and Luis Angel Firpo went down not to rise again. The greatest fight in history was over.

1944

When Corbett Fought Jeffries

May 11

One of the strangest fights in the history of the ring ended with dramatic abruptness forty-four years ago today, and old-timers still talk of it in tones of awe. It was the bout at Coney Island between Jim Jeffries and Jim Corbett for the world heavyweight championship. Even at this late date it seems worth a backward glance.

Corbett had been dethroned there years before by spindly Bob Fitzsimmons, and powerfully muscled Jeff subsequently had knocked the crown off the Cornishman's head. Jeffries was then only 25, a massive man at his physical peak. Corbett was a has-been, approaching 34, with his star already set.

But Gentleman Jim was convinced that he could regain his throne if he ever could inveigle the Boilermaker into a match. First of all, though, he worked himself into condition in an arduous four-month preparatory session at Lakewood. He walked and he rowed and he swam, but for a while did no boxing whatsoever. By the end of his secret training he was as hard as the proverbial nails.

Not until then did he approach Bill Brady, the theatrical man who had managed him in his own championship days but now handled the affairs of Jeff. The cagey Corbett pleaded that he was desperately in need of money—even the loser's end of the purse. Still fond of his former charge, Brady finally capitulated despite his fear that the younger and stronger Jeffries would administer a terrific beating to Gentleman Jim.

Ten weeks before the match Corbett went into formal training. His chief sparring partner was Gus Ruhlin, a top-ranking heavyweight, and the program did not call for mild skirmishes, love taps or shadow boxing. Behind locked doors the two of them went at it in earnest for as many as twenty rounds a day, Ruhlin simulating Jeff's famous crouch while the hair-trigger brain of Corbett was working out battle plans. Perhaps there never was a finer trained athlete than the former champion when he stepped into the Coney Island ring. The Boilermaker, on the other hand, had drilled most casually. Corbett looked easy to him.

They were a study in sharp contrasts as they squared off, Gentleman Jim, a trim, pantherish figure at 185 pounds and Jeff, a shaggy grizzly bear at 210. And it was a fight between a panther and a grizzly, too. The panther flitted in and out, stabbing away with blinding speed. The grizzly stalked him menacingly, trying to get in close and never catching so elusive a foeman.

Corbett jabbed and jabbed. His fancy footwork and extraordinary defensive skill kept him out of range. Jeff never missed a punch by a wide margin. He missed by fractions of an inch. Gentleman Jim being so tantalizingly clever that he barely moved his head to duck out of harm's way. By the sixth round the fight had become so lopsided that Corbett smashed home seven straight punches to Jeff's chin without getting a single return.

In the ninth the ex-champion switched from jabbing to hooking, almost sending the dazed and blinded bear to the floor. Then he reverted to his previous jabbing tactics as the youthful giant he faced began to bleed copiously from the nose and mouth. The spectators could hardly believe their eyes. A victory for Jeff had seemed so certain that attendance was small and those who came hoped against hope that the still glamorous

Corbett would not be too badly mauled by the steel-sinewed Boilermaker. Instead, they found themselves on their feet, frantically screaming "Corbett, Corbett!"

So it went through the fifteenth and through the twentieth of this twenty-five-round bout. Jeff's handlers were getting desperate. Here was the man who was being hailed as the greatest champion of all time, unable to hit a 34-year-old ghost. They told him frankly that his only hope lay in a knockout.

Corbett was only seven minutes away from one of the most astounding victories in ring history when it happened. He was tiring fast and the grizzly bear opposite him had unflinchingly absorbed everything thrown in his direction. Relentlessly Jeff bore in as Gentleman Jim tried to end it by a knockout, much as Billy Conn tried to flatten Joe Louis instead of covering up for a couple of rounds and the inevitable decision in his favor.

In the twenty-third round the grizzly pinned the panther against the wall. Thrice in succession Corbett drove his left hook into the bloody mask in front of him and the crowd, loving him for his brilliant fight against seemingly insuperable odds, pleaded fervently for the crusher. But Gentleman Jim's uncanny seventh sense failed him.

Jeff maneuvered him over against the ropes and feinted with his right. For the first time Corbett was unaware of his proximity to the strands. He pulled back sharply only to have the ropes catapult him straight into a pile-driver left, delivered with the full fury of a hitherto frustrated fighter.

It was the end. Corbett dropped as limply as a wet towel, his head hanging grotesquely over the bottom strand of the rope while Referee Charlie White called off the fatal ten seconds. If that gallant battle proved anything, it proved this: That when a bout is terminated in a knockout, the only punch which counts is the last one.

The Whizzer Is Still a Whizzbang

July 3

There was an item in the paper not so long ago which may have escaped your attention. It mentioned that sixteen officers and men of the "Little Beavers" destroyer squadron received Bronze Star medals for courageous service in the Pacific last fall and winter. Among them was Lieutenant (jg) Byron R. White. Upon receipt of his decoration, Lieutenant White was quoted as saying, "I just got in on the gravy train. The other guys deserved the medals, but I came to the squadron from a PT job in November after the biggest work was done."

Maybe so, but that ain't the way I heard it. Lieutenant Byron R. White, in case the name eludes your memory, is none other than Whizzer White, the All-America halfback from Colorado, who went on to become the highest priced player in the National Football League ($15,000 per season) for Pittsburgh before finishing his abbreviated career for Detroit. If the Whizzer didn't rate the decoration for that particular task, he has at least a couple of other fancy medals coming to him for the other job he was on before he joined the destroyers.

As far as this reporter knows, the Whizzer received scant acclaim for what he did while attached to the fast little torpedo

Byron "Whizzer" White, an All-American selection from the University of Colorado, in his playing days.

boats. Yet, when he was in the Solomons, a dispatch from that area declared, "Lieut. Byron R. White's work in the central Solomons may never be publicized, but he may some day become the outstanding hero of this war."

Later a high naval officer enthusiastically stated on returning from the Southwest Pacific, "Byron White is the No. 1 candidate as THE hero of this war." Just what the Whizzer was accomplishing in that corner of the world has been cloaked in mystery and naval secrecy. Apparently, though, he has been doing his usual bang-up job.

A most remarkable young man is Whizzer White. When he played football for Colorado he was in a rather obscure spot because rarely has anyone considered the Rocky Mountain Conference as an ideal jumping-off place for All-America ranking. Yet he made it. However, his real test was still to come. Nothing deflates an incorrectly named All-America faster than the professional league, and nothing will more quickly establish one justifiably chosen.

All the Whizzer did was become the leading ground-gainer for two of the seasons he played while gaining a place on the 1940 all-league team, the super All-America. He had power in off tackle drives and the elusiveness of his native Rocky Mountain goat in an open field. He could do everything and he could do it all superbly well.

But the Whizzer's claim to fame was not based only on a strong back and strong legs. He had a mind to match them. At Colorado he was Phi Beta Kappa and won himself a Rhodes scholarship. For just one year he became a Yank at Oxford but, with the outbreak of the war, he returned to the United States and matriculated at the Yale Law School. The rumor, never completely confirmed, was that he finished first in his class. Since the Whizzer was such an intellectual wizard, everyone merely accepted it as gospel truth without bothering to check its accuracy.

Perhaps his last game in professional football was the proper farewell salute. He gained 81 yards for the Lions on November 30, 1941, and faded from sight only to bob up in another section of the world, doing the same slam-bang job he had been performing on the gridiron.

That must have been a most memorable game for three members of that Detroit squad. One was White. Another was a big tackle, Johnny Tripson. The third was an end, Maurice Britt. White and Tripson may play football again. Britt never will.

Tripson hit the headlines first during the invasion of North Africa. For "dauntless courage and fearless devotion to duty," the giant tackle received the treasured Navy Cross. Ensign Tripson piloted one of the landing craft in the first wave to go ashore, braving terrific enemy fire until his "mission was accomplished."

Then, there was the 210-pound, 6-foot 4-inch Britt. This Army lieutenant led a force of fifty-five men in Italy and was surrounded by a German detachment twice that size. In the ensuing battle the Detroit end fell with grenade, shrapnel and bullet wounds in side, chest, face and hands. Refusing medical aid, he arose to pitch thirty grenades, fire seventy-five rounds of ammunition and wipe out a machine-gun nest. His own inspiring leadership won that fight. But in the next one he lost his right arm and almost lost a foot. Never again will he be able to appear on the National Football League roster. But his name will be immortal in the history of our country, since he was decorated with the Congressional Medal of Honor.

What Whizzer White has done to become an even greater hero than either of his teammates is one of those hush-hush propositions with which the Navy cloaks its intelligence officers. His lone forays behind Japanese lines in the Solomons have been shrouded by utmost secrecy. But he is quite a lad is Whizzer White. And so are the hundreds of other National Football League stalwarts, professional sports' leading contributors to the war. More power to all of them.

Byron Nelson Does Most of the Talking

October 12

Byron Nelson and Jug McSpaden have been on a golfing marathon since the first of the year. The two of them were caught between trains not so long ago in company with Ed Dudley and Freddie Corcoran.

"It's been a wonderful year for me," said Lord Byron in his soft Texas drawl, "but I sure will be glad when it's over and I can relax."

"Before we're through," sighed Jug, "we'll have played golf about 300 days out of the 366 in the year."

"I wish I only knew how much money you two raised for charity," said cheerful Freddie. "It must be well up in the hundreds of thousands."

"Everyone knows who Nelson is now," said Big Ed, a reminiscent gleam in his eye. "Do you remember your first tournament, Byron?"

"I sure do," grinned the tall Texan. "Lawson Little was the big star that year and I was the most unknown of all the unknowns in the tournament. So they matched me with Little in the first round. Although I was pretty scared, I decided I'd have to teach him who I was on the first hole. His tee shot was a beauty, but I took me the biggest-headed driver in my bag, teed the ball way up high and I really lit into it. I must have passed his drive by twenty or thirty yards. They had a circle marked around the green as a restraining line for the crowd and I put my second shot inside the circle.

"I'll spare you the sad details. But Lawson went out in a par 36 and I had a 33. What won the match for me was the eleventh hole. Little rammed in a birdie and I came up with an eagle. Eventually I beat him, 5 and 4. Several months later I was on the same train with Lawson—me in an upper berth and him in a drawing room—when I dropped in on him.

" 'Before our match in the Sacramento Open,' he told me, 'I was going around asking everyone, "Who's Nelson?" and everyone said that you were just a long, hungry kid from Texas. But those first two shots of yours opened my eyes.' "

"Henry Cotton asked the same question in the Ryder Cup matches," contributed Dudley. "Byron and I were playing him and Alf Padgham in a Scotch foursome. Cotton said, 'Who's Nelson?' and Byron showed him with a tremendous approach shot that dropped only twelve feet from the pin. Then Byron turned to me and remarked, 'Put it in.' So I did."

"Later on, though," confessed the Texan, "I pitched up a lousy one, thirty-five feet or more from the hole. Not very hopefully, I turned to Ed and said again, 'Put it in.' He did, too."

"How about the time Ty Cobb had us out to his house?" asked Corcoran. "We'd hardly stepped in the door before Ty told us he didn't want baseball to be mentioned, but he only wanted to talk about golf."

"So we talked about baseball all night," commented McSpaden laconically.

"I asked Ty what he did to get out of a slump," drawled Nelson, "and he said he'd start bunting with a fungo bat and work his way up to where he was swinging with all his old power. Then he asked me the same question. I answered that I'd begin pitching 100 yards until I had that shot under control. Then I'd move up to 150 yards and so on. 'Swell,' shouted Cobb, 'that's just the system I'm going to use myself from now on.' "

"Tell us about your venture into organized ball," prompted the helpful Corcoran.

"The year I won the National Open," said Lord Byron, "the Saint Louis Browns were coming to Toledo to play an exhibition game and Fred Haney, the manager of the Mudhens, thought it would stimulate the gate if I played right field for him. I went at it seriously, practicing for about ten days beforehand.

"I discussed the situation with Luke Sewell and suggested that his starting right-hander pitch low to me so that I could make use of my golf swing. In the first inning I fielded a hit and threw to second to hold the man on first. I also caught a fly ball. I did all right in the next inning, too. But when I got to bat the right-hander wasn't there any more, but the meanest looking lefty I ever saw. 'I gotta talk to Sewell,' I said to myself, but there was no time.

"I took a cut at that ball. If I'd ever hit it, the ball would be traveling yet. I took another cut. And another one. In brief, I fanned as the crowd booed me roundly. They booed me again in the field when Chet Laabs hit one of those wicked liners that keep rising. I backed against the fence, but it caromed off for a double.

"My next time at bat Haney said, 'I'd like to win this game if I can. Would you mind sitting out the rest of it?' So he used his regular right fielder as a pinch-hitter. Maybe I loused up the position because he fanned, too. Then the crowd booed him and hollered, 'We want Nelson.'

"I had to play golf the next day at Cleveland. But I was so stiff and sore from the baseball that I was swinging like a rusty gate. But golf is such a silly and unpredictable game that I merely went out in 29, came back in 34 and shot me a 63."

Quite a golfer is Byron Nelson. And quite a guy, too.

1945

A Mild-Mannered Gentleman

September 2

Ty Cobb had the reputation of being one of the snarlingest, fightingest ball players that the game ever has produced. He denies it all in his present-day mild-mannered fashion. In fact, if you listen to him long enough, you leave with the inescapable conclusion that butter wouldn't melt in his mouth and that the swashbuckling Tyrus Raymond Cobb was the original Casper Milquetoast.

"I never had as many fights as they said," he protests and then adds, "As far as spiking anyone is concerned, I doubt that I deliberately spiked more than one or two players in the entire twenty-four years I was in the big leagues." The big sissy! It's kind of late to be destroying all those illusions. But let's listen to his story for a moment.

"When I came up to Detroit," he recounts, a dreamy look in his eyes, "I was just a mild-mannered Sunday school boy. Sam Crawford then was the big dog in the meat-house and I was just a brash kid. But, as soon as they started to put my picture in the papers and give me some publicity, the old-timers began to work on me.

"They practically put a chip on my shoulder, hazed me un-

Ty Cobb, left, and Arthur Daley, 1955.

mercifully and every time I'd put down my hat I'd find it twisted into knots on my return. But now that I look back on it, I think that's a better system than the gentlemanly treatment the rookies get these days. If I became a snarling wildcat, they made me one.

"Another thing was that the manager didn't correct mistakes. He never had the chance. Your team-mates climbed all over you first of all. I remember that famous seventeen-inning game with the Athletics in 1907, the very game that won the pennant for us because we used up three or four of Philadelphia's star pitchers. We should have won in the eleventh, except that Davey Jones shied away from the crowd and let a ball fall safely for two bases. When he came back to the bench our players were so mad that they practically tore the uniform off his back. That's the way we played ball in those days."

Ty paused and glanced nostalgically out the window. "As for all those stories that I went around spiking people," he continued, "that's nonsense. I tagged a base just with my shoe tip and there are no spikes in the toe of your shoe. Did you ever hear of Cobb getting spiked? No. You just heard of Cobb spiking some of our more illustrious citizens. Look!"

Tyrus Raymond pulled up his trouser legs and displayed the most amazing collection of scars ever seen outside of a dissecting room. "Of course, I never before admitted any of these," he said. "There never was any sense in tipping off the opposition on how black and blue or damaged I was.

"I never tipped them off on anything. Wait a minute. Yes, I did. Remember Billy Sullivan? There was a truly great catcher and I never could steal a base on him. So one time I'm up at bat and I decide to try a little psychology on him because I've absolutely nothing to lose. 'Billy,' I said out of the corner of my mouth, 'if I get on base I'm going down on the second pitch.' He didn't know whether or not to believe me. At any rate, he became rattled and I stole second as promised.

"So the next time I'm at bat, I'm so tickled at the way that system worked that I told him the same thing again." Ty looked a little sheepish. He glanced around as if expecting to see Billy Sullivan peering accusingly over his shoulder and then continued his tale. "I lied to him," he said shamefacedly. "I stole on the first pitch. But, at least, I was one of the very few base runners who ever stole on Sullivan."

Cobb's record of ninety-six stolen bases in a season probably never will be broken, because modern ball has virtually eliminated the steal as a method of progression. Why risk a steal when the next guy is liable to hit one into the seats? His record of having a lifetime average of .367 never will be broken either, because a Cobb comes along about once every century.

"There was only one infielder who ever bothered me," he stated. "That was Bobby Wallace. He just straddled the bag and waited for me to come into him—as I had to do. With the rest of them, though, it merely was a case of waiting for the last possible moment before committing yourself. Then you had the initiative, and not he. With the fall-away slide that I worked on and developed, the infielder had nothing more than the tip of a shoe to tag. You could neither spike nor be spiked with that slide, either."

Ty was just as much a student of batting as he was of stealing bases. The man who may be baseball's only millionaire practiced place hitting so intensively that he always sought the holes left open by infielders covering bases. "The secret of hitting," he explains, "is the stance at the plate, an open stance for pull hitting and a closed one for pushing the ball—just like golf. If you're a left-handed batter, never try to pull on a left-handed pitcher."

But why try to explain Cobb's method of doing things? He was so far beyond the average that what might seem simple and fundamental to him would be out of the reach of the ordinary athlete. The fiery Georgian—pardon me, he is a very meek chap—made so much baseball history that his like never will come again. It's too bad about Cobb, though. Can you picture what a ball player he would have been had he only a modicum of fight and spirit in his make-up? Ahem!

Louis and Conn Back by Request

October 17

The war definitely is over. Or hadn't you heard? It was perfectly proper for you to disregard the formal surrender ceremonies. What makes the termination of hostilities absolutely and unqualifiedly official is that Uncle Mike Jacobs not only has signed Joe Louis to defend his world heavyweight championship next June but airily talks about a three-million-dollar gate. That settles it.

Uncle Mike, his store teeth clattering contentedly, was discovered strolling along Jacobs Beach yesterday in company with his meal-ticket, the Brown Bomber himself. "That three-million bucks is a cinch," he said amid disconcerting clack-clacks. Then he added naively, "You don't mind if I talk big, do you?"

"But, gosh," he continued. "I've already enough ticket requests at hand to choke a cow. Guys write in for seats and they don't give a hoot what the price is or where the fight will be held. After all, they've been waiting four years for this. Toss in the sale of television rights and there's no telling what the gate will be." Uncle Mike paused and gazed dreamily into the air, trying to spot a few more invisible millions.

The Dark Destroyer cast an amused glance in the direction

of Uncle Mike, grinned and remarked, "Ah got nuthin' to worry about now." Apparently he isn't worried about Billy Conn—not yet anyway. Even though he never said a word about it, his main concern has been the accumulation of enough folding money for back taxes, an amount those in the know say is $117,000. This trifling sum (ahem!) is due within six months after he was mustered out of service. Uncle Mike probably will pick up the tab owed Uncle Sam and accept an I.O.U. on it in return. So much for the immediate financial problems involved.

Yet one really can't get completely away from the financial aspects of this fight since it promises to be the greatest single event in the entire history of sport. It has the power to dwarf into insignificance and chase back to the "small change" department the second Tunney-Dempsey imbroglio which still is the record gate at a modest $2,658,660. Remember when that seemed a large sum of money?

But when Uncle Mike gazes dreamily into the air, he doesn't see the sky. He's looking plumb into the stratosphere—movie rights, radio rights, television rights and a solid chunk of cash for tickets. There just is no limit to what the "take" might be, particularly if television develops with the rapidity everyone expects.

As for the fight itself, no one can tell. If you rate it off the last one, it will be brilliant and spectacular. But you just can't be certain of such things. Many a repeat performance of a savage bout has degenerated into a slow waltz. Yet as long as one of the contestants packs as much dynamite in his fists as Louis does, it never can be too dull. In fact, that's its guarantee of sensationalism.

Five long years will have passed since their last meeting on June 18, 1941. And time never adds more weapons to a fighter's equipment. The Dark Destroyer will be 32 when he puts his crown on the line once more. The Conn Man will be crowding 29 and packing at least a dozen more pounds than the 174 which made him razor-sharp and a will-o'-the-wisp the last time out.

One angle which the publicity-purveyors will not overlook is that Billy the Kid will use that extra weight to add power to his punches. But his punch won't do him the least bit of good if he's lost one iota of his speed. It was that blinding speed which whirled the handsome Pittsburgh Irishman to the very verge of victory the last time.

Louis looked slow and cumbersome in comparison to the flashy Conn. He was heavy-footed and heavy-armed. You can't hit what you can't catch and the Brown Bomber rarely could catch the dancing master who spun about him in growing confidence and—unfortunately for him—in growing disdain.

As they moved into the twelfth the cocky Conn threw caution to the winds. What a contrast this bold youth made with some of the timid souls who had mingled fearfully with the Dark Destroyer in the past! Near the round's end he crashed over a pulverizing left hook to the jaw and the uncertain Louis actually clinched while pandemonium broke loose out in the darkness beyond the ring's dazzling lights. No one had ever seen that before.

Into the thirteenth round Conn progressed, the fight won. Two of the three officials had the challenger ahead on points and the other scored them on even terms. Billy had only to stay away for the rest of the way and William David Conn would be the new champion of the world. But he is a stubborn and proud youth. He didn't want to win by a decision. He wanted the flourish of a knockout.

In he stampeded for the kill, swarmed over Louis—and it happened. Conn left a tiny opening and the Brown Bomber found it. A right cross rocketed through, a mite too high on the head for an instant knockout. But Billy's knees buckled and he was on his way. A murderous barrage sent him toppling and a gallant bid had come to a sudden end, a scant six minutes and two seconds from the scheduled finish.

Whenever these two rivals are discussed my mind inevitably goes back to a conversation the two of them had overseas. It's been told before but it still is such a descriptive gem that it can bear repeating. Conn was telling Louis how he had planned to hold on to the championship for two years before giving the Brown Bomber a chance to reclaim his title.

"How could you have held the title two years, Billy?" drawled Joe. "You couldn't even hold it for two more rounds."

The Boy Grew Older

December 21

The frail little caddy wearing the sun visor was thrilled to death. He finally had the opportunity to see the great Walter Hagen in action. It was back in 1927 that the 15-year-old youngster hitch-hiked from Fort Worth to Dallas to watch the fabulous Haig battle for the PGA championship. With admiring eyes he studied every stroke and never left his idol's side for an instant.

Eventually Sir Walter reached the final against Joe Turnesa. By then he had begun to notice his worshiper with the sun visor. He even spoke to him and the caddy soon was walking on clouds. No more rabid or devoted follower did Hagen have than the kid from Fort Worth.

The match had reached a crucial point and Hagen had to shoot into the sun. The glare bothered the hatless Walter and he glanced over at his new, young friend. That gave him an idea.

"Hey, sonny," he said. "How about lending me that sun visor of yours?"

Would he lend it to him? The boy would have given it to him. With the visor shielding his eyes, the Haig whipped off a magnificent shot and went on to win the championship.

Last week the lad in the sun visor was back at the Glen Garden Country Club in Fort Worth, where he once had been a caddy. A large gallery followed him just as breathlessly as he had once followed the mighty Haig. And in that gallery was Walter Hagen himself. The boy had grown older and had become golf's most spectacular figure, Byron Nelson.

Lord Byron was tickled pink to be back at his old club. He took the other professionals over to a wall and proudly showed them a shield which dutifully noted that Byron Nelson had won the club championship in 1930. He also showed them another shield which listed the club's caddy champions. Two kids had tied for the honor in 1926. One of them was Nelson and the other was, oddly enough, Ben Hogan. It's quite a coincidence, isn't it, that one golf club could simultaneously produce two such superlative links operatives.

It was old home week for the pair of them when they returned to Fort Worth, but this time little Ben couldn't tie big Byron. He wasn't even close, finishing well down the list while Nelson won his nineteenth tournament of the season and increased his winnings to more than $66,000 in war bonds.

Nothing gave Lord Byron more satisfaction, however, than the sight of his old idol, Hagen, in the gallery which followed him. Nelson doesn't teem with color the way the Haig did but he's just as tremendous a figure in the sport as the Haig was. One reason for his lack of color—if he actually lacks it— is that his golf is too perfect, too mechanical. He never gets into trouble, while Sir Walter would flub one shot and then extricate himself from his difficulties with an incredibly spectacular recovery.

Fred Corcoran, the high panjandrum of the PGA, had a chance to talk to Hagen at Fort Worth. As a matter of fact, all the professionals did. Once the Haig stalked into the lobby, a wide grin on his face, all conversation ceased and everyone made a beeline for him. He hasn't lost that magnetic appeal one bit.

They fell to discussing great shots and someone asked Hagen which was the greatest one of his career. "It was one that never came off," he answered with a chuckle. And then he went on to tell about it.

It happened in the British open of 1926 and the Haig came up to the last green, needing a 2 to tie Bobby Jones for the championship. His tee shot was a full 160 yards from the green and nothing less than a full-blown miracle would enable him to make it.

Just before he approached the ball he whispered to his caddy to go on the green and hold the pin—just in case. Since there were some ten or fifteen thousand persons in the gallery he didn't want them to think that he was deliberately making so bold a move as to go all out for the hole.

But up on the clubhouse porch the Emperor Jones, the title virtually in his hip pocket, was watching nervously.

"Do you think he'll make it?" someone asked.

"It would be just like him to make it," answered Bob, a trifle petulantly.

Hagen stepped up quickly to the ball and swung his club. The pellet rose in a majestic arc and soared straight for the green. It landed on the near edge, trickling toward the cup. Just as it reached it, though, it took one of those funny little bounces and playfully jumped over it, coming to a rest inches beyond. That was the shot Sir Walter believes was the greatest he ever made—except that he didn't quite make it.

It was rather appropriate that Corcoran should return to town at this time and turn one's thought to golf—and particularly to Hagen. For today is Walter's fifty-third birthday and the old codger has reached such a state of antiquity that his next competitive start will be at Dunedin in Florida a fortnight hence in—of all things—a seniors' tournament.

Until the Haig turned up at Fort Worth, few of the professionals had ever seen him in five years. "But he still is the dominating figure in a room," says Fred. "In that respect he's just like Babe Ruth. Not only was he one of the greatest of all golfers but he easily was the most colorful. Take the time he played in a Red Cross benefit exhibition at Nassau with Bobby Jones, Gene Sarazen and Tommy Armour with the Duke of Windsor refereeing. At one point Hagen turned to His Grace and casually remarked, 'Hey, Eddie, will you hold the pin?' And darned if the Duke didn't rush, beaming, to hold the pin. But that was Hagen for you. Is it any wonder that he was in a class by himself?"

There could be no answer.

1946

South of the Border

April 3

Do you remember that advertisement which caught every eye a decade or so ago? It read: "They laughed when he sat down at the piano." Presumably, the "he" was a party cut-up who had been taking secret piano lessons. Then he played with the skill of a Paderewski and they laughed no longer. It was pretty much the same way with the Mexican baseball league. Everyone in organized ball snickered condescendingly when the brothers Pasquel "sat down at the piano." But they, too, are laughing no longer. It's getting serious.

Developments of the past couple of days, when a trio of Giants, George Hausmann, Roy Zimmerman and Sal Maglie, joined Vernon Stephens of the Browns across the border and soon were followed by Mickey Owen of the Dodgers, hardly are reassuring. Yet there is no cause for real alarm. Talk that the Mexican promotion is as much a threat to the two majors as was the Federal League is just so much poppycock. The parallel doesn't exist.

The Federals set up shop in major league cities and not only fought the existing circuits for players but for patronage as well. Our Good Neighbors (ahem!) to the south are supplying their own patronage, such as it is. Their battle is only for players, a battle that's being waged in a player-glutted market. Otherwise they wouldn't have the foggiest chance of meeting with success.

As far as quantity goes, the Mexicans haven't done too badly but, as far as quality goes, they've snared only three top-flight players, Stephens, Owen, and Luis Olmo. In nuisance value they have been looming large enough to give American magnates a sharp pain in the neck, but the actual damage they've done has been negligible, unless you want to include the stirring up of feelings of discontent among some of the players and feelings of uneasiness and indignation among the owners.

The indignation is understandable. The Pasquel brothers have corralled a couple of hundred thousand dollars worth of ball players for nothing. And organized ball will wince noticeably when hit in the pocketbook. The threat of the Mexican league undoubtedly has caused the payment of larger salaries than expected to some slaving chattels. From that standpoint, it's serious

However, there is no chance of the Mexican League developing into another Federal League. Last winter the majors sneered at the Pacific Coast circuit and its ambition to attain major league status. They said that the Coast—Los Angeles and San Francisco excepted—didn't have the populations nor the proper size ball parks to merit advancement. Yet south of the border there is only one center, Mexico City, big enough to have a paying clientele.

Furthermore, the clientele won't pay much. Mexico doesn't hand over the fancy salaries to its citizenry that the Yanquis do. Therefore it can't command ticket prices comparable to our own nor has it the seating facilities to accommodate them at lesser prices—for only three days a week, too. The entire proposition looks so economically unsound—from this distance anyway—that one has to wonder how the project is being financed. It can't be done by gate receipts the way we do it up here.

What is the answer? Can it be, as so many have said, gambling? Latin-Americans are inveterate gamblers. Baseball writers, who have visited Cuba, have reported that a native earning $10 a week will bet $10 during one game—$20 if he can get the credit. Bookies patrol the stands, changing odds and taking wagers on every pitch. With so much money at stake feelings run inordinately high.

Not so many years ago the Philadelphia Athletics and the Pittsburgh Pirates played an exhibition game in Mexico City. Al Simmons was serving as the pro tem manager of the As and Frank Frisch, the proverbial blushing violet, was handling the Buccaneers. Beans Reardon, an outspoken gent, was the umpire.

Beansie summoned Messrs. Simmons and Frisch to the plate before play began. "Listen to me, you muggers," he snapped. "Do you see that hot-tempered bunch in the stands? They'll kill me if they think I made a mistake. But today I don't make any mistakes. If I hear as much as a peep out of either of you in protesting any decision I quit on the spot. I'll just walk off the field and catch the first train back to the States. No gripes today, boys, or Beansie takes a powder."

There were no gripes or protests. Messrs. Frisch and Simmons writhed inwardly at times but suffered in silence. Beansie finished the game in one piece.

Rogers Hornsby, one of baseball's immortals, took a fling at Mexican ball when he managed a team there a couple of seasons ago. But he quit in disgust and disillusionment. The popular story is that the promoter complained when the Rajah hit a game-winning jackpot homer as a pinch-hitter in the ninth. The complaint was—or so the tale goes—that he thus ruined the next attraction. Maybe that yarn is made of whole cloth. But the grim-lipped Hornsby quit then and there.

When players of the caliber of Stephens, Owen and Olmo jump the big leagues it's pretty much of a left-handed indictment of the owners who let them slip away. As for the athletes, only time will tell whether or not they were foolish in making the break since they are barred for five years, which virtually means for life.

The penalties are so severe that not many will dare take the leap. Mainly they will come from the group of stars who are almost over the hill or run-of-the-mill players whose hope for success in the big league is negligible, the Danny Gardella stripe. That Mexican grab-bag hardly can hold a Joe DiMaggio, a Ted Williams, a Bobby Feller or the like.

The talent raids are serious enough to give the magnates a certain amount of concern, but not serious enough to be a threat to their existence. At least they won't be this season. If the jumpers can come back next fall with glowing reports of their stay, with messages that money grows there more plentifully than the cactus plant and with word that a new major league is in the making, it will be time to give heed. Meanwhile the harried moguls are asking each other how a town like Nuevo Laredo (population, 10,000) can support ex-major leaguers in better style than that to which they are accustomed.

End of an Era

November 29

The Army–Navy game at Philadelphia's cavernous Municipal Stadium tomorrow marks the end of one very distinctive era in American football. It's the grand climax to a period when the Great Autumnal Madness was absolutely dominated by the service academies in general and West Point in particular. When Doc Blanchard, Glenn Davis & Co. toss aside their golden helmets and peel off their black jerseys after the final gun, the age of the super teams will have run its course.

For three consecutive years Messrs. B. and D. have run over, around and past all opposition without ever meeting with defeat. The scoreless tie with Notre Dame was the only thing resembling a blot on that glittering escutcheon. There may be some scoffers who mumble that the West Pointers were operating against kids and 4–Fs during the war years. Perhaps they were. But the flawless machines that Red Blaik sent out on the gridiron would have been tremendous teams at any time against any opposition.

Army had everything when Junior and Doc were patrolling the Plains, particularly a year ago when this Kaydet juggernaut was at its absolute peak. Blaik had two teams of almost equal strength then, sparked by the finest pair of backs ever to operate together. Blanchard hit the line with the careening impact of a berserk water buffalo and Davis fled to the outside with the speed and guile of a frightened gazelle. They had hard-charging linemen to open up the holes for them and always had a passing attack to make the foe honest—and cautious.

Personnel changed considerably through those years, but B. and D. were the two constant factors, the heart of the team. Even when the squad strength dwindled so alarmingly this campaign that the redhead was forced to send out his varsity eleven for virtually sixty minutes each Saturday afternoon. Davis and Blanchard were the rallying points not only on the offense where their skill always had been obvious but also on the defense where they performed yeomen deeds.

So this game tomorrow is more than an ordinary game. It's the exit march for the two best publicized backs the sport has had. Even if the rest of the Army squad were returning intact next year—which it isn't—the cadets still would tumble down the scale without Blanchard and Davis. They belong in the once-in-a-lifetime category, so rare that the only duo in even the same approximate class with them—if the memory of the oldest living inhabitant still is trustworthy—is Pfann and Kaw of Cornell.

The beauty of B. and D. has been that each of them has been able to do so much so well. Until this season when Doc injured his leg, he did all of the Army punting. But with Blanchard functioning on unsteady underpinning in the early going, Blaik merely transferred the kicking assignment to Junior without ever noticing any difference in effectiveness. Both can pass, Davis better than Blanchard, and both can receive. In the Notre Dame donnybrook big Doc made a two-handed, overhead catch of one of Junior's tosses with all of the careless grace of Joe DiMaggio collaring a simple fly ball.

They're such polished players that they block smartly and neatly. Blanchard has the weight advantage in that department, of course, his robust 205 pounds leaving Davis far behind at 168 or so. In fact one of the most vivid recollections this reporter has of them is the picture of Doc taking off against John (Tree) Adams, the huge Notre Dame tackle, a season or so ago. Blanchard hit him amidships and, like a giant redwood, snapping in two as it topples, Adams collapsed. The first terrifying thought was that Doc had broken him in half.

Regularly during the past three campaigns they were simultaneously at their peaks of effectiveness. But occasionally one would have a better day than the other. Perhaps the defensive set-up would jam the middle alleys and Davis would romp. Or perhaps the defenses would spread to protect the flanks and Blanchard would have a field day. Yet the only time they were both contained was in the gruelling Yankee Stadium battle this year when they worked without rest. Prior to that no one believed it, but they actually are human.

It's sad that they're departing, because watching them in action always was a pleasure. It's sadder yet to realize that the sun also is setting on Army dominance. Not very long ago Bill Corum shrewdly commented that the Navy team of 1946 was, in effect, the Army team of 1947.

It was a keen observation. The midshipmen have been stripped of their tremendous wartime talent much sooner than had been expected along the banks of the Severn. Such stars as Smackover Scott, Tony Minisi, Hunchy Hoernschemeyer, Ralph Ellsworth, Bob Kelly and the like departed for greener pastures. It left Tom Hamilton with an almost insuperable rebuilding job to do.

Army is going to find things pretty much the same way next year. Practically the entire varsity team graduates. Since there isn't too much depth of talent in back of them anyway, the Kaydets will drop from a supercolossal billing to merely good. Back they'll fall to the same level as most Ivy League foes, many of them smarting under humiliating defeats.

Smarting most will be Penn, twice vanquished by some sixty points. It was Penn, you know, which was responsible for starting the cadets up to the top when Gen. Robert Eichelberger, then superintendent of the Academy, witnessed the Quakers crush the West Pointers, 48 to 0. Instantly he brought Red Blaik in as coach and the war brought in the talent.

That era ends tomorrow, though. Messrs. Blanchard and Davis bow out. No football story ever will seem authoritative again, not without the cute use of those initials. B. and D. It just won't be the same without them.

1947

Sleepy Jim Reverts to Type

January 6

Frank Frisch expressed it best, perhaps. Not very long ago the Flash was discussing the situation which had confronted him at Pittsburgh last season and the listener wondered why his hair wasn't snow white instead of being merely liberally spinkled with gray. "But I love to manage a team," he said musingly and wistfully. "There's something to it that gets into your blood, an excitement to meeting problems and a fascination to handling men despite all their complexities. It drives you nuts but I still like it better than anything else in the world."

The presumption is that Sleepy Jim Crowley once was bitten by the same bug which now holds Frisch. The Old Horseman has resigned as the Commissioner of the All-America Conference to accept part ownership of the Chicago Rockets in that same organization. More important still is the fact that he returns to his old trade as the coach of the team.

Those who have been close to Somnolent James were aware of the fact that he was restless in his executive post and anxious to return to the bench. However, it did come as a surprise that he remained in pro ball instead of taking a job on some campus. Sleepy Jim almost could have had his pick of available college berths because he is one of the best coaches in the profession.

Yet the mere fact that he remained in the Conference is an

immense tribute to his faith in it. Crowley is assuming a herculean job with his eyes wide open. Not only is he bucking the mighty Chicago Bears with their magnificent organization and faithful following, but he also has to buck the up-and-coming Chicago Cardinals with the witty and likeable Jimmy Conzelman at the controls. Furthermore, the Bears and the Cardinals have the infinitely superior stadia in Wrigley Field and Comiskey Park. The Rockets are stuck with the huge but otherwise unattractive Soldier Field.

This newest move will be the supreme test of the Rocket franchise. If Sleepy Jim can't make a go of it, no one can. He's a shrewd and clever coach, one of the most respected in the business. And he has a compelling personality, forceful and yet always leavened by a delightful sense of humor. The Notre Dame old timers insist that he is the nearest approach of them all to the immortal Knute Rockne, whose prime favorite he was.

Many a battle of wits did they have in the old days of the Four Horsemen some twenty-odd years ago and Rock didn't always come out best. In fact, he used to delight in telling the tale of one prize rejoinder delivered by Somnolent James, whom he'd once described as "a sleepy eyed lad who looked as though he were built to be a tester in an alarm clock factory."

One afternoon Rockne grew increasingly annoyed by Crowley's inability to follow his assignment on one particular play. But Jim didn't grumble at "the Swede" as they called their Norwegian-born coach. He took the Rockne tongue lashing without complaint until Rock let go with a final burst of asperity.

"Can you name anyone," he taunted, "who's dumber than a dumb Irishman?"

Sleepy Jim just couldn't resist. "Yes, coach," he said sweetly. "A smart Swede." Rockne loved it.

The Crowley wit never was cruel but it often was barbed. After one particular close and tough game, Sleepy Jim found himself strolling off the field with the referee who hadn't given Notre Dame the better of things.

"You were lucky to win today," growled the official.

"Yes, Cyclops," snapped Somnolent James. "Judging by the way you refereed today, we certainly were lucky to win."

On rare occasions he was not above tossing a flippant bon mot or two at the opposition. In the Rose Bowl game Solomon, the Stanford safety man, fumbled one of Elmer Layden's tremendous booming punts and Ed Huntsinger, scooping up the loose ball, converted it into a touchdown.

The towheaded Solomon was beside himself with grief. In furious frustration he pounded the turf with his fists. "What a dope I am!" he moaned. "What a butterfingered lunkhead! What a stupid slob!" And he was just warming up. He grew more and more violent in his self-condemnation. Then Sleepy Jim eased alongside.

"Why not shut up, Solomon?" he said with tender consideration. "No one's disputing you."

Once one of the priests at Notre Dame caught Crowley off limits at South Bend, an approximate three miles from the school.

"Crowley," he said sternly, "I'll give you exactly three minutes to get back on the campus."

Sleepy Jim gazed soulfully down the road and sadly shook his head. "I don't think I can make it, Father," he said. "Not against this wind."

He's been a gay, quick-witted operative all his life. When he first became Commissioner of the All-America Conference his old Four Horseman buddy, Elmer Layden, was serving in a similar capacity for the National Football League. Layden had derided the idea of the new circuit in its then unformed, blueprint stage by making the crack: "They haven't even got a football."

Both of the ex-Horsemen attended a banquet in Chicago soon afterward. Layden was on the dais but Crowley's chair was vacant. When the hall was full, however, Sleepy Jim made a dramatic entrance, a football under each arm.

"Look, Elmer," he quipped. "We've finally got a football—two of them in fact."

Somnolent James is returning to a more familiar post now, back in harness as a coach. The Chicago Rockets couldn't have gotten a better man for what appears to be the toughest uphill job in football. Good luck, Jim.

The King Is Dead

November 5

The King is dead and he leaves no successor. Man o' War, the mightiest thoroughbred the turf has known, was affectionately laid to rest yesterday beneath the blue grass pastureland where he romped so majestically during his declining years. It was a heart attack which caused the death of Big Red. At least that's what the veterinarians said. But it could have been more than that. It could have been a broken heart, too.

Will Harbut had died a few weeks before and Man o' War loved his devoted Negro groom in one of those strange attachments that animals sometimes get for humans. Old Will would coax and cajole and spoil and baby Big Red. Pridefully he'd reel off the long string of turf accomplishments turned in by his brilliant charge while the beautiful chestnut seemingly would listen and nod knowingly as Old Will described him as "de mostest horse." Then Harbut would plead, "Stand still, Red." And Red would stand still.

Their relationship had been a wonderful one down through the years and the big stallion missed him sorely when his faithful companion took ill. Nor did he last long after Harbut died. Perhaps the most touching tribute paid Old Will was contained in the obituary notice printed by The Blood Horse, the official publication of the thoroughbred industry. It contained this final, breathtaking sentence: Among his survivors are his wife, six sons, three daughters and Man o' War."

According to the theologians, there is no afterlife for animals. But heaven would never be heaven for Old Will unless he had his beloved Man o' War at his side. Then he'd be able to turn to the open-mouthed celestial sightseers and rattle off the old story, ". . . and War Admiral looked over at Pompoon and he said, 'Pompoon, my daddy broke John P. Grier's heart.' . . . Stand still, Red. . . . He broke all the records and he broke down all the horses. So there wasn't nothin' for him to do but retire. He's got everything a horse ought to have and he's got it where a horse ought to have it. He's just de mostest horse. . . . Stand still, Red."

There never was quite as remarkable a steed as Man o' War. Will Harbut wasn't at all extravagant in his claim that this was the greatest of them all. Big Red was everything he said he was and more. No horse ever stirred the emotions or gripped the imaginations of the public the way he did. He was the symbol of racing perfection. He set records almost every time he started and such was his supremacy that he thrice was held at the astronomical odds of 1-to-100, including the classic Belmont Stakes, supposedly the most severe 3-year-old test of them all.

He lost only once in his brief racing career. Every schoolboy knows by now that he was upset by Upset as a juvenile. An inexperienced starter sent the field away when Big Red was prancing sideways and Johnny Loftus never did get him unwound. He closed like a thunderbolt but finished a half length back.

Only once was he really pressed—if you want to disregard that Upset misadventure, as you should—and that was against the lightly weighted John P. Grier in the Dwyer Stakes at Aqueduct. The big golden horse, whose coat seemed to shed fire in the sunlight, carried 126 pounds to his rival's 108. They broke together and they raced together, stride for stride, bobbing head alongside of bobbing head while screaming thousands watched amid mounting excitment.

At every furlong pole there was a gasp of incredulity. At every furlong pole Man o' War was setting a new record. And still he could not shake loose from John P. Grier. Into the homestretch they roared together and, suddenly, the dark head surged out in front of the one with the rich, reddish glow. Man o' War had met his master at long last. Or had he? Will Harbut was right. The "mostest" horse let go with a mighty blast to win by a length and a half. They said then that Big Red had broken the heart of the gallant and swift John P. Grier because the beaten colt never was as good again.

When Samuel D. Riddle retired Big Red to stud after his 3-year-old campaign and after he'd set a then world money-winning record of almost a quarter of a million dollars, Man o' War brought his glamour with him. Not only did he never lose one iota of it but he even gained more as his fame as a stallion soared to unbelievable heights. At any rate, his home at Faraway Farms just outside Lexington became a "must" for every visitor to Kentucky's Blue Grass country.

It was a visit that had to be unforgettable. Perhaps it seems a trifle silly and naïve for anyone to admit that he actually approached the stall of Man o' War with feelings of awe and humility. But that was the way this observer reacted. It was a genuine thrill to see him, that regal head lifted imperiously and that powerfully built body shimmering aristocratically in the sunlight.

The rays of the sun darted through the window over his stall and seemed to fondle the rich, red mane on his neck. He was big, too, at 16.2 hands, a heroic figure of a horse. Ah, Big Red. The nickname was obvious. And he was truly a king in his royal court, condescending to glance with soft brown eyes on the 2,000,000 hero worshippers who made, at least, a mental obeisance to his equine majesty.

If Man o' War appeared to sense that he was something above the common plane, the royal chamberlain, Will Harbut, was positive of it. If Old Will ever had a complaint, though, it was this—and sadly he said it—"He was born in Kentucky, he lives in Kentucky and he'll die in Kentucky." He'd sigh and add,

"But he never raced in Kentucky." To a hardboot from the Blue Grass that was unforgivable.

And now Big Red is gone. It creates almost a feeling of personal loss, incomprehensible but true. However, Man o' War was no ordinary horse. His like may never be seen again.

Arthur Daley asked for only one autographed baseball in his career and got it—from Babe Ruth. The following three columns make up a series written in tribute to the Babe.

1948

Last Out for the Babe

August 17

It had to come sometime, of course. But Babe Ruth seemingly had acquired a cloak of immortality as if he were a demigod who had sprung from Zeus. He was not an ordinary mortal even in life. Now in death he will assume still more grandiose proportions as an almost legendary figure. The Babe was a truly fabulous man, the best beloved and the best known person of our times, greater even than the sport which spawned him.

Here are two striking and most illustrative incidents. One Sunday morning last March the Babe was kneeling in church when a prim, bonneted old lady timidly tapped him on the shoulder. "Mr. Ruth," she whispered, "I just want you to know that I pray for you every day." Obviously she had never seen a baseball game in her life. Yet her imagination had been so captivated by the Bambino that she remembered him in her prayers. And that undoubtedly was multiplied by hundreds of thousands throughout the country.

The other incident happened during those grim days at Guadalcanal in the early stages of the Pacific war. The Americans and the Japanese had come to grips at long last in their fight to a finish. Among other things they exchanged were insults on hastily lettered placards. Important personages on each enemy side were vilified until our boys reached their insult supreme. "Emperor Hirohito is a stinker," the card said—except the last word was considerably stronger. Thereupon the Japs countered with their insult supreme. Their retaliatory card said: "Babe Ruth is a stinker."

Their choice is illuminating. It could have been Roosevelt or MacArthur. But the Nipponese mind seemed to sense that the Babe was a greater figure to Americans than either of them. Of course, many of the Japanese had seen the hulking figure of this baseball god on his trip to Japan and they, too, had idolized him just as he had been idolized in the United States.

The hold that Ruth had on the public never has been matched by anyone in sport or out of it. He commanded it by just being himself, the most natural and unaffected man in this wide world. He lived a full and lusty life. He did incredible things, some of which have seen print and some of which never will. In a way it is unfortunate that the entire story never could be told, because it would make the Babe a still more unbelievable person than he actually was.

The King of Swat was much more than a magnificent baseball player. Experts will argue themselves blue in the face as to whether Ruth or Ty Cobb was the greater performer. It doesn't particularly matter. The Babe was in a class by himself when it came to color. He teemed with it, vibrated with it and exuded it from every pore. He could strike out and excite a crowd infinitely more than Cobb hitting a grand slam home run with two out in the ninth.

As a left-handed pitcher at the beginning of his career he was one of the very best and his record for consecutive scoreless innings in the world series still stands. As an outfielder he also was one of the very best, a beautiful thrower and a more than adequate ball hawk. As a batter he was superb. That was his forte. If he had concentrated on singles instead of homers, he would have left hitting marks which never would have been approached. But his fame was to come as a distance slugger and he scorned the trifling single as beneath his dignity.

There can be no questioning the fact that he saved baseball when that structure was rocked to its very foundation by the Black Sox scandal of 1919. And along came Ruth with the distraction of his thunderous bat. The fans thronged to see him and the scandal was brushed aside. He hit more home runs and longer home runs than any man had ever fashioned before. He even contributed a new adjective to the English language. Titanic hits invariably would be described as being of "Ruthian" proportions.

Everything about the man was "Ruthian." His appetites were prodigious. His physique was prodigious. His feats both on and off the field were prodigious. He made money on a massive scale and he spent it as fast or even faster than he made it. One year he technically was rooming with Ping Bodie, although Ping picturesquely described it as rooming "with Babe Ruth's suitcase." The Babe had parked himself in a $100-a-day suite in another hotel and growled in defense of that procedure: "So what? a guy's gotta entertain!"

Even his famous stomach ache at the end of the 1925 spring training was of truly Ruthian proportions. After consuming enough hot dogs and soda pop to have killed a horse, he was rushed from the train to the hospital as a shocked nation waited anxiously for every bulletin as to his condition. Only the tremendous vitality of that tremendous body enabled him to fight off his illness.

His failures also were cut from the heroic mold, such as his .118 batting average in the 1922 world series and his disastrous season of 1925 when he hit only .290 and lost his rebellion against the authority of Manager Miller Huggins. But his failures were so few that only his glorious successes will be remembered. Even the record book, ordinarily dull and statistical, takes on a certain enchantment and glamour where it lists the fifty-four marks that the mighty Bambino left behind him.

His most extraordinary contribution to the game, however, rests in the fact that he alone changed its complexion and contour. It had been a game of "inside baseball," a tightly played contest for single runs—stolen bases, squeeze plays, placement hitting. But the booming bat of the Babe demonstrated that runs could be gathered like bananas—in bunches. He soon had everyone swinging from his heels, shooting for the fences and trying to follow his lead.

Not only did he transform its strategical concepts, but he revitalized it in the box office, making new fans in untold numbers. He raised the general salary scale of all major leaguers until rookies now get higher wages than stars received before he brought his boisterous bat and boisterous personality on the scene.

Babe Ruth's records may all be broken some day, but the imprint he left on the game can never be erased. He was baseball's greatest figure and the sport never will see his like again.

Down Memory Lane With the Babe

August 18

Writing about Babe Ruth is akin to trying to paint a landscape on a postage stamp. The man was so vast, so complex and so totally incredible that he makes mere words so puny and insufficient. They say that truth is stranger than fiction. So was Ruth. No Hollywood scenarist would dare borrow fragments of the Babe's life for use in a plot. They would seem much too fantastic for belief.

Take, for instance, his famous home run off Charlie Root in the 1932 world series. The grinning Bambino impudently pointed to the very spot in the bleachers where he intended to hit the ball—and then did it. Afterward someone mentioned to him that it had been a most rash act. "Suppose you had failed?" he was asked. "Gosh," boomed the Babe, a startled look on his face. "I never thought of that." To him the impossible always was within reach.

Less publicized than that breathtaking episode but practically a companion piece to it was a feat he performed in Chicago. The Yanks were locked in a seemingly unbreakable 1-to-1 tie with the White Sox and Mark Roth, the traveling secretary, was beginning to sweat blood. Train time was rapidly approaching

Babe Ruth—"the sport will never see his like again."

and the station master had promised to delay the train only for a comparatively short period of time. The game dragged through the twelfth inning and into the thirteenth with Roth squirming in feverish anxiety.

Just as the fourteen inning began, the Babe spotted the haggard secretary. "Whatsa matter, Mark," he bellowed, "you sick?"

"Yes," moaned Mark, "if you bums don't finish this game soon, we'll blow the train."

"Why didn't you say so sooner?" boomed the Babe. "I'll get us outa here."

Need it be said that he won the game with a homer in the fourteenth? And the Yanks caught the train.

There was another time when Ford Frick, then a baseball writer but now the president of the National League, brought his aged father to see his first baseball game, an exhibition fray in Fort Wayne. Late in the contest the Babe wandered over to where the elder Frick was sitting. "Getting tired, pop?" he roared. "Tell you what I'll do. See those railroad tracks over there?"

Mr. Frick gazed at a maze of tracks beyond the center-field fence some 400 feet away and nodded. "Pop," said the Babe, "I'm gonna hit one onto those tracks."

He did, of course. But he also destroyed the faith of Mr. Frick in the game of baseball. He figured there must be something fundamentally wrong about a sport which permitted its players to call the turn with such uncanny accuracy.

Everything about the man was on the incredulous side. He once hit a ball with such velocity that it went screaming through the pitcher's legs and went sailing serenely over the head of the *center fielder*. Imagine that, if you can. He once hit a ball so high that Jimmy Dykes, circling frantically underneath, couldn't catch it as the grinning Babe chugged into second with the shortest—but highest—double on record.

"Nice work, James," said the mild Connie Mack. "If that ball ever had landed on your skull, it would have killed you."

Incidentally, Ruth's one great fear was that he would kill a rival player with one of those projectile shots off his bat.

Somehow or other, though, not many fans realize what a remarkable pitcher the Babe had been earlier in his career and some of the unbelievable things about this remarkable child of nature apply with equal force to his feats on the mound. Twice he won twenty-three games and he holds the world series record of $29\frac{2}{3}$ scoreless innings. Ironically enough, the man he nudged out of the mark was the great Christy Mathewson.

Among the things never seen in print about the Bambino is one incident that old-timers still discuss with awe. When Ruth was a kid pitcher for Baltimore, he spent one entire night industriously burning the candle at both ends. Sleepless and a trifle shaky, he reported to the ball park and was hurried under a cold shower. Thereupon he spun himself a gaudy two-hitter and won his own game, 1-0, with a home run in the ninth. The fictional Frank Merriwell wasn't worthy to have carried the Babe's bat.

It was wise Ed Barrow, then manager of the Red Sox, who converted him from a pitcher—where he might have ranked with Matty, Walter Johnson, and the other hurling immortals—to an outfielder. Symbolically enough, Barrow made this historic change on his birthday, May 10, 1918. The report of that game carried a line which seemed both inconsequential and unimportant then but which was to have monumental significance later on.

With painful simplicity the sentence read: "Babe Ruth, the pitcher, played in the outfield for the Sox, but went hitless."

He wasn't to go hitless very often thereafter. Except when he faced Hub Pruett, a left-handed pitcher with a jug-handle curve and a sharp-breaking fadeaway. For some reason that no one ever has been able to explain, Ruth least of all, the left-hander had the Indian sign on the Babe. Eighteen times Pruett faced the Babe one season and sixteen times he struck him out. During that entire campaign Pruett threw the Bambino only one fast ball. Oh, yes. Ruth hit it out of the park.

When Eddie Rommel, now an American League umpire, was tantalizing the Babe to death with his annoying knuckle-ball, the big fellow kept getting madder and madder with each missed swing. In one turn at bat Ruth almost broke his back swinging at the first two knucklers. Then as Rommel wound up, the Sultan of Swat suddenly shortened his grip and punched at the ball with a choked-up technique. Believe it or not, he sent it sailing into the stands for a homer. No other ball player ever could do that.

Memories of this baseball Superman are so profuse that they fairly flood the brain. Books have been written about him and even they hardly could do him justice. As he himself remarked sadly and remorsefully just before his death, "I guess I should have written two books of my life, one for the adults and another for the kids."

Still More on the Babe

August 19

No matter how hard a fellow tries to get away momentarily from the subject of Babe Ruth, he soon finds that it is impossible. At the Giant-Braves ball game yesterday the players discussed nothing except the Babe. In the press box it was the same. And that amazing stream of humanity which swept past his bier in the Yankee Stadium lent added evidence of the unshakeable grip that the King of Clout held in the imaginations and affections of his adoring public.

"Gosh," said Johnny Mize, a note of awe and reverence in his voice. "When I kept getting closer and closer to the Babe's home run record last year, I kept getting more and more nasty letters. 'Who do you think you are, you bum?' they'd ask, 'trying to break Ruth's record?' Some of them were downright profane in their indignation. They just scorched the hide off me. No one ever wrote to wish me luck. They all called me names. Maybe they were right, though." He sighed. "I guess it would be sacrilege to hit more homers than the Babe."

Over on the other bench, the Braves were talking about him in hushed tones. Big Frank McCormick, a New York native, actually had seen the Bambino play, which was more than his teammates could say. "When I was a kid," he said softly, "I went to the Stadium every chance I could get just to watch the Babe in action." The other Boston players gazed on him with renewed respect. Here was a man who actually had seen an idol in the flesh.

They talked endlessly of his prodigious slugging feats and it was odd in a way that not one of them ever thought to mention his superb performances as a pitcher. Yet even the Babe himself was wont to select one of his hurling achievements as one of the big thrills of a career which must have supplied thrills by the bushel basket. That moment came after he had filled the bases with none out against the feared Detroit Tigers, the most dangerous hitting team in the entire league.

And the next three batters were Ty Cobb, Wahoo Sam Crawford and Bobby Veach, three of the very best in the game. If this had been fiction, Frank Merriwell would have fanned the entire side and readers would rightly have sneered at so fantastic an improbability. But that's precisely what Ruth did. He struck out Cobb. He struck out Crawford and he struck out Veach. Bingo! It was more of a sensation in that era than Carl Hubbell's later-day feat of fanning Ruth, Gehrig, Simmons, Foxx and Cronin in succession.

It was as a pitcher also that the Babe gained the dubious distinction of pulling an egregious blunder of mistaken identity. In a clubhouse meeting before he was to take the mound against the Cubs in the 1918 world series, Manager Ed Barrow went over all the Chicago hitters with him.

"Watch out particularly for Leslie Mann, Babe," he said. "He's a dangerous right-hand hitter in the clutch and I want you to be careful with him. In fact, it won't do any harm to dust him off a bit. He takes a heavy toe hold at the plate."

The first batter he faced was a left-handed hitter who crowded the plate. The Babe insouciantly decided to back him away by throwing at his head. He accidentally plunked him in the middle of the forehead.

When the inning ended Ruth strode proudly into the dugout and remarked to Barrow, "I guess I took care of that Mann guy for you."

Barrow laughted so heartily he almost fell off the bench.

"Babe," he chuckled, "you wouldn't know General Grant if he walked up there with a bat."

It seems that Ruth had hit Max Flack instead of Leslie Mann.

Although the Home Run King was to receive a salary of $80,000 a season, he loved the game so intensely that he'd gladly have played for nothing, if that had been necessary. When he first entered organized baseball with the Baltimore Orioles, Jack Dunn offered him a salary of $600 for the season.

Ruth's jaw dropped and a look of incredulity leaped into his eyes.

"Do you mean," he stammered, "that you're gonna *pay* me to play ball?" Payment for doing something he loved was entirely beyond the comprehension of this rawboned youth.

He smartened up, of course. When he held out for the $80,-000 in the depression year of 1930, his sportswriting friends advised him to take it easy because, after all, he'd be making more money than the President of the United States, Herbert Hoover.

"What's Hoover got to do with it?" he growled and then thoughtfully added, "Besides, I had a better year than he did anyway." He was right as rain on that one.

The Babe could never be repaid in money for his glorious contributions to the sport. If he has left a monument behind him, it's the place where he lay in state yesterday, the trace of a thin and seemingly appreciative smile on his tanned face. That place is the Yankee Stadium, the "House That Ruth Built."

The time has come now, it appears in this corner, to make it official. The House That Ruth Built should bear his name, Babe Ruth Stadium. That would be the final and supreme gesture, the acknowledgement of the debt that the Yankees owe to the Babe. Before he came along the Yankees were a run-of-the-mill team in our town, a baseball stepchild to the favorite son, the Giants.

His tremendous drawing power as an attraction, however, provoked the jealous John McGraw into forcing the Yanks out of the Polo Grounds. The Stadium was the result and the Yankee dynasty was born. Ruth fathered it and his paternalistic pride in it never ceased. All sorts of wild-eyed suggestions have been pouring in as a means of paying tribute to the Babe. The simplest, the easiest and the one he'd prefer above all others would be to change the name to Babe Ruth Stadium.

How about it, Messrs. Topping and Webb?

1949

Honoring the Old Arbitrator

August 31

Umpires are human, contrary to popular belief. Most of them also are very nice guys. But there is none nicer than Bill Klem, the self-styled Old Arbitrator, who served as a National League umpire for thirty-six years and then acted as Chief of Staff—he made up the title himself—for the senior circuit's Boys in Blue for the next eight years. This lovable old tyrant is being brought up from his Florida retreat on Friday to the Polo Grounds, where the New York Chapter of the Baseball Writers Association will pay him honor at special ceremonies before the Giant–Dodger game.

The typewriter pounders always have been tremendously fond of Sir William. It isn't only because he is the best umpire who ever lived. They rub shoulders with the great much too constantly and casually. Greatness alone never impressed any of them. They love the old fellow because—well, it's hard to say. He has the class of a thoroughbred, that indefinable something that lifts him above the rest. Most of all, perhaps, they admire him because of his sincerity.

Although the Old Arbitrator is a God-fearing man who practices his religion faithfully, he comes close to being a backslider on occasions. "Baseball is more than a game with me," he once thundered, "it's a religon." He might have added in his shiny-eyed zeal that Klem is its high priest. He continuously preaches its gospel. "Baseball is the greatest thing that ever happened to this country," he boomed in his foghorn voice on still another occasion. Old Bill is an ardent patriot, too. He wasn't born on Washington's Birthday for nothing.

The diamond game owes Klem a debt it never will be able to repay. The foundation stone of our national pastime is its umpires. And the foundation stone on which that foundation stone rests is William J. Klem. He brought a dignity to the job that it never had had before. He brought it respect and authority. He brought it a certain element of infallibility. "I never missed one in my life," he roared. And meant it.

Take this example. The Giants were playing the Cubs early in the Klem career. Part of the scoreboard was in fair territory, part of it in foul. A line was painted to designate which was which. But it stopped at the bottom of the scoreboard, leaped across it and then continued upward from the top. As luck would have it, a Giant drive caromed off the scoreboard at almost the precise spot where the line should have been but wasn't. It was a tough decision but Klem never hesitated.

"Foul ball!" he intoned, giving it emphasis with a majestic sweep of his hand. John McGraw shot out of the dugout, raging and storming. The Giants were apoplectic in their wrath. Only Klem remained calm, unshakeable as usual.

The next day the shamefaced park superintendent approached the Old Arbitrator. "Bill," he said, almost apologetically, "McGraw demanded that I examine the scoreboard to see where that hit landed. I found the dent where the ball struck. Would you believe it? It was foul by only three inches."

"Naturally," said Bill, a quiet gleam of satisfaction in his eyes. "I never missed one in my life." Thus did the legend of his infallibility begin.

No more ruthless antagonist did he ever have on the playing field than the hot-tempered McGraw. In one of the first games he ever worked in the National League he called one against the Giants, and by way of making things worse, thumbed the most notorious umpire-baiter of them all out of the game. "I'll have your job for this," threatened the Little Napoleon.

"Mister McGraw," said Klem quietly, "if it's possible for you to take my job away from me, I don't want it."

Oddly enough, though, these two were firm friends away from the diamond, frequently dining together. In a way, they formed a Mutual Admiration Society.

"McGraw was the greatest manager of them all," Klem still will tell you.

"If there ever was a good umpire," McGraw grudgingly admitted, "it was Klem."

Until the Old Arbitrator came along, umpires were in the habit of dressing at their hotels. But Klem reasoned that it was unfair and hazardous to expect a Man in Blue to mingle with the departing crowd, a conspicuous figure in his working clothes. He changed at the ball park, even though he frequently had to use the grounds-keeper's shed with a bucket of water instead of a shower. So insistent was he on dressing rooms for umpires that every ball park in the country eventually built them quarters of their own.

Once he viewed the architect's plans for remodeling a ball park. "Where are you putting the umpires?" relentlessly demanded Klem. "Here," pointed out the architect, showing him a room next to the home team.

"I don't want it there," roared the Foghorn. "I don't want to be listening to clubhouse discussions through the walls. I want our room apart. I want it behind home plate."

"But that would be too expensive," protested the architect.

"I don't care," shouted Klem. "I insist that it be placed behind home plate." And he stalked majestically away. That's just where they put it, too.

If you ever bothered to notice it, you would observe that American League umpires stand directly in back of the catcher while National Leaguers are off line, crouching over the shoulder of the catcher, the side depending on whether the batter swings right or left. Klem discovered this by accident in order to avoid having his view blocked by huge receivers. It now is part and parcel of National League umpiring technique, the better technique in the opinion of most experts.

The Old Arbitrator was so good that he umpired in eighteen —count'em—world series, a number that never has been even approached by anyone else. He didn't quit his active role until he was approaching 70 and now, a serene 75 years of age, he's the Chief of Staff for the National League arbiters. He's the lad the Baseball Writers will induct as an honorary member of the chapter on Friday. There is no one they like and admire more.

The Advantages of Playing Hookey

September 21

This is a story without a moral. Except for the ending it could be held up to the youth of America as a horrible example. So allergic was Pancho Gonzales to school and so deep-seated was his love for tennis that he spent most of his boyhood ducking truant officers who soon learned that the one place to catch the culprit was on the tennis courts. As a penalty for his misspent youth Gonzales should have been destined to a life of poverty and regret. Instead, he is likely to make between $60,000 and $150,000 within the next few months at the ripe, old age of 21. That ain't the way Horatio Alger would have written the yarn.

The colorful California phenomenon yesterday signed a professional contract with the Jack Kramer–Bobby Riggs interests and will make his play-for-pay debut against Kramer at Madison Square Garden on Oct. 25. That match and the hundred or so which will follow should smash to smithereens the record gross of $400,000 that the Kramer–Riggs tour accumulated in five of the six continents. Perhaps the extremely youthful Gonzales hasn't the mechanical proficiency and skill of a Riggs. But he so teems with color—an attribute Bobby never had—that the turnstiles will spin a merrier tune than ever before.

As a success story the tale of the explosive-hitting Pancho is quite without parallel. He has violated all precedent. The ex-amateurs who blazed the trail ahead of him all had toiled long years to reach stardom before they succumbed to the lure of the dollar. Look 'em over—Bill Tilden, Vinnie Richards, Ellsworth Vines, Fred Perry, Don Budge, Riggs, and Kramer. But Gonzales shot up from nowhere.

The rest of them were destined for top rank from the very start and had a tennis racquet as an early nursery toy. The dynamic Pancho never tried the game until he was 13, played little (except hookey) until he was 17 and then enlisted in the Navy where he at least was free from those pesky truant officers. Three days after his discharge he was back playing tennis, bigger, stronger, and better than ever. Eliminated in an early round by Gardnar Mulloy at the National championships in 1947 he later went on to vanquish in the almost equally rugged Pacific Southwest championships such undisputed stars as Jaroslav Drobny, Bob Falkenburg, and Frankie Parker on successive days before Ted Schroeder polished him off in the final.

But the then 19-year-old kid was coming along like a house afire. The tennis fathers ranked him seventeenth, a rather lofty rating for so inexperienced a youngster. However, he was to astonish them even more the next year. The rankest of outsiders in preliminary discussions, he went through the National championships in quite meteoric fashion to win it, much to the delight of the gallery which had unashamedly adopted him as its very own.

The professional promoters had begun to cast covetous glances in his direction because here was the natural they had been seeking for so long. So what does the unpredictable Pancho do? He starts to ruin the act. He let his normal weight of 182 balloon up over 202 and tennis is one sport where fat folks just don't belong. Gonzales lost at Wimbledon to Geoff Brown, a run-of-the-mill Australian. He returned to the states and lost more than he won. When the diabetic Billy Talbert took a shot of insulin and blasted Pancho off the Southampton courts to retrieve a match that was seemingly lost, everyone figured Pancho was the proverbial flash in the pan.

The experts calculated that even if the colorful Californian reached the final of the nationals—and not a one of them expected that to be possible—he'd be a sitting duck for Schroeder, the best amateur in the world. No one was more glum and disconsolate at that prospect than Riggs, the chief talent scout for the professionals. Bobby already had approached Ted on his availability and had been given a most emphatic no. But Pancho, like Barkis, was willin'.

The recipe for rabbit pie begins thusly: First, catch the rabbit. So Gonzales caught the rabbit by reaching the final against Schroeder. But the biggest part of the pie making still had to come. With blistering ferocity they tore at each other in the first set and established a tournament record before Schroeder won it, 18-16.

Any top-flight tennis player will tell you that there is nothing quite as discouraging or as heartbreaking as losing a marathon set. The imagination begins to run wild at recollections of a score of missed opportunities. It's a psychological blow from which few recover. By way of compounding the injury, Schroeder also took the second set, 6-2.

Pancho probably never lingered in school long enough to have remembered the stirring words of John Paul Jones, "I have not yet begun to fight." Instinctively, though, he had the idea. He wrested away the third set, 6-1, and the fourth, 6-2. Unbelievingly, he also took the last one, 6-4. A flash in the pan, eh? He'd showed 'em.

"I've often wondered how much I weighed at the end of that match," mused Pancho yesterday. "I was 182 when I started and my tennis shorts fitted me snugly. But by the end of the third set, I had to put pins in them to keep them from falling down. By the last set I was using a chain to hold them up. Did I lose weight!"

That happened, of course, before the devaluation of the pound and poundage lost was absolute. But his stirring victory will enable him to pick up many a dollar, a pound, a franc, a lira, and whatnot in the future. Despite his two-time victories in the nationals, Pancho is still a relative novice. He will learn from Kramer just as big Jack learned from little Riggs. Once he's brought his game to the rounded peak of the big blond there is no reason why their series can't be continued indefinitely.

Professional tennis never quite had any pairing such as this one. Usually it's a fading pro star pitted against a fully developed amateur. This time it is a pro star who still hasn't reached his peak against an undeveloped amateur whose potentialities are enormous. And both are tremendous hitters, as well. If more kids use truancy as a sure-fire road to riches, Pancho should be blamed for it. He has set a very bad example.

1950

The Eighth Wonder of the Age

February 21

The chances are that few readers of yesterday's sports pages even noticed the headline and fewer still caught its significance. It read: "World Cue Title Is Kept by Hoppe." The story from Chicago related in quite prosaic fashion that Willie Hoppe had retained his three-cushion billiards championship. After all, the cue game hardly ranks as a major sport and the winner would not rate more than passing attention except for the fact that he is Willie Hoppe. That makes it something special because the graying Boy Wonder of yesteryear is something special. He must be at least the eighth wonder of the age.

When this most remarkable man won his first championship the world of sport was populated by many other athletic demigods. Ty Cobb was then a rookie outfielder on the Detroit Tigers; Jim Jeffries had just retired as heavyweight king; Frank Gotch was the top wrestler; Jim Thorpe had not yet traveled football's glory road; Alex Smith and Jerry Travers were the rulers of the golf domain and Johnny Hayes was about to win his memorable Olympic marathon championship from Dorando.

Not only have all of them faded from sight but countless sports generations following them have come and gone. Yet

Hoppe has ruled his domain from 1906 until today, an unbelievable stretch of forty-four years. There were undoubtedly a few brief periods when he was temporarily without a title but they were so brief that his consistency takes on added luster. The world of sports has never seen his equal and he alone has been able to thumb his nose at the Old Gentleman with the Scythe.

Hoppe had been playing billiards for an even dozen years when he brashly challenged the almost legendary Maurice Vignaux of France, the Lion of Billiards, for his 18.1 balkline championship. The 18-year-old Willie astonished the experts by dethroning him and he's been astonishing the experts ever since. In view of the fact that the one-time Boy Wonder is now 62 years of age, it almost takes your breath away to realize that he's been at it for fifty-six years, or since he was a toddler of 6.

Back in the distant past Hoppe's father owned a hotel in Cornwall-on-Hudson and the 6-year-old boy climbed on boxes or chairs in order to stroke cue balls across the green baize surface of the pool table located there. At the still tender age of 9 he gave an exhibition of his skill before a group of Princeton University professors. It wasn't his skill which flabbergasted them as much as the fact that he seemed to have an uncanny, superhuman ability to measure angles with mathematical precision. In other words he could solve billiard problems at a glance.

To those dilettantes who occasionally pick up a billiard cue and stroke a ball it might appear that there is nothing particularly arduous about the sport. But when it becomes a life profession, it's an awful lot different. The nerve strain of championship play is just as exhausting as a golf championship and crack golfers such as Byron Nelson have quit rather than subject themselves to it. Like golf, one faulty stroke can be fatal because it opens up the table to the other fellow.

So exacting a taskmaster is billiards and so ceaseless is the search for perfection that Hoppe has been practicing five hours a day for more than half a century. Can any other competitor in any other sport even approximate that? The physical strain can't quite match the mental strain but it is there none the less. Willie has walked a total something like 25,000 miles around the baize tables, or the equivalent of the circumference of the earth.

It has not been an easy life, especially since he has been a one-man road company living out of suitcases. But it has been a singularly rewarding one. The chances are that Willie has earned $25,000 a year since he reached maturity. Only twice has his income been seriously cut, once during the depression and again during the war, when he devoted most of his energies to entertaining the troops.

The one-time Boy Wonder discovered early that the soldiers had little interest in three-cushions or balkline play but were rabid about pocket billiards, the fancy name for pool. A late-comer to one of his exhibitions, ignorant of Willie's identity, muscled his way alongside of the table and arranged the balls.

"Let's see you make that," he challenged.

Wilile studied the layout. "That shot is impossible," he said quietly.

"You ain't so hot, bud," snapped the youth, scornfully. "Many a time I seen Willie Hoppe make that shot. Maybe you oughter take lessons from him."

The graying Boy Wonder hasn't been so embarrassed since he was sent to a little Pennsylvania town as a replacement for the ailing Welker Cochran.

"You Cochran?" asked the sharp-visaged poolroom owner.

"I'm Willie Hoppe," explained the gracious little fellow. "I'm substituting for Cochran."

"Willie Hoppe, eh?" snorted eagle-beak. "I never heard of you. I hope you kin give our local boy a battle. He's a purty slick article with a cue."

Hoppe slaughtered the local pride, of course.

One of the most amazing things about this amazing man is that he still is an eager beaver for winning. He has held every championship at one time or another and the flame still burns just as fiercely now as it did in 1906. That's the most implausible feature of his reign and it marks him as one apart from the ordinary individual. And that's why he is so tough to beat.

At the age of 62 he is vanquishing fellows who weren't even born when he began his extraordinary career. There have been various polls of late on the outstanding athletes of the last half century. In one respect at least none of them can compare with Willie Hoppe. He's still rolling along, better than ever, after the rest of them have long since retired. And the moralists used to tell us that fellows who hang out in poolrooms will come to no good end.

Old Jake Goes Home

November 15

They laid the body of Jake Weber tenderly at rest yesterday in the magnificent $25,000 mausoleum he had built in Woodlawn Cemetery. To Jake it was always his "muzzlem" and he viewed it with a fierce pride. Often he'd visit his beloved "muzzlem" and stare in fascination at the bronze plaque which bore the rather startling words, "In memory of Jake Weber, trainer of American Olympic Track and Field Teams." Then followed the years and sites from 1920 through 1948, six in all. His heart would warm at the sight of it and that heart would glow even more at the American flag above the mausoleum. He loved his country as few men have loved it.

To Jake there was never anything incongruous about his final resting place. "Whatcha do y'self, y'know is done," he'd explain with an airy wave of his hand. Deep was his resentment when no statue was erected in honor of John McGraw. "A great man," he said bitterly. "But they never built a statchoor to him. Right?"

Jake was as lovable a character as ever traveled along the road of sports. But he was distinctly a character. Everyone was his pal and he was a man who never had an enemy in his life. Whenever he became particularly enamored of anyone, he'd invite him to consider one of the vacant crypts in the "muzzlem" as reserved for him. But if the object of his affections joshed Jake about it, Jake would point a stubby finger at him and announce firmly, "Ye're out."

For all of his eccentricities, however, Jake was the best trainer in the country for the better part of his life. This chunky, bow-legged little fellow would always get coy whenever his age was mentioned. No one ever did know exactly how old he was. If you don't mind a personal intrusion, here's a hint. He trained my father as an athlete and that's more than fifty years ago. Jake must have been kneading muscles for sixty years and his age had to be in the vicinity of 80.

Many a time in his prime he could have written his own ticket. But he was a man of intense loyalties. He served at Fordham for three decades and repeatedly spurned offers to go elsewhere. McGraw wanted him to switch to the Giants and Jake refused. Yet the Little Napoleon never faltered in his high regard for Jake's abilities. When McGraw's face swelled with an attack of erysipelas, he sent for Jake and Jake's magic cured him.

He massaged stage and screen actors but left unheeded their pleas to set up shop on his own so that he could minister to all comers. Even the suspicious Paavo Nurmi would let no American hands touch him except those of Jake Weber .

Although Jake's formal education was limited, he had a keen native intelligence. He devised more gadgets, baking machines, and the like than any other man, even though some of them looked to be borrowed from Rube Goldberg.

His trademark during the football season was his flit gun, with which he liberally sprayed the wearied heroes at every time out. Inside the gun was some magic elixir that Jake had concocted, a Fountain of Youth preservative which restored tired muscles to pristine strength.

What was in the gun? No one ever did find out. Nor would Jake tell. He'd just wink ponderously and his body would shake with an explosive chuckle.

"Trade secret, y'know," he'd say and roar laughing.

On one memorable occasion Jake even coached the Fordham football team. Tom Thorp was the regular coach but he had an important refereeing assignment that coincided with a game with Holy Cross. So he turned the team over to Jake.

"The same guys start this game what started last week?" announced the pro tem coach to the thirty-five-man squad. "What guys started?"

Jake gasped. All thirty-five men had raised their hands. He used eleven at a time but it didn't make any difference. Holy Cross won, 60 to 0.

"I quit after that," related Jake with considerable relish. "Right?"

Jake always punctuated all remarks on a crescendo note with the word, "Right?" He was the world's worst public speaker but there never was a Fordham gathering that didn't bring forth the chant, "We want Jake." The harassed toastmaster always had to acquiesce although he knew that there'd be no more speakers that night. Jake was a nonstop talker, so hilariously funny in either his words or his delivery that he had the boys laughing until they cried. He wasn't making an exhibition of himself, either, because his audience truly loved him.

The favorite was the story of the time he wrestled the bull in Madison Square Garden—he actually was a top-flight "rassler" in his youth—and made off with the receipts from the box office ahead of the raiding police.

"This Dutchman promised them athletes he'd pay them," he'd chortle, "and I hid out until I'd paid 'em every cent. Right?"

And now this wonderful, ageless little guy is gone, at rest in his beloved muzzlem with the beloved American flag atop it. It won't be easy to forget him. Right?

1951

Listening to Stengel

December 9

Charles Dillon Stengel, the distinguished nonstop conversationalist, wandered into press headquarters one night during the world series and promptly began a filibuster. There usually is neither beginning nor end to Stengel's discourses. Sometimes there isn't any middle either. He just rambles away, tossing people off the sled at every turn.

Just as a listener has decided that the Ol' Perfessor is talking about his Yankees, he drops a careless hint that this happened when he was managing Toledo. Then he brings in John McGraw or Wilbert Robinson and confusion descends with an enveloping cloak upon the gathering.

By diligent sorting out of Stengel's words and phrases for two months, this bewildered listener thinks he finally has pieced the whole thing together into something resembling coherency. This is done from memory. There's no advantage gained by taking notes. They never make sense afterward. Sometimes they even becloud the issue.

"We wuz in Terre Haute," Casey was saying. This was a striking concession on his part. Although he never identified the "we," he at least said where they were.

Casey Stengel tells all to Arthur Daley.

"Didja ever hear of Ralph Miller," he asked. "He was a real strong guy." So help me, he never mentioned Miller again.

"Let me tell yuh somethin'," he said, musingly. "I coulda been a comedian. A baseball clown, I mean. There are only sixteen major league managers. But there's no ceilin' on comedians. How many have there been? Al Schacht. Nick Altrock. The field is unlimited. I know I coulda been one. I'll tell yuh why."

A broad grin creased his weatherbeaten face. He drew his chair closer to the table.

"Like I said," he resumed, "we wuz in Terra Haute for an exhibition game. I guess it musta been the spring of 1915 when I'd joined the Phillies."

Ahem! The record books show that Stengel became a Phil in September of 1919. So this had to be the spring of 1920. It's really rugged trying to pin this guy down with his facts.

"We were a terrible ball club," he croaked on unconcernedly, "and I decided to have some fun. So I let Lee Meadows in on the plot. I let the rest of the team go out to the ball park and I pay my way into the centerfield bleachers. I'm dressed like a rube. I got on big farmer's boots and blue jeans and a fancy jumper. The Phils are just finishin' practice when I start to work.

"I stand up in the bleachers and I holler—I got a real strong voice—'Bush leaguers!' After I've yelled that long enough and loud enough, the players are beginnin' to look around and notice me.

"So I holler louder: 'You guys is so lousy that we got guys in the stands who can play ball better'n you bums.'

"I kin see that I'm gettin' under Art Fletcher's hide. He's hot headed anyway. 'Ya bum, ya,' I shouts. 'Bush leaguers,' I jeer. 'I kin play better'n any of ya.' I scream.

"Finally Fletcher turns around, blazin' mad. 'If you're so good,' he yells, 'Come on down here and play.'

" 'I ain't got no spikes,' I shout. 'I'll lend you mine,' sez Meadows. At first the cops won't let me outa the bleachers. But I finally make it and I really ham it up good at first base for Terra Haute, makin' catches like this, see?" Stengel contorted himself into grotesque positions in demonstration.

"They ask for my name to put it on the line-up card. 'Ponzi,' I tell 'em. You remember Ponzi the guy in Boston who swindled everyone? Well, I wuz swindlin' the Phillies. Never in all my life did I want to make a hit more than in my first time at bat. I took a clown stance but, brother, I wasn't foolin'. It was embarrassin'. I struck out and I didn't mean to.

"But the next time up I hit a triple and I made such a fancy slide into third that everyone on the team took a closer look at the rube in the clown outfit and realized it was me. But the local yokels didn't know it and they wrote real glowin' stories about the hometown phenom, Ponzi, who had been signed to a big league contract by the Phillies.

"Like I said, I think I coulda been a clown in this business if I'd really put my mind to becoming one. Only sixteen managers, but no limit on clowns. I'm not saying that I have any regrets. I ain't. But I didn't want you birds to think Stengel is just a one-career guy."

Regret it? Heavens to Betsy! By sticking to the more serious side of baseball the amusing and amazing Stengel was able to take a side trip to Texas and Oklahoma on his way back to California after managing the Yankees into their third straight world championship. Know what he stopped to inspect? Some oil wells he owns.

That 56-Game Streak

December 13

Joe DiMaggio confessed at his farewell press conference the other day that the high spot of his career was his fifty-six-game hitting streak in 1941. It almost had to be, because it's a major league record which may never be broken. The Yankee Clipper never was the luckiest of ball players but he is frank to admit that Dame Fortune accompanied him to the plate all during his hit harvest. Then she abruptly gave him the cold shoulder to end it.

The streak began, unostentatiously enough, off Lefty Al Smith of Cleveland on May 15 and it ended on July 17. Ironically enough, Smith was one of the pitchers to stop him, Jim Bagby having been the other. More ironically still, it halted despite two of the hardest hit balls of the entire splurge, a pair of ripping "doubles" down the third-base line that Ken Keltner miraculously converted into outs. Otherwise the streak would have reached close to seventy.

This was a period of mounting excitement and continual crises. There were dramatic moments by the score. There was humor and there was pathos. And there was one heart-warming aftermath that the Jolter never will forget.

The first big crisis, perhaps, came when DiMag needed one hit to break Wee Willie Keeler's longstanding record of forty-four games. The Yanks were playing the Red Sox and Heber Newsome was the Boston pitcher, a circumstance which filled the Clipper with a strange feeling of foreboding. He never had hit Newsome well.

In his first time at bat the Jolter jolted out a tremendous blast. But Stan Spence made a circus catch and DiMaggio's heart sank. He didn't figure to hit Newsome that well again. But he hit him even harder on his next trip to the plate only to have the Red Sox center fielder make a supersensational spear of the drive. The Red Sox center fielder was Joe's little brother Dom.

A wayward thought flitted through the Clipper's mind as he jogged glumly back to the bench.

"It speaks very well for the integrity of the game," he sighed to himself, "but it certainly wasn't diplomatic—especially when Dom is coming to my house for dinner tonight."

Joe wasn't very happy. Two rousing shots off Newsome and two loud outs. It would be impossible, he thought, for him to improve on that off his Nemesis. Clutch performer that he is, though, he next hit one where no outfielder could catch it—a home run into the stands.

The Jolter had a narrow escape against Eldon Auker, the submarine-ball thrower, early in the string. He went hitless into the ninth and was the fourth batter. Someone else had to get on base before he even could get in his licks. Someone else got on base. DiMag rifled the first pitch over third for a double.

There was a close call also against Johnny Babich of the Athletics. The right-hander was determined not to give Joe a decent offering, forcing him to swing at a bad pitch or else accept the penalty of a walk. In this case it was truly a penalty and DiMag was really worried. He walked once and he walked again. Then Babich threw three wide ones. The Clipper automatically glanced at Joe McCarthy on the bench. His eyes widened. His heart skipped a beat.

"Good old Joe McCarthy," he said jubilantly to himself. The

ever-helpful Marse Joe had flashed him the sign to hit away, a violation of the unwritten rule.

Once more it was a bad pitch, high and outside. But the angry DiMag swung anyway, the fat part of his bat reaching for the ball. It exploded as it took off. Babich hadn't even completed his follow-through when the liner whistled between his legs and into the outfield. Joe glanced at him as he scampered to first and then laughed. The color had drained from Babich's face, leaving him a sickly green.

The strangest part of the streak was that Joe always got at least one genuine hit in each game. For instance, he scratched out a safety against the White Sox one day when the ball hit a pebble as Luke Appling reached for it, caroming off Luke's noggin for what had to be scored as a base hit. But Joe later hit a homer to take the curse off the freakish safety.

Not long after the fifty-six-game streak had ended, the Yanks were in Washington. "Wait for me, Joe," called out Lefty Gomez, his roomie, in the clubhouse. The other Yankees dressed quickly and departed while Gomez dawdled. Impatiently DiMaggio waited, his annoyance growing at his slow-poke pal. Finally they reached the hotel. The lobby was deserted.

"I gotta see Johnny Murphy," said Lefty. "Come up with me. I'll only be a minute." The grumbling DiMaggio reluctantly accompanied him.

Lefty threw open a door. "Hiya, Joe," thundered fifty voices. The entire Yankee team, the club officials and the newspaper men were there for a surprise party. They presented to the Clipper a magnificent silver humidor with a big "56" engraved on it as a treasured memento of his hitting streak.

That record, by the way, may outlive Babe Ruth's home-run mark.

1952

The Dutchman Retires

February 28

Honus Wagner hung up his spikes the other day, formally retiring from baseball to take a deserved life of ease on a pension. Actually he had come and gone pretty much as he pleased in his role as Pirate coach. In effect, he already was on a pension, merely going through the motions of coaching whenever he felt like it and rarely deigning to take an out-of-town trip with the ball club. Around the time of his seventy-eighth birthday, however, the famed Flying Dutchman decided to make the break a clean one.

One day in St. Pete a couple of years ago Casey Stengel got to talking about Wagner.

"It's a funny thing about ball players," he mused. "Folks go around picking top players in every position and they say: 'He was great but * * *' Then they'd mention some weakness. However, no one ever could use any 'buts' about old Honus. It had to be, 'He was great. Period.' He had no weaknesses and could do everything superlatively well. I know that John McGraw said the Dutchman was a greater player than Ty Cobb or Babe Ruth. Ed Barrow said the same. Sometimes I wonder if they aren't right."

It really is an extraordinary tribute to the grizzled septuagenarian that he is the acknowledged king among shortstops. There always is dispute as to who belongs at first base, Sisler, Gehrig or Terry. Fans will argue about Lajoie, Collins, Frisch, and Hornsby at second and so on down the line. But Wagner has no rivals and no shortstop is mentioned in the same breath with him.

The experts will rave about Joe Cronin as a hitting shortstop, Phil Rizzuto as a fielder, Travis Jackson as a thrower and so on. But Wagner, eight times the batting champion of the National League, was a better hitter than Cronin. Old-timers will tell you he was a better thrower than Jackson, a better fielder than Rizzuto and, on top of all that, he was the base-stealing champion of the league for five seasons. What is more, he could play any position, being a wide-ranging, rifle-armed outfielder and an adroit first baseman. He lasted twenty-one years in the big leagues and hit more than .300 for seventeen of them, never dropping below that mark until he was more than 40 years old.

The Flying Dutchman was a massive man in his youth, a shade under six feet in height but a solidly packed 200 pounds. He had tremendous shoulders, bowed legs and huge hams of hands that hung to his knees. When he fielded a ball, it was like a steam-shovel operating because he also came up with dirt and pebbles.

Once in his early days he was playing first base. He took off his glove and reached into his back pocket with his left hand for a plug of eating tobacco. The pitcher threw, the batter swung and the shortstop fielded the ball while Honus tugged to get his hand out of his pocket. But that big paw was firmly imprisoned. Wagner caught the throw in his bare right hand and had to have the pocket cut off his uniform in order to free his left one.

However, he was as gentle as he was big. Fred Clarke, his first manager, noticed that Wagner, a rookie, wasn't getting any batting practice and asked why.

"The regulars won't let me hit," said the mildmannered, uncomplaining Wagner.

"Get up there and hit or get off the ball club," roared Clarke.

Those were the cutthroat days when veterans never gave a rookie a break. But when Wagner shouldered his way to the batting cage, they let him hit.

Then came a game against the fabulous Baltimore Orioles, the roughest and toughest crew of them all. Wagner hit a "triple" to right. The Oriole first baseman gave him the hip. Hughie Jennings, the shortstop, made him circle wide around him at second and John McGraw, the bellicose third baseman, tagged him in the teeth with the ball.

"Are you gonna take that from them?" raged Clarke.

A few innings later the Dutchman duplicated that drive. He raced to first like a careening water buffalo and bowled over the first baseman. Jennings saw the glint in his eye and gave him room at second. McGraw tried to block the bag at third and Wagner knocked him almost into the grandstand. He'd learned fast.

"The biggest thrill I ever got," old Honus once told me, "came when a Giant batter hit a home run. As he passed me, I said: 'Nice hit.' He snapped, 'Go to hell.' I liked that. I'd been in the big leagues three years and he was the first player ever to speak to me." Life was indeed rugged in those days.

There is so much more to Honus Wagner, though, than his astonishing feats as a ball player. He was—and is—a delightful storyteller and the most incorrigible liar of them all, a wonderful person in every respect.

About ten years ago a wide-eyed rookie, entranced by the Dutchman's fantastic tales, shook his head in disbelief.

"Mr. Wagner," he said, "I find it hard to believe all your stories."

"At least, sonny," answered the old man gently, "I never told you one you couldn't repeat to your mother."

Three of a Kind

December 12

Samuel Adrian Baugh, the cattle rancher from Texas, will throw his last forward pass for the Redskins in Washington on Sunday. It will be a new National Football League record because Slingin' Sammy automatically sets a new mark every time he slings the ball. The wiry Texan with the whiplash arm was the best passer of them all. This isn't merely an opinion. The record book proves it.

Sammy has thrown more passes than anyone else, has completed more passes, has tossed more touchdown passes, has gained the most yardage (approximately thirteen miles), has the highest over-all efficiency (56.6 per cent) and has the highest one season efficiency, an incredible 70.3 per cent. And he has scads of in-between records as well. Not the least impressive of his marks is the fact that he has served sixteen years, an endurance comparable to Eddie Collins' twenty-five seasons in the big leagues.

Nor is Baugh the only illustrious performer bowing out on Sunday. Frankie Albert, the wizard of the San Franscisco Forty-Niners, also has announced his retirement. So has Bob Waterfield of the Los Angeles Rams, although Waterfield is likely to

Sammy Baugh displays his passing form.

have extra playoff chores of some description before he can formalize it.

These are three great players for the pro league to lose in one fell swoop. In an era of specialists all three proved themselves rounded football players. Baugh proved it perhaps more than either of the others because his amazing career virtually spanned two gridiron generations, the era of the sixty-minute player and the era of free substitutions.

All three have been tremendous punters. Waterfield also has been a superb field goal kicker, a talent the others never had. All three ran well with the ball in younger days while Waterfield was the most adroit and deceptive T-formation quarterback the league ever has had. Replacing all three superstars will be a long, tedious and maybe even impossible operation.

Sammy has played little this year. The indestructible man who had seemed made of whipcord and wire springs discovered that a 38-year-old is prone to injury. He has been sidelined for most of the season.

When George Preston Marshall introduced the Slinger to the Washington press corps in 1937, Baugh didn't even own a cowboy hat. But the Magnificent Marshall was thoughtful enough to outfit his pseudo-cowboy in complete cowboy regalia, including high-heeled boots. The most significant remark the laconic Texan uttered as he squirmed uncomfortably at his first press conference was not even to the point.

"Mah feet hurt," drawled Sammy.

But he was to become so famous that he was earned upwards of $300,000 in salary, endorsements and by-products. What did he do with the money?

"Half went in taxes and half went in Texas," slyly remarked Sammy.

He owns a ranch of more than 5,000 acres and amuses himself by competing in rodeos, a genuine cow-puncher at last. He once won a calf-roping contest in 17 seconds, so proficient has he become at his new trade.

Sammy was even more proficient as a football player. As a tailback in Washington's old single-wing formation, he never had a peer. He could run and he could throw. He also was the best straightaway punter in the league and a fiend at exploiting the quick-kick. He holds the record there, too, a titanic boot of

85 yards. On punting ability alone he could turn a game topsy-turvy.

The oldest and most widely used Baugh story demonstrates the Slinger's uncanny passing ability more vividly than any adjectives. In the first blackboard drill he ever had with Coach Ray Flaherty, a play was outlined.

"And when your receiver reaches this point," indicated Flaherty with a chalk mark, "I want you to hit him in the eye."

"Which eye?" asked Slingin' Sam.

He was virtually that accurate, too. In fact, he was so accurate that he just about revolutionized the sport all by himself. Until the Slingshot came along, passers rarely passed in their own territory. They threw only on what were known as "passing downs" in obvious pattern.

But the first pass Baugh threw against the Chicago Bears in his first play-off game was from his own end zone. This unorthodoxy caught the Bears completely by surprise. A moment after they'd been backed against the goal-line, the 'Skins were free from the trap in midfield. Principally through Baugh's deadly passing Washington upset the Monsters, 28 to 21.

In this game Baugh also met Bronko Nagurski for the first time. The legendary Bronk had broken loose in an open field, rumbling down on slim Sammy, the safety man, like a runaway brewery truck tearing downhill. Sammy spilled him to save a touchdown. A mighty fine tackler and defense man was Sammy.

Slingin' Sam threw a football like a catcher pegging to second base. A flick of the wrist did it. He threw bullets which defied interception and he also could waft an occasional long, gentle pass for telling gains.

Baugh, Waterfield and Albert are all heading toward retirement. But don't let anyone tell you differently, Sammy was the best.

1953

Welcoming Ol' Diz

January 25

Things should be a lot livelier in the Hall of Fame from now on. The brash, impudent and ever-laughing Dizzy Dean has arrived as a full-fledged member and the joint never will be the same again.

Ol' Diz was inordinately modest when he first heard the news that he had been elected. Said he: "It's doggone nice for an old cotton-picker from Arkansas to be up there with them fellers."

Yet that formal statement was hardly in character. It would have been much more like him to have declared airily:

"What wuz them writin' fellers takin' so long for! They shoulda knowed from the start that Ol' Diz was the greatest pitcher who ever lived." Nope. There never was anything modest about Mr. Dean.

The Great Man once wrote a discreet autobiography of sorts and merely stated the facts. With remarkable self-restraint he set down these words:

"Anybody who's ever had the privilege of seein' me play ball knows that I am the greatest pitcher in the world. And them that ain't been fortunate enough to have a gander at Ol' Diz in action can look at the records."

Unfortunately, though, the records do not quite present an accurate picture. For five blazing years the buoyant Mr. Dean was exactly what he said he was, the best. But then he was hit on the toe by a line drive in the 1937 All-Star game and his days of true greatness were at an end. With his easy pitching motion, his overpowering fast ball, his courage, his skill and his utter disdain for all hitters, he probably would have lasted another decade "effen I hadn't of tried to pitch too soon while my toe was still broke."

Flaming competitor that he was, he just couldn't wait for his toe to heal. He began to pitch, favoring the toe, and the new, unnatural muscle strain permanently injured his arm. What an arm that was!

Branch Rickey, his discoverer, couldn't believe his eyes the first time he saw Diz in action at a tryout camp. Each tyro pitcher tossed to three batters. But Diz gave the Mahatma hardly a glimpse of him. The big fellow fanned the three on nine pitches. So he was summoned back for a longer look. Nine more pitches added up to nine more strikes. Rickey assigned Diz to Saint Joseph in the Western League despite the Great Man's protestations.

"Don't waste time sendin' me to Saint Joe, Branch," urged the gangling Dean. "I kin win you twenty games for the Cardinals."

"By Judas Priest!" ruefully roared Rickey afterwards, "I now believe Diz could have done it." As it was, he won seventeen for a last-place team.

Dean was a rookie out of the pages of Ring Lardner when he first reported to the Cards. His boasting drove Manager Gabby Street to the verge of distraction. And in one exhibition game in the Spring the Cards were being clobbered by a fearsome Athletics team.

"I jes' wisht Ol' Diz wuz a pitchin'," muttered Ol' Diz on the bench.

"Get in and pitch," screamed Street. "And I hope they beat your brains out."

The bases were filled when the Great Man stepped in, almost without a warm-up. He was grinning jauntily in complete unconcern. He struck out Al Simmons. He struck out Jimmy Foxx. He struck out Mickey Cochrane.

Diz was a charter member of the famed Gas House Gang and one of the ringleaders.

"Don't you worry none, Frankie," he told his astonished boss, Frank Frisch. "You string along with Ol' Diz and he'll make a great manager outa you."

That was in 1934, the year he announced to the Flash that "me 'n' Paul" would win forty-five games. It was the only time Dean underestimated himself. His younger brother, Paul, won nineteen. But Diz won thirty.

Late that season the brothers pitched a double-header against the Dodgers. Diz opened with a three-hitter and then Paul twirled a no-hitter. Diz was furious.

"Effen you'd only a tole me you wuz gonna pitch a no-hitter," he growled, "I'da pitched me one, too." He probably would have at that.

Against the Braves one day he strolled past the Boston dugout and made his announcement.

"I ain't pitchin' no curves today, fellers," he drawled, "Nuthin' but fast balls." He shut them out with three hits.

Diz was a fantastic performer. When Eldon Auker of Detroit was warming up before the seventh game of the 1934 World Series, Dean planted himself behind Cochrane, catcher and manager of the Tigers.

"He won't do, Mick," he said sadly. "He jes' won't do." He didn't. The Cards shelled him out early as Diz, laughing and clowning his way through, won 11 to 0. He got so playful that Frisch threatened to yank him.

"They ain't nobody yankin' Ol' Diz," announced Ol' Diz serenely, "when he's got hisself an eleven-run lead."

The self-confessed Great Man is a welcome addition to the Hall of Fame, though he lowers the humility quotient of the immortals down to virtually nothing.

"Tree-mendous!" Says Casey

March 24

Saint Petersburg, Florida, March 23—No one can give the same intonation to the word tremendous that Casey Stengel gives it. He lands on that first syllable with both feet. But when he applies the adjective to Master Mickey Mantle his rasping voice becomes caressing.

"If that kid only hit right-handed, he'd be tree-mendous," barked the Ol' Perfessor. "If he only hit left-handed, he'd be tree-mendous. But since he does his hittin' both ways, he's . . . ." Casey groped for a superlative and couldn't find one better than his favorite. "He's just tree-mendous," he said simply.

"He kin drag bunt with two strikes on him," continued Stengel. "The distances he kin hit a ball, hittin' with power to all fields. I saw him belt one right-handed into the upper right field tier at Detroit. He hit one left-handed over the left center field wall in—wait a minute. Rizzuto was on base at the time and he kin tell you. Come here, little man."

Phil Rizzuto pattered over.

"Remember the time you were stealin' second and Mantle hit one?" asked Stengel.

"Holy Gee, Case," said the bubbling Rizzuto, awe in his voice.

Mickey Mantle as a rookie, 1951.

"I never saw a ball hit so hard. Did that shoot, I even stopped to look at it and that's something I never did before. Oh, boy, the Mick sure can ride that ball."

The conversation was slightly more than Mantle could bear. He fled to the safety of the batting cage in sheer embarrassment. He's a shy, modest boy of 21. He's still a mite bewildered by the fact that even the most cynical of baseball men readily admit that the kid is destined to become one of the truly great stars of the game. He's so quiet and reserved that he's the despair of interviewers, particularly strangers. His main trouble is that the fellow least impressed by Mantle is Mickey Charles Mantle himself.

"I'll never forget my first spring training," he said. "I stayed over when Casey had finished the preliminary camp and the regulars began to arrive. Gosh, I felt that I should be asking them for their autographs. The odd part about it is that I still feel the same way." He grinned boyishly.

"Gee, but I have so much to learn. I know that I hit .311 last year but I struck out too much. I can't get it through my thick head that I should let certain pitches alone. I swing at them and it gets me into trouble."

"Next hitter," sang out Ralph Houk, who was catching batting practice.

Allie Reynolds fired in a high, hard one. It streaked across Mantle's shoulders. Mickey swung and missed.

"That's the one you should take without swinging, Mick," said Houk quietly. Mickey finished his turn at bat and returned to the back of the batting cage.

"Did you notice that miss?" asked the boy wonder. "If I had been batting right-handed I would have hit it. I'm the same guy but I'm a different hitter depending on which side of the plate I'm on and I have different weaknesses. Let me show you."

Mantle took his position at an imaginary plate as a left-handed batter, crouching slightly. Then he swung around into a right-handed pose and stood almost straight up with no crouch at all. It's something that never would be noticed ordinarily. Only a personal demonstration revealed the difference. The same Reynolds pitch was a ball to the left-handed Mantle but a hittable strike to the right-handed Mantle.

"I've often wondered if I could have made good with any other team but this one," he said. "This is the grandest bunch of guys anyone could want.

"The first fellows I met were Hank Bauer and Johnny Hopp. Then Jerry Coleman and Bobby Brown took me in hand. I'll always be grateful to Doc Brown for what he did when my Dad died. He got me off in a corner and talked to me for hours. I felt an awful lot better after that."

Master Mickey stared off into space for a moment and shuddered.

"I don't think I ever will experience a day like opening day of 1951," he said. "The world series didn't bother me none. I wasn't even excited. But opening day was the worst day of my life. I don't think I slept a wink the night before and I was trembling all over from the moment I reached the Yankee Stadium.

"To tell you the truth, I don't remember much about that game. It's all a blur to me. I think I grounded out to third in my first time at bat and I did get a hit that drove in a run. That might have been my second time at bat but I'm not sure of it. I take no credit for it. I was so scared that I just shut my eyes and swung. I didn't see a pitch all day. I was too scared. The world series was a breeze after that."

With his phenomenal speed of foot, his power hitting, his strong arm and constant improvement afield, Master Mickey has everything he needs, including a burning love for the sport.

"This don't seem like no job to me," he says earnestly.

"The kid's tree-mendous," says Stengel.

The Rajah Speaks His Mind

March 25

Tampa, Florida, March 24—"I don't like to sound egotistical," said Rogers Hornsby, who couldn't sound egotistical if he tried, "but every time I stepped up to the plate with a bat in my hands, I couldn't help but feel sorry for the pitcher."

Coming from anyone else that would be a rather startling statement and it probably would be an egotistical one to boot. But the Rajah is a blunt, outspoken chap who always tells the truth. If the truth forces him to admit that he is the greatest right-handed batter who ever lived, Hornsby will frankly admit it, not in the spirit of vainglory but merely as an unavoidable fact.

The record book proves it, of course. The Rajah had a lifetime batting average of .358, second only to Ty Cobb's .367, and had one utterly incredible five-year span when his average was a mite under .402. Here's the way he did it—.397, .401, .384, .424 and .403. No wonder he felt sorry for the pitchers!

In many respects Hornsby was a more fearsome hitter than Cobb. The Georgia Peach was a deft batter. The Rajah was a brutal one. Cobb made the most of his hair-trigger brain and his lightning speed. A consummate faker, he'd pull infielders out of position and punch the ball through the holes he created. Or he'd bunt or line the ball to the outfield.

Hornsby was brute power. He slashed line drives to all fields, some of them screamers which were still rising when they smashed into the stands for home runs.

"I never deliberately tried for a homer in my life," he said scornfully. "I merely met the ball where it was pitched." Yet he hit as many as forty-two in a season.

The old-timers will tell you that Hornsby had no weakness as a batter. So the question was asked of him.

"No," he said simply. "I had no weaknesses."

But he must have had some when he first came up to the big leagues. What was his major weakness then?

"Pitching," he said laconically. He didn't smile. He's too deadly serious about baseball for that.

"I had to learn to hit curves and stay away from bad balls," he explained. "That's why I always believed a good hitter didn't have to be born that way but could acquire the knack. These modern players should be able to hit and it's a mystery to me why they can't.

"The rawest rookie of today gets opportunities that the rookie of my day never had. The regulars wouldn't let us get near the plate when they were taking batting practice. I can remember when Bob Connery, the scout who brought me up to the majors, pitched batting practice to me after the regulars had left the field.

"How many kinds of pitches are there, anyway? There's a fast ball, a curve, a knuckler and a slider. And a slider ain't nothing but a soft curve. In my day there were so many other pitches—the spitter, shine ball and all that sort of stuff. Let me tell you that the curve ballers of my time could really bend a curve."

The Rajah chewed reflectively on a toothpick, his cold hazel eyes staring off into space.

"No one has seen a curve ball," he continued, "until he's seen Jug Handle Johnny Morrison throw one. Aldrich had a good curve. So did the Barnes brothers, Nehf, Rosy Ryan and Rube Benton. Notice how many of those guys I just mentioned worked for John McGraw. McGraw always insisted on having curve ballers. If a curve breaks down and away from the belt buckle, there's nothing a batter can do with it but hit it into the ground for a double play."

How about the Hornsby position in the furthermost back corner of the batter's box? Was that a help to him as a hitter?

"It helped me," said the Rajah, "but that don't mean it would help everyone. I didn't stand back there when I first came up. But I soon learned that by laying back I had a longer look at the ball. I could follow it better and I guess it did make me a better hitter. I strode in toward the plate to cover outside pitches and I just had to learn to let the inside ones go by because they were balls."

What was his remedy for batting slumps?

"Can't say I ever had any," he snapped. "When a fellow has a lifetime average of .358, there ain't much room for slumps. Maybe I had some for a two or three-game period. But never much more. We used to get out of a slump by bunting. It gets your eye back on the ball. Then you swing more freely and soon you're going full tilt again."

The manager of the Cincinnati Reds watched his players with searching gaze. What were his prospects for the season? By golly, I forgot to ask him.

Traveling Along Dream Street

May 31

Jack Sharkey was walking outside the Yankee Stadium with Johnny Buckley pattering silently and sadly by his side. Suddenly Sharkey stopped, tilted his head upward and peered intently at the dark sky.

"I don't like the looks of that sky, Johnny," said the fighter to his manager. "It might rain and I'd hate to have my fight postponed."

"What fight?" asked Buckley.

"Are you crazy, Johnny?" said Sharkey impatiently. "My fight with Jack Dempsey. Are you my manager or aren't you? I don't want to surprise you but I'm fighting Jack Dempsey at the Stadium tonight." He laughed hollowly.

"No, you ain't," said Buckley. "Listen, pal. This may be news to you but you've already fought Dempsey. He knocked you out in the seventh round."

Devious are the routes that fighters take when they begin to travel along Dream Street. A solid punch on the whiskers can jar a man loose from his memory and even set up a strange behavior pattern. Jersey Joe Walcott's sitdown strike against Rocky Marciano conceivably could be a case in point because ring history is loaded with such peculiarities. Uncharted indeed is Dream Street.

Mickey Walker was one of the great ones. He won both welterweight and middleweight championships and was so tough that he eventually campaigned among the heavyweights. The first professional fight of the fabulous Toy Bulldog was against Phil Delmont. When the bout was over, Walker was quietly soaping himself in the shower. Then he turned on the cold water and squealed.

"Hey, Georgie," he called out to Georgie Ward, his second. "What round did I knock out that guy?"

"You didn't knock him out at all, Mick," tearfully responded Ward. "He knocked you out. In the very first round, too."

Jimmy Johnson, the fabled Boy Bandit, once sent Ted (Kid) Lewis, one of his better fighters, into the ring against a lad whose name has been forgotten here. Just before the bell sounded for the first round, Jimmy tossed one last reminder at his tiger before starting down the steps.

"Watch out for his left hook," warned the Boy Bandit.

Johnston reached the bottom step and was startled to hear the heavy thud of a falling body. He looked in horror. It was Lewis who was on the deck. That left hook had been ignored and had therefore connected. Lewis was in an obvious fog when he staggered to his feet at the count of nine. But his head seemed to clear as he progressed. He boxed beautifully and hit smartly. In fact, he hit so smartly that he flattened his foe for keeps in the eleventh.

In the dressing room afterward, Lewis was strangely silent and morose. He took his shower and emerged with tears streaming down his face.

"This is awful, Jimmy," he wept. "I've let you down. I've let down all my friends. I'm in disgrace."

"Why?" asked the puzzled Boy Bandit.

"A guy I should have licked knocked me out in the first round with a sucker punch," moaned Lewis.

"Wait a minute," snapped Jimmy. "You knocked him out in the eleventh."

Lewis, it would seem, had scored a victory on instinct alone.

Hardly had the third round of the Jack Sharkey—Tommy Loughran fight begun when Sharkey landed a terrific right on the jaw. Down went Loughran. But at the count of five he leaped to his feet and walked over to Referee Lou Magnolia, fists dangling at his side.

"Let me sit down, Lou," said the gentlemanly Tommy. "I don't know where I am."

Magnolia let him sit down—in his corner as a knockout victim.

Much more chummy was Eddie Simms with Referee Arthur Donovan on the occasion of a bout with Joe Louis. The Dark Destroyer had exploded a left hook on Simms' jaw. Eddie arose and smiled in sickly fashion at Donovan.

"Let's you and me take a walk on the roof," suggested Simms to the referee. At least that was one way of getting away from Louis. Donovan led Simms to his corner, the fight over.

There was once a kid from Philadelphia—his name isn't particularly important—who came to New York for an outdoor fight. After the weighing ceremonies, the youthful gladiator returned to his hotel and took a nap. By early evening a heavy downpour had postponed the fight but the kindhearted manager let his hero slumber away undisturbed. That kid slept as though he had been drugged.

At midnight his hotel phone rang. The boy groped in the darkness for the phone, his mind still fogged by his sleep. It was his girl friend, calling from Philadelphia.

"How did we do, honey?" she chirped sweetly.

"I guess I musta been knocked out *again,*" he said despairingly, "because there ain't nobody here but me."

At least he recognized the symptoms, which is more than most of them do. Strange are the behavior patterns a knockout produces and unpredictible is the meandering journey down Dream Street.

1954

A Visit With Bob Jones

January 22

Bob Jones was rambling away in a reminiscent mood yesterday when he put the finger with unerring precision on the one factor that lifts a golfer to greatness. He didn't mean it to apply to himself because he's much too modest and gracious to do that. But the principle also fit the Emperor Jones as if hand-tailored for him.

"A great champion," he said, "has to have a willingness to take the mental punishment you have to take. That's why Ben Hogan is so great. He tries harder than anyone else."

The Georgian stopped short and a look of surprise flitted into his eyes as if he'd discovered something for the first time.

"I guess I tried harder than anyone else, too," he said, almost as if he were reluctant to believe it.

He sure did. Bob Jones retired from competitive golf at the age of 28 after he had made his historic Grand Slam—"the impregnable quadrilateral of golf" as George Trevor once described it—by winning British amateur and open championships and then the United States open and amateur crowns, a feat without parallel.

The Emperor Jones was in town to be the guest of honor at

Bob Jones as he appeared in 1930, the year of his Grand Slam.

the Metropolitan Golf Writers Association annual dinner at the Waldorf-Astoria. It was natural, of course, that he'd do some traveling down memory lane with some of his old friends of the press tents.

"Sam Snead once asked me," he said with a smile, "which championship I wanted to win most.

" 'Whatever one I was in at the time,' I told him.

" 'I think you got something there,' said Sam.

"When I was competing, I concentrated on each tournament as it came along. Each was of equal importance. But in retrospect I guess I'd have to select the British amateur of 1930. There are two reasons for that choice. One was that it was the only time I ever won the British amateur. The other was because it was the start of the Grand Slam."

The Emperor Jones smiled, ruefully shook his head and resumed.

"I'll never forget my first match. It was with a fellow named Sid Roper, a Welsh coal miner. 'How good is he? I asked someone who knew. 'Not much,' I was told. 'He'll get all 5s and 6s.' But when I saw him drive off the first tee I whistled softly to myself. 'This guy's a whale of a golfer,' I said.

"Fortunately I was off to a hot start and had a 3-up lead at the end of four holes. But I couldn't win another hole from him and he didn't score higher than a 4 on any hole. After I'd disposed of him, I was lucky in that I then had to face almost every good golfer in the tournament. So that put me on my mettle and I went all out against each of them because none was a sleeper who might trip me if I permitted myself to get careless.

"But there was nothing extraordinary about my golf in that tournament and I thought I played badly in winning the British open a short time later. Yet it was in the British open of 1926 that I played about as perfect a round of golf as I ever did in my life. You remember that, don't you?"

That magic round of 66 on Sunningdale is still mentioned in awed and reverential tones by the Scots and the British. It was a fantastic round. Jones scored a 33 going out and a 33 coming back. He took 33 putts and 33 other strokes. He didn't have a 2 on his card or a 5. He had six 4s and three 3s on the outgoing holes. He had the same on his return.

"The strange part about golf," said Bob reflectively, "is that even on a good round I doubt that I ever hit more than six shots exactly where I wanted to hit them. But this was uncanny. I holed one putt of 18 feet but I didn't have another difficult putt all day. My two mistakes were trifling. On the short thirteenth I hooked my tee shot into a bunker. But I blew out to within 3 feet of the cup. On the seventeenth I twisted my drive some 5 feet off the fairway. But the grass wasn't deep and I put my next shot on the green. What a round that was!"

It was a much less embarrassing round, no doubt, than the one he played with the mighty Harry Vardon of Britain at Inverness in the United States open of 1920. The Emperor Jones looked up quickly and grinned.

"I know what you mean," he said. "I was only 18 and utterly awed by Vardon, the greatest figure in the game. He was phlegmatic and spoke not a word to me. On one hole we both were in front of the green. He chipped up neatly and properly. I tried a fancy cut and foozled it horribly.

" 'Did you ever see a worse shot, Mr. Vardon?' I asked, trying to hide my mortification by making conversation. He then spoke to me for the first and only time of the tournament.

" 'No,' he said."

Between 1923 and 1930 Robert Tyre Jones won the United States amateur five times, the United States open four times, the British open three times and the British amateur once. That record speaks eloquently for his greatness.

Listening to a Four-Minute Miler

May 14

Roger Bannister lounged carelessly in a chair at the Yale Club yesterday and talked with rare graciousness, penetration and charm. He is sandy-haired, tall, slim and ever-smiling. Pictures of him in action while running a mile in 3:59.4 are a mite flattering. When he strides in a track suit, he looks barrel-chested and overpowering. Street clothes make him shrink to more boyish proportions.

The first man to break past the barrier of the four-minute mile was the luncheon guest of Col. Eddie Eagan, the one-time Rhodes scholar at Oxford, the one-time Olympic boxing champion and the one-time chairman of the State Athletic Commission. Eddie invited a few old friends to break bread with him and his fellow-Oxonian, Bannister. And Roger captivated everyone in a lot faster time than 3:59.4. He did it in nothing flat.

In the course of the conversation the 25-year-old medical student said something which epitomizes the art of record-breaking.

"It's the ability to take more out of yourself than you've got," he said.

While listening to him, a fellow got the impression that the idea for the four-minute mile was born at the Olympic Games in 1952 as a long-range vindication program of sorts.

"I trained for the Olympics with a light program," Roger explained. It was clearly an explanation, too, and not an alibi. "A fortnight beforehand I ran a three-quarters in 2:52.9 and * * *." He stopped because at least one listener had caught his breath and then whistled softly in amazement.

"That's correct," said Roger laughing lightly. "It's four seconds faster than Arne Andersson's record. That convinced me that I was in rare form.

"But I never realized until too late that there were so many entries for the Olympic 1,500, that heats, semi-finals and finals would all be hard, all-out races on successive days. I just didn't have the stamina for so sustained a program. If I could go back and do it over again, I'd make sure that I not only was the fastest but the strongest.

"Don't misunderstand me. I'm taking no credit from Josy Barthel, the winner. He's a great competitor and I have only the most profound respect for him. But when five of us drew up almost abreast at the bell lap, he seemed to say, 'Let's go.' And he went. I was worried.

"I found that I was under a heavier nervous strain than running the four-minute mile. All England wanted me to win the Olympics. The responsibility was great. The English felt that their champion should be the champion of all the world. I jolly near collapsed when I finished fourth at Helsinki. After crossing the finish line, I barely jogged to where I could fall on the grass.

"After the Olympics I found everyone interested in the four-minute mile. So I got interested. I also had a theory of training that I wanted to vindicate. If I could vindicate that theory I could see no fun left in track as a sport. I could see no sense or purpose in running vast distances in order to build up stamina. Besides, I didn't have time for it.

"So I'd race a quarter mile and then jog a quarter mile, doing six or ten such quarters in a workout. It's not too different from the system Gunder Haegg and Andersson used of putting the body to stress and then relaxation. They did it in the open country. I did it on a track."

Bannister paused, smiled and then addressed his next remark to Col. Arnold Strode-Jackson, the Olympic 1,500-meter champion of 1912 and the first of the great Oxford milers.

"It might interest you to know, Colonel," he said, "that I was president of the Oxford A.A. when we decided to tear up that third-of-a-mile track you once ran on and rebuild it as a standard quarter-mile track. The old one, as you know, was more like a cross-country course since it was through trees and down hill. I need not add that this modernization drew severe disapproval from the Old Blues who wrote indignant letters to *The Times* for weeks afterward.

"But we used to run in the wrong direction on the old track, clockwise. I guess you've all heard the theory that the right leg is stronger than the left leg since most folks are right-handed. But Oxonians, running in the wrong direction on the Oxford track, pushed hardest on the left leg and made that as strong as the right leg. That's why Oxford always had so many great milers, Strode-Jackson, Jerry Cornes, and Jack Lovelock among them. But that's neither here nor there.

"On the day of the 3:59.4 mile it was blowing a gale at lunchtime but it was only a gusty breeze at race time. I was worried about that and I was worried because the track felt hard to my spikes. But once I started to run I forgot everything. My plan, roughly, was to run even quarters—a 60-second first quarter, a 2-minute half and a 3-minute three-quarters. But I'd hoped to shade a minute for the first quarter, relying on gaining a second by bursting off the marks fast and getting rid of nervous energy. It was a psychological comfort to find myself doing 57.5 for the first quarter and I felt comfortable until right near the end. Then I went all out. No. I had absolutely nothing left at the finish."

He almost made it sound easy.

Out in the Open

June 18

Springfield, New Jersey, June 17—It undoubtedly was the most talked about shot of today's opening round of the United States open golf championship over Baltusrol's lush, green pastureland. Naturally enough, Sam Snead made it. The Slammer didn't want to make it, despite his flair for the spectacular. He just had no choice in the matter. If he had failed, his open bubble might have burst almost before he had started to blow some air gently into it.

The millionaire hillbilly normally hammers out drives of 300 yards or thereabouts. But his first shot in the tournament was a clinker. It was a feeble hook that traveled little more than 210 yards or so and caromed off the mesh fence that marks out-of-bounds. It might have gone through the fence and Sam was lucky that it remained on the premises.

But when Samivel surveyed the lie, he was horrified to discover that the ball was resting within a foot of the fence. He had no room to swing. So he decided to play it left-handed. He held a No. 8 iron with the toe of the club down and the heel up and whacked away. Samivel didn't know his own strength. The ball shot out 190 yards diagonally across the fairway into the rough on the far side. He did extraordinarily well to get a bogey 5 and a solid round of 72.

"T'warn't nuthin'," said the Slammer modestly in discussing his southpaw effort. "I remember onc't before when I hadda play left-handed. I was frozen against the tree and I boomed it out into the rough that time, too. However, I didn't hit it as far."

"That's a shot Ben Hogan should be making," said Jimmy Demaret. "Everyone seems to have forgotten that Ben started out as a left-handed golfer."

"That's correct," said Hogan with a shy smile. "I threw a ball left-handed and did everything lefty. I owned only one club, a left-handed mashie. Let's see. That would be when I was about 13 years old. I couldn't afford to buy any left-handed clubs and so I bought me a set of right-handed clubs, one at a time for a dollar in the dime store. And I've been right-handed ever since."

"I didn't see Sam make his shot," said Demaret, "but I know I'll never see a better one than Lew Worsham pulled against me in a P.G.A. championship. I had him 1 up and one hole to go. He was smack against a tree. So he took a No. 2 iron, held it upside down and belted one 200 yards to within twenty feet of the pin. It rattled me so much that I three-putted. So he tied me. I was doggone lucky I beat him on the second or third extra hole."

"If you fellows are going to tell tall tales," said Gene Sarazen, with an impish grin, "I'll have to bet my money on my boy, Walter Hagen. Come on, Walter. I'm sure you can top that."

"Lemme see," began the Haig reflectively. "It was in the North and South open one year and I'm leading by two strokes into the last hole."

"Which course?" asked long Jim Barnes.

"The No. 3 course," said the Haig. "As I stepped to the tee I said to myself, 'It's time to show these folks what a great champion you are.' "

"That's Hagen for you," said Sarazen delightedly.

"So I decided to belt the daylights out of it," continued Hagen unconcernedly. "The ball went four miles—but into the woods at the left of the fairway. I fight my way through the underbrush and I'm quite surprised to discover a clearance there. And I also see an old mammy on a porch, calmly peeling potatoes.

"I say to her, 'Mammy, did you see a golf ball come in here?' she shakes her head. 'No, sir,' she said. 'There ain't nobody plays golf in here. They plays over thataway.' And she points in the general direction of the fairway. But I look around and look and look. Finally I find my ball. It's perched as pretty as you please on top of a pile of leaves but against a tree so that I can't get at it properly. There's nothing else to do but hit it left-handed. I whip out my No. 7 iron.

"I'm a litle mad at myself by now, thinking that I've blown the championship by showing off at the wrong time. 'I've gotta get this back on the fairway,' I keep telling myself. I say it every time I address the ball and every time I take my position I know I'm going to flub it. I must have backed away a half-dozen times.

"Finally I just step up and swing. Far beyond the trees there's a roar from the crowd. I get out of the woods myself and discover that the ball is on the green ten feet from the pin. So I win after all."

"There's only one Hagen," said Sarazen admiringly. He can say that again.

More Honors for Willie

December 20

Jimmy Dykes, the unfrocked manager of the Orioles, and Tom Sheehan, the chief trouble-shooter for the Giants, were exchanging pleasant lies during the baseball meetings a week or so ago, when Willie Mays edged his way into the conversation. That was inevitable. No member of the Giant official family can talk for five full minutes without mentioning Willie the Wonder.

"Wait a minute, Tom," said Dykes, a needler without a peer. "You're not going to stand there and tell me that Willie Mays actually exists."

"Of course he exists," said Long Tom, starting to splutter in indignation. "Didn't you see the catch he made on Vic Wertz in the world series?"

"I saw it," said Dykes firmly. "But I still don't believe it. That catch had to be an optical illusion. It was the greatest catch I ever saw in my life."

"A fair-to-middling catch—for Willie, I mean," said Sheehan with studied casualness. "I've seen him do better."

"What?" shrieked Dykes.

"I'm skipping over the play he made against the Dodgers in

Willie Mays, as a New York Giant, and Arthur Daley.

1951," said Sheehan. "The one involving Carl Furillo and Billy Cox. Remember it?"

"Vaguely," said Dykes, completely shaken out of his pose of indifference. "I might as well ask you to repeat it because I suspect you intend to do it anyway."

"Now you're cooking with gas," said the appreciative Sheehan. "The score is tied with one out in the eighth and Cox is at third with the winning run. Furillo slams a line drive to right center and Cox tags up. Willie races seven miles before spearing the ball with his glove, a marvelous catch. But he's facing the right-field wall and there's no way he can stop, wheel and make the throw home to head off the runner.

"At this time Willie is merely a 20-year-old kid who's been in the big leagues only a couple of months. He don't know nuthin' from nohow. So he figures out a new way to do it. He spins around, away from the plate in a reverse turn, and the ball is on the way to the plate before he's finished spinning. It goes on a line in the air for a perfect strike to Wes Westrum and Cox is dead, tagged out ten steps down the line."

"Whee!" whistled Dykes, properly impressed.

"But that wasn't his best catch," said Sheehan. "Here it is."

It isn't often that the urbane and slightly supercilious Dykes gets trapped into resembling an open-mouthed rube. But Long Tom had him trapped.

"This catch was so wonderful," said Sheehan, "that even the fellows in the press box didn't appreciate it because Willie made it look so easy. We were playing the Braves at the Polo Grounds and I was watching from Horace Stoneham's office above the clubhouse in deepest center field. It gave us an unusual vantage point.

"Bill Bruton was at bat and he's not a long-ball hitter. So Willie played him shallow. From where we sat it almost looked as though he was almost standing on second base. Well, sir, Bruton hit the longest ball he ever hit in his life. He hadn't even brought the bat around before Willie had started running. It was a screamer down that center-field alley.

"Willie kept racing toward us. He looked over his left shoulder. He glanced over his right shoulder. And all the time he's going full tilt as he turns his head, right or left, to follow the ball.

" 'He'll never make it,' says Horace to me.

"Don't bet on it," I says to him.

"Willie looks to the left for the last time. He looks to the right. Then he reaches out his two hands in front of him with his back to the plate. And that ball sails smack over his head into his outstretched hands. One more step and Willie is on the cinders below us, which should show you how far he had to run.

In my book that was the greatest catch he ever made."

"Shut up," said Dykes weakly. "I've heard enough for one day."

At any rate, something that everyone had suspected has finally been made official. Willie the Wonder Mays, 23, has been named the Most Valuable Player in the National League by a special committee of the Baseball Writers Association. How could he miss?

For half a season the 'Mazing Mays had been hitting homers at a pace far ahead of Babe Ruth's record. Then he abruptly quit his distance clouting and concentrated on singles, doubles and triples until he won the batting championship with a rousing .345.

He can hit, field, run, throw and inspire. And this happy-go-lucky kid with the infectious laugh excelled in every department. The M.V.P. trophy is an honor he richly deserved.

Arthur Daley was awarded the Pulitzer Prize for the following six columns.

1955

A Letter From Ty Cobb

February 22

The postman's ring is never more welcome than when he brings a letter from Ty Cobb, whose .367 lifetime batting average makes him the greatest hitter who ever lived. The Georgia Peach took pen in hand—he wrote with his fist, too, and not with a typewriter—to put in a generous word for an old teammate.

"No doubt you will be surprised to hear from me again," he began. "But there are two matters I'd like to discuss with you.

"The first is Sam Crawford, the old outfielder for Detroit, who is being overlooked by the voters for baseball's Hall of Fame. He's one of the old-timers who really did so much for the game. Yet far too many of the old boys find it much more difficult to gain entrance than some of those from the present era.

"Sam Crawford is one of the many who have dropped out of circulation and who have lost their publicity channels. In no way do I mean to try to influence you, but you may feel inclined to write about Sam some day and bring him to the attention of others.

"Sam was a natural pull hitter and drove a tremendously long ball. He did this in spite of the fact that he had to contend with the dead ball and with trick pitching. If Sam ever had the chance to operate today he'd have murdered the lively ball. The moving in of the fences, the establishment of Greenberg Gardens and the wire fence in Cleveland have made home-run hitting much easier.

"His misfortune was that he played big-league ball fifty years too early. If he were swinging away today he'd be up with the all-time home-run leaders. He led the league with Detroit in 1908 when he hit only seven. And he also led the other league with Cincinnati in 1901 when he hit sixteen. But they pinned the label of 'Home Run' on Frank Baker when he struck only twelve in 1913.

"Now Sam wasn't fast because he was such a large man. But I'd like you to note that he stole as many as forty-one bases in 1912 and thirty-seven the year before. Compare this with the tops of today, Minoso, I think. [Editor's Note: Bill Bruton of Milwaukee was tops with thirty-four and no one else was higher than twenty-two.]

"Sam had a quite unusual record in the rapidity with which he made good. He broke in with Chatham, Canada, and played forty-two games. Promoted to Grand Rapids, he played sixty games before being promoted to Cincinnati, where he played thirty-one games—all of it in the same season of 1899.

"All in all, he had four seasons with Cincinnati and fifteen with Detroit. His best batting average was .378 and his record for the most triples, 312, will probably never be broken. I'm hoping earnestly that Taylor Spink's special committee of old-timers will examine Sam Crawford's credentials and elect him to baseball's Hall of Fame."

The rest of Ty's six-page letter is personal. Yet the letter itself demonstrates how much the once fierce and bellicose Cobb has mellowed and softened with the years. He discreetly never mentioned it but it long has been an open secret among baseball men that the Georgia Peach and Wahoo Sam did not speak to each other for many years even though they played side by side in the Detroit outfield.

It wasn't Ty's fault except by indirection. When Cobb joined the Tigers in 1905, Crawford was the king. He was the team's best hitter and most popular player. And along came the youthful firebrand from Georgia to take the headlines away from him. If Wahoo Sam resented Cobb his attitude at least was understandable, especially in that dog-eat-dog era.

A rookie's life today is all peaches and cream. The old-timer, whom he'll eventually replace, shows him all the tricks of the trade and gives his successor-to-be a speed-up course. A half century ago a rookie was elbowed out of the batting cage by the regulars. He had to learn his trade the hard way.

Cobb once told this reporter of finding his bats sawed in half. He never mentioned who the culprit was—if he knew. But it was pretty rough going for baseball's greatest hitter when he was breaking in. And Wahoo Sam was no help. That's for sure.

Harry Heilmann used to say that Crawford would have hit fifty to sixty homers a year if he'd swung against the jackrabbit ball.

"Even with the dead ball," said Harry, "Wahoo Sam used to back the center fielders up against the fence at least twice a day."

E. S. Barnard of Cleveland installed a 45-foot screen atop the right-field wall in the League Park bandbox. Sam hit the ball over the screen.

As the clean-up hitter behind Cobb the big, brawny and handsome Crawford drove in countless runs. Unfortunately for him, they didn't tabulate runs-batted-in then. Wahoo Sam would have had a hatful.

It's a magnificent gesture on the part of Tyrus Raymond Cobb to urge Crawford's election to the Hall of Fame. It shows what a generous old softie Ty has become.

The Silent Mr. Stengel

March 6

Saint Petersburg, Florida, March 5—"I ain't talkin'," said Charles Dillon Stengel. The Yankee manager folded his arms across his manly bosom and stared stonily across Miller Huggins Field, just like a sphinx. But soon his vocal chords began to simmer and seethe in the fashion of a volcano that has been suppressed too long. An eruption was inevitable.

"I'm kinder dead this year," was his feeble explanation. "I can't talk."

So the tourist merely sat in the dugout with him waiting patiently for the hot, molten lava to come cascading forth. It was to be the Last Days of Pompeii, total engulfment.

"Now you can take Cerv," began Stengel for no particular reason at all. It wasn't surprising, though, because Ol' Case frequently starts his conversations in the middle.

"Like I wuz sayin', you can take Cerv and I'll explain it to you. At one time or another we had the three most valuable players in the American Association. One wuz Cerv, one wuz Skowron and one wuz Power, which I got rid of, and none of them did nuthin' the followin' season. But he can hit left-handed pitchin' and he can hit right-handed pitchin' and he can pinch-hit, a very handy feller to have on your ball club I don't mind sayin'."

There now will be a slight pause for station identification.

The last chap he was discussing was not Cerv or Skowron or Power but Enos Slaughter. How did Enos get into the discussion? Who knows?

"Now just look at that kid, Carter, on third," said the virtually mute manager. "He's gotta good arm. You can tell by the way he throws."

A tourist is bound to learn something if he listens long enough to the Ol' Perfessor. If a man throws well, he has a good arm. Betcha never knew that before.

"For the first time and I'd better knock wood on this," Stengel droned on, "Mantle comes to spring trainin' in good health and he's a first class man in so many ways which he did like he got power, speed and an arm but strikes out too much. What's wrong with Bauer and it seems a lotta clubs desire him which you know and Noren had a very good year although I don't like to have a left-handed thrower in left field. Hey, Mantle, thatsa way to bunt you might hit .400 and beat Berra out."

The last sentence was shouted to Master Mickey after the erstwhile boy wonder had deftly dragged a bunt down the first base line.

Stengel's roving eyes stopped at sight of a mob of ball players clustered near first base, all candidates for the job there. The leading candidate, at the moment, is Bill (Moose) Skowron, a reformed football player from Purdue and a powerful right-handed hitter.

"The reason Skowron stayed in the outfield his second year," said Casey, picking up a conversational thread from the tangle, "is that I delayed him. You can look it up but I think he led the American Association two years in hittin' although I may be wrong. Yankee success at first has been with lefty hitters but when you mention Gehrig you take in a lot of time.

"Mr. Kryhoski played on our ball club part of the year and he lives in New Jersey where a lotta writers and ball players live. He once hit sixteen home runs in the American League which ain't the American Association but the big leagues although he only hit one homer last year with Baltimore which is a bad ball park.

"He's thrilled to be back with the Yankees and one of the things which annoys the management is the salaries of all the first basemen we've got which is more than the rest of the league combined. We have the most first basemen, the largest and they eat the most which you should see their hotel bills.

"And now we come to Collins which may be an outfielder. He played center field in Newark and also played right field for me in the world series. You can look it up but he had Novikoff on one side of him and some one else whose name I've forgotten on the other but you can look it up. That should prove he's a great outfielder in order to be able to do it with them guys on either side of him.

"There's a kid infielder named Richardson who wuz in our rookie camp which he don't look like he can play because he's stiff as a stick but—whoost!—and the ball's there and he does it so fast it would take some of them Sunshine Park race track handicappers with the field glasses to see him do it so fast does he do it. He never misses. As soon as he misses a ball we'll send him home.

"We start out to get us a shortstop and now we got eight of them. We don't fool we don't. I ain't yet found a way to play more than one man in each position although we can shift them around and maybe make outfielders outa them or put 'em at ketch like we done with Howard but if some of the second division teams don't start beatin' Cleveland we may be in trouble.

"Like I said, though, I wanna see some of these guys before I start passin' comment and that's why I ain't talkin'."

Sorry, folks. That's why it's impossible to offer any quotes today from Charles Dillon Stengel, the sphinx of Saint Pete.

Dressen's Tower of Babel

March 28

Saint Petersburg, Florida, March 27—Charlie Dressen breezed into Saint Pete the other day with his Washington Senators. But it wasn't as a zephyr. Charlie is more of the tornado type. Lots of wind.

The unfrocked manager of the Dodgers, 1953 vintage, hasn't changed a bit and is totally unchastened by his year's exile to the Pacific Coast League. He's as effervescent as ever and fairly bubbles with enthusiasm, even though his Senators bear only the skimpiest resemblance to the Brooklyn team he once handled so successfully. The Washingtons go through the same general motions but not nearly as well.

Yet Charlie is so high-spirited he'd be convinced that the Peoria Rinkydinks—if they were his Peoria Rinkydinks—could beat the Giants four straight in the world series. In other words, this disillusionment with the Senators hasn't set in thus far. Maybe it never will because that eternal optimist, Mr. Dressen, wears only rose-colored glasses. But there's a contagion to his enthusiasm and he may even do better than anyone expects.

The ever-cheerful Charlie has an odd assortment that includes Cubans, South Americans, Italians, and citizens. He can't even talk to a third of his squad and, when Dressen can't talk, its like shutting off his supply of oxygen. His chief interpreter at the moment is Camilo Pascual, one of his better pitchers.

"I don't know where all these guys come from," said the grinning Charlie, enjoying himself hugely. "A couple more rolled in today. There's a guy named Crespo. His first name? I dunno. Wait a minute till I ask my man. Hey, Pascual."

The pitcher trotted over to the bench and Charlie began to guffaw in brisk merriment.

"Get a load of this," said Charlie in an aside. He turned to Pascual. "Crespo," he said deliberately. "Primo Nombre, huh?"

A smart fellow, that Pascual. He understood in practically no time. But his reply was unintelligible.

"Don't give me that," said Dressen, "write it out." So Pascual wrote it out as "Alejandro." Don't bother to remember the name, though. Alejandro Crespo won't be around that long.

"And then I got the two Italians," said Charlie. "I think the State Department wished them on me. They're kinder using us as a farm club. One's from Rome and the other from Bologna. They didn't eat for the first three days. But they've been eating real good ever since Cookie Lavagetto joined me.

"We'd hardly opened camp when Clark Griffith said to me, 'Charlie, we ought to have our own interpreters.'

" 'You're doggone right, Griff,' I says to him, 'how do I know them guys are interpreting correctly?'

"It's a fact, too. I can't understand what they're saying. They all sound like rattlesnakes to me. Even when I was with Brooklyn, I never was too sure that Campy was giving the right instructions to Amoros. You know what Casey Stengel told me. He said that the first two words any foreign ball player learns is ham and eggs. He says I should hold up a slice of ham for the bunt sign and a fried egg for the hit sign."

Charlie whistled shrilly. All his Latins seem able to understand that without the aid of an interpreter.

"Bucky Harris said this ball club would give me a rude awakening in midsummer," airily announced the chipper Charlie. "Ha, ha. I never had a more rude awakening than when Bobby

Thomson hit that home run. It was a long, long walk to the clubhouse that day.

"But the only time I ever thought I was asleep on a ball field was when I was managing Oakland and had Billy Martin of the Yankees playing for me. He wasn't on the Yankees then, of course, but he was on his way. We were getting a sound shellacking and it was a long inning. But there was one out when the batter hit the ball to Wilson, my shortstop.

" 'Hurray,' I say to myself. 'We'll make a double play and get this inning over with.' Wilson tosses to Martin at second for the force-out. Then I sit up straight and blink. Instead of whipping the ball over to first for the double play, Martin rolls the ball in toward the mound, slings his glove away and everybody runs for the dugout.

" 'Wait a minute,' I whisper to myself and you'll notice I didn't say it out loud. 'Am I crazy? Or are there more than two outs?' But the umpires don't say nuthin' and the other team goes onto the field. I've been in baseball for a long while but that's the first time I ever saw an inning finished with only two outs."

Cheerful Charlie will need a lot of two-out innings if he is to budge the Senators from sixth place.

For Whom the Bell Tolls

March 29

Tampa, Florida, March 28—The slickest trader in the baseball business has always been Branch Rickey. Whenever the Mahatma starts his spiel, other club executives stuff cotton in their ears, clutch their wallets and look frantically around for the nearest exit.

The Top Branch has made so many advantageous deals down through the years that most folks think he never has made a mistake. He has, though.

The worst deal he ever made, perhaps, was the one in which he traded Gus Bell from Pittsburgh to Cincinnati for three nonentities. In thunderous tones the Deacon announced that Bell just didn't have what it took to be a major leaguer. That season Bell tolled away with a .300 batting average and thirty home runs while winning nomination as the starting center fielder in the All-Star game.

For some reason which defies comprehension, the Mahatma didn't take to the likeable young man from Louisville, suh. Yet Bell seemed to fit to the letter Rickey's prescription for a young ball player. He could run, he could throw and he could hit with power. What's more, his personal habits were beyond reproach and he was a devoted family man. Rickey dotes on that because he, himself, is the nearest thing to a marriage broker the big leagues have had.

"Are you married, boy?" is the first question he tosses at a newcomer. "No? Are you engaged? Do you have a girl? There's nothing like marriage, my boy. Find yourself a nice girl and marry her. Best thing in the world for you."

Not only was Bell married but he was madly in love with his wife. When she lost her mother in an accident, he was especially attentive to her, taking her on some of the road trips.

En route to training camp one year, one of the children took sick and the worried Gus reported late. Rickey should have had more of an understanding and appreciation of the situation than anyone else. Somehow or other, he didn't.

The Mahatma had the impression that the young outfielder wasn't as absorbed in baseball as he should have been and didn't hustle enough.

"Young man," said Rickey to him one day, transfixing him with a steely glare. "I've a good mind to send you to Hollywood in the Coast League."

"Go ahead," said Gus with indifference. "I can be closer to my family there." After two weeks of banishment, however, he was recalled to Pittsburgh.

Finally Rickey took a personal hand in teaching Gus—his real name is David Russell Bell—how to hit to right field. A special class was held one morning, Prof. Rickey barking instructions to his left-handed slugger.

"By gosh, boy!" exhorted Rickey, "you're big and strong. You're losing all your power when you slice to the opposite field. You must learn to pull. Let's work on it." So they worked for a couple of hours and Bell was soon lashing booming drives to right, never to left. The Mahatma beamed.

In his first time at bat that afternoon Bell doubled down the left-field line. Perhaps that's when Rickey gave up on him.

It was in October of 1952 that Gus received a 'phone call from a baseball writer.

"What do you think of the trade, Gus?" the typewriter-pounder asked.

"What trade?" said Gus. He was told how Gabe Paul of the Redlegs, the youngest David Harum in the business, had hornswoggled Rickey.

"That's wonderful," said Gus, delighted to escape.

It was a break in more ways than one. It brought Gus into contact with the hard-bitten Rogers Hornsby, the Redlegs' manager. The Rajah made a hitter out of him.

"I don't care what anyone else says about Hornsby," says Gus. "He was great. I had been overstriding and he shortened my stride. I'd been waggling my bat too much. He steadied me. Most of all, he concentrated on my timing, teaching me to forget about pulling the ball and to aim through the box. 'Once you get your timing down,' he told me, 'you'll get your share of homers.' And that's just about the way it worked."

Now Bell is toiling for Birdie Tebbetts, a quick-witted and understanding man. Birdie thinks the world of him—and vice versa.

"I don't know how Gus ever got the rap of not being a hustler," says Birdie scornfully. "He's a perfect ballplayer for a manager. He has the right temperament and he's a real hustler. His one fault is that he's a worry wart. If he isn't hitting, he lets it eat him out inside.

"I'd say he rates with the best center fielders in the game, right up with Duke Snider and Willie Mays. But the New York writers give them all the publicity."

It's astonishing to think that Rickey didn't cotton to so admirable a youngster as Bell. He has all the physical, mental and moral attributes the Mahatma seeks in ball players. Apparently the Top Branch just goofed. There's no other explanation.

A Visit With the Challenger

September 8

North Adams, Massachusetts, September 7—Archie Moore lolled back in an overstuffed easy chair in the living room of his quarters at Camp Kenwood. His hands were clasped on the back of his head and a glint of perpetual amusement was in his eyes. Even in repose there is something strikingly regal about this king of the light-heavyweight division. The one jarring note, however, is the pixie look he has. It seems a trifle unkingly.

At the admitted age of 39 Archie has been a part of the fist-fighting dodge for some twenty-odd years. Nothing about it is new to him. Somewhere and at some time it's happened to him before—except the fact that he now is training to meet Rocky Marciano for the heavyweight championship of the world at the Yankee Stadium on Tuesday, Sept. 20.

"It's the same thing, though," Moore insisted, a slight smile curling his lips. "Everyone puts emphasis on it but me. I'm training the same as I've always trained. However, this is longer, more monotonous." His grin widened. "So I keep myself entertained by shooting my target pistol, playing softball, driving my car, fishing, gliding and . . ." Whoa! What was that last one?

Archie had neglected to mention that early in his training he decided to take flying lessons. As chairman of his own entertainment committee, he thought it would be fun. It didn't faze him, but it scared the daylights out of Julius Helfand, chairman of the New York State Athletic Commission; Jim Norris, the boxing promoter; Harry Markson, the managing director of the International Boxing Club, and almost everyone else. It almost took a presidential decree to slow down the stubbornly independent Moore, but he was grounded. Then he took to scorching the roads at 100 miles per hour in his racing thunderbolt. It was a tough job but they slowed him down there, too.

Gliding? Was this a mysterious new device to demonstrate that he wasn't scared of anything up to and including the rock-fisted Rocky?

"Not quite," he laughed. "I have a glider pilot here, Tony Crivelli from Switzerland. He ties onto the plane of my regular pilot, George West, and then cuts loose. It looks as if he'd crash into a mountain but he knows those updrafts and wind currents so well that he glides off. He even does loops. That looks like fun. I haven't been in that glider yet but I will soon."

Archie is the most relaxed challenger this tourist ever saw. It's not a pose with him, either. However, he's so smart that a fellow might be justified in being a mite suspicious. No. It's probably genuine.

His visitor made the mistake of mentioning Lucky Thompson, the band leader, whom Archie has been backing.

"Wait," said Archie, bounding to his feet, one finger upraised and the amused gleam in his eyes flickering still brighter. He ducked into the next room and emerged with a tape recorder. He hooked up the gadget, turned the dials and gazed dreamily at the ceiling as he waited for music to emerge. It was plaintive music, the melody masked by a fancy arrangement.

"It's 'Embraceable You,' " translated Archie. After great ear-straining the tune was recognized. "That saxophone you hear is Lucky's," Moore added, speaking reverently. "Now he's playing 'How Deep Is the Ocean?' " At that moment the ocean barely swam into focus—or whatever the aural equivalent of focus is.

Ahem. Archie obviously was a musician. What instrument does he play?

"I'm no musician," said Archie cheerfully. "I just like music. I have been accused of playing the bass fiddle but I deny it. My relation with Lucky? No, I wouldn't say I've been his manager for the past five or six years. Call me his mouthpiece." The Great Mouthpiece, eh? Archie sure knows how to talk.

Fascinating as this ancient gypsy is, it was imperative that he be detoured to the business at hand. Had he ever seen Rocky fight?

"Twice," he said, holding up two fingers. "Once against Walcott and once against Charles, the first fight with each. I was tremendously impressed by him." This was a startling statement in itself. Most challengers are inclined to say that the champion is an ineffable bum. Never can it be stated that Archie falls into any orthodox mold.

"I'll tell you what impressed me most," he said. The amused glint had disappeared from his eyes. He'd stopped his feinting and fancy footwork. He'd become serious. "I was impressed by his determination to win. Any time a champion goes out as if he's destined to win and doesn't sit back to wait for someone to give it to him, he must impress you.

"And that's why ours will be such a great fight. I'll match his determination with my own."

Archie sounded convincing. And in the background Lucky Thompson was still beating out a tune.

A Visit With the Champion

September 11

Grossinger, New York, September 10—Rocky Marciano pushed himself firmly away from the dinner table, he had the strength for it, too, because he'd just polished off a steak in most expert fashion.

"How about our usual after-dinner walk?" he said to his companion. For the visiting fireman this was part of the ritual, dinner with Rocky in his cottage on the edge of the mountain top airport here and then a long, conversational stroll up and down the runway.

"Just a second," said the heavyweight champion of the world. "How do you like my new cap?" He said it proudly as he donned a Red Sox baseball cap. A small boy with a new toy couldn't have looked more pleased than Rocky with the Bosox bonnet clamped firmly down over his black hair.

"Ted Williams sent me this," he added prouder still. "What a wonderful bunch of guys those Red Sox are.

"I visited their dugout just before I came up here and I never met more enthusiastic boxing fans in my life. Just before I left them Jimmy Piersall came over and whispered in my ear: 'Hey, Rock,' he said, 'would you mind having your picture taken with

Arthur Daley in 1955 with the heavyweight champion of the world, Rocky Marciano.

me? I want it for my scrapbook.' Gee, would I mind? It was an honor for me to have my picture taken with a player like Jimmy Piersall."

There even could be some significance to the fact that the Red Sox cap was size 7⅛, the identical size Rocky had when he was a crude unknown in Brockton, struggling to gain recognition. His head hasn't swelled a fraction since he became heavyweight champion because he is still the same warmly human, gentle, modest and humble man now as he was then.

A week from Tuesday the Brockton Blockbuster will be making his sixth defense of his crown when he meets Archie Moore at the Yankee Stadium. A few days ago Archie had tossed one casual remark over his shoulder. Perhaps it was a booby trap of some sort because Moore is a very cute guy who may even be trying to start a war of nerves.

"I understand," he had said slyly, "that Rocky has started to take dancing lessons at Grossinger's."

"Who me?" exclaimed Marciano when the statement was relayed to him. His face crinkled into a grin and he stopped short on the airstrip as if Archie had just popped him in the solar plexus and taken all the wind out of him.

"Gosh," said Rocky, "I can't dance and I never could. I'm the world's worst dancer and if you don't believe it, you can ask my wife."

Maybe Archie was merely making a left-handed suggestion that the champion should try to improve his footwork.

"A very amusing fellow is Archie," said the smiling Marciano. "I never met him until we signed for the fight and I must admit that I got a big kick out of him. He arrived wearing a yachting cap and a Van Dyke beard. The photographers asked him to pose while winking. He winked for five minutes and along came a guy who pleaded for just one more. 'I can't,' said Archie. 'I must be dignified.'

"But I never have been concerned with my footwork, even in the ring and I've never attempted to be quick on my feet. My only interest was in having the proper balance in order to give the leverage to my punches. I'm no Fancy Dan and it would be silly for me to pretend to be one."

That might be considered the understatement of the century. It's Rocky's crudeness which is one of his greatest assets although that bull-in-a-china-shop style also has brought him scathing denunciation as a dirty fighter.

"Maybe I'm too sensitive for my own good," he said earnestly. "But I want people to like me. I want to be a popular champion. I was hurt real deep by the blasting I got after the Cockell match. I've never thrown a dirty punch in my life deliberately. You have to be clever to thumb a man or pull illegal tricks on him. I'm not clever.

"In the first place, I have the shortest reach of any heavyweight champion in history. So I have to get in close. I put so much into every punch that, even when I miss, I'm still attached to the glove and my body follows through. I realize that still pictures make it look as though I hit Cockell after he was down. I was horrified when I saw them. But I studied movies of that punch, frame by frame, and was relieved to see that his knee hadn't touched when I threw that punch.

"I worked hard to get where I am. When I was first starting I used to box in the Y.M.C.A. in Brockton every single day. Since the Y was closed on Sundays, I made friends with the janitor so that I could sneak in even then for workouts.

"Charlie Goldman made me what I am today and I noticed he no longer hollers instructions to me while I'm sparring. So maybe I'm learning. Charlie tells me that he used to make like Svengali to force me to move my arms. Now I do it by instinct."

Dusk had settled over the airstrip before the walk was ended. By the time the cottage was reached, the serene Rocky was talking freely about the subject uppermost in his mind, the pennant chances of the Boston Red Sox.

1956

Bad-Ball Hitter

March 23

Bradenton, Florida, March 22—The Milwaukee pitchers had been in training camp for more than a week before the rest of the squad reported. The strong-arm boys were sharp, fast and confident when they faced the hitters, winter rust still on their bats.

Henry Aaron stepped into the batting cage for his first look at a thrown ball since the previous autumn. He swung three times and rifled three balls over the distant center field fence.

"Ol' Henry is ready," he announced emphatically.

It seems that Ol' Henry—except that he's actually Young Henry—is always ready. Three years ago this amazing performer was a 19-year-old second baseman for Jacksonville in the Sally League. A year later he was a regular outfielder on the Braves. And now, a venerable 22, he's attaining stardom with such speed that none would be too surprised if he won the National League batting championship this season.

Henry is a deceptive youngster with a wry sense of humor. He likes to give the impression that he doesn't know who is pitching and that he cares less. And he also hornswoggles the pitchers into thinking that he drowses off between pitches. He merely relaxes in sleepy-eyed languor.

Rain held up a Giant-Braves game at the Polo Grounds last year and the athletes idled in the clubhouse with cards and whatnot. Henry got involved in a red-hot checker game with Charlie White, the catcher. White studied the board with great deliberation and finally made his move. He looked up at Henry, who seemed sound asleep.

"Wake up, Henry," he said sharply. "It's your move."

"Oh," said Henry. He reached for a checker and made a triple jump.

That's the way Henry bats, too. He's always ready and on the alert, appearances to the contrary. Furthermore, he'll swing at anything. The experts say that Yogi Berra, once the champion bad-ball hitter in the big leagues, no longer is in Henry's class.

"Henry's strike zone," says the laughing Jolly Cholly Grimm, his manager, "is from the top of his cap to his shoes. I haven't seen anyone like him since Joe Medwick was in his prime."

"I make up my mind to swing at a pitch," drawls Henry with a careless shrug of his shoulders. "So I swing. I don't look for no walks."

The pitcher who gives Henry the most trouble is Robin Roberts of the Phillies. Part of that difficulty, however, Henry may have brought on himself. One day he tagged Roberts for a home run and jogged disinterestedly to the bench where happy teammates pounded his back.

"Great stuff, Henry," one of them chortled. "I hope you realize you hit that off the best pitcher in baseball."

"Not to me, he ain't," Henry replied. The grapevine carried that crack back to Roberts and he's been trying ever since to convince Aaron of the inaccuracy of the appraisal.

The youngster's propensity for wild swinging practically ruined Bill Bruton as a base stealer for much of last season. The fleet center fielder would break for second and Henry would foul one off. This continued so repeatedly that the weary Bruton finally gave up.

Not until the batting order was changed and Bruton stopped hitting in front of Aaron did he take off the brakes. Then he wound up with twenty-five steals, the high for the league.

Henry is essentially a wrist-hitter. He's not big enough for power. An inch under six feet and weighing 170, he snaps into a pitch with whiplash effect. Yet his twenty-seven homers indicate he can get distance. As a 20-year-old freshman he batted .280 and then advanced to .314 last season. The end is not in sight.

The biggest break Henry got—no pun is intended—occurred when Bobby Thomson broke his ankle in spring training. So the ex-infielder from the Sally League became overnight a big league outfielder.

"Even before that happened," said Grimm, "I knew I had to find a spot somewhere on the ball club for him. He runs well and is real quick in his throwing, snatching at a ball like Willie Mays. He hit well from the start but it was the injury to Thomson that gave him his chance. He sure did capitalize on it."

"I was ready," said Henry, a faint smile erasing his deadpan expression. "I had spent that winter playing the outfield in Puerto Rico. I hit good there and I was still hitting good when I reached training camp."

He shrugged his shoulders again, almost as if that explained everything. Nothing seems to bother him. Aaron was having a salary wrangle with the front office when Lou Perini, the owner of the Braves, attended a Milwaukee baseball writers dinner. His praise of Henry bordered on the extravagant and Henry looked as though he was sleeping through it all. But when he finished, the youngster nudged Grimm.

"Does he mean that before I sign or after I sign?" he asked. A wide-awake operator is the sleepy-eyed Henry Aaron.

Listening to John Landy

May 22

John Landy of Australia is so intelligent, clear-thinking and logical that his words should never be ripped away from the general background of his conversation. It's when they are taken from context that they seem shocking or vainglorious or both. Want a sample?

"Breaking through the four-minute mile barrier is a stock performance," he said casually. "I could keep doing it indefinitely."

But he's also the chap who frankly admitted that Roger Bannister of England had more ability as a miler and that there were a half dozen milers in the world today who had far greater potential than he had himself.

The curly haired Aussie has the rare knack of being able to stand off and view himself in cold, analytical detail. Although he has turned in more fast miles than any man in history—six that range from 3:58 to 3:59.6—the world record-holder for the classic distance harbors no illusions. He realizes full well his limitations. He knows that he is a runner who always will be vulnerable to the sprint finish of a fast-closing racer.

"I'd rather lose in 3:58," he once philosophized, "than win in 4:10."

The phenomenon from Down Under was in our village over the weekend—naturally this can be described only as a "flying visit"—for a television appearance on Sunday and a luncheon that *Sports Illustrated* tossed for him at Leone's yesterday. At least it gave him a chance to express his thoughts and hopes and fears. Perhaps he could explain his theories about the defeat in 3:58 as being preferable to the victory in 4:10.

"There's just no point in running a 4:10 mile," he said with a ready and disarming smile. "To break new ground is a thrill. If I run, I want to run well and it just isn't worth the effort unless I can do my best. I've been beaten twice under four minutes and on both occasions I thought I could put it over."

Bannister outsprinted him once, 3:58.8 to 3:59.6, and Jim Bailey upset him stunningly a fortnight ago, 3:58.6 to 3:58.7.

Landy is a man of infinite charm and graciousness. He has borne up exceedingly well under the strain of mass interviews, personal interviews, radio interviews, television interviews and what-not on both coasts. He's just a slim 146-pounder who has been asked to assume the crushing burden of serving as Australia's Olympic ambassador.

"I'm smartening up to your techniques," he said with a sly smile when hustled from one button-holer to another.

In a moment of despondency in Finland during the spring of 1954, he spoke after he had approached the four-minute barrier for the umpteenth time but had been turned back once again. That's when he made a most unprophetic statement.

"The four-minute mile is impossible," he said dejectedly. "If I ever do it, it will be a fluke." Ahem! Did he still feel that way?

"After I did it," he said with a grin, "I realized that it was not a physical feat of high caliber. Some of the things I said then were not reasoned out. After a race I'm in an emotional state and not always responsible."

Okay. Since he was in a responsible state at the moment, perhaps he could answer another question. How much faster can he run a mile?

"I'm within two or three seconds of my physical limits," he said, carefully measuring his words. How about Bailey, the

Australian-born student at Oregon? Could he again upset Landy in a rematch?

"Yes, without question," said Landy in matter-of-fact fashion. "He's a much stronger runner than I ever was."

Landy undoubtedly will be favored in the 1,500-meter run, the Olympic mile, at Melbourne in November. How highly did he regard his chances?

"There are a half dozen or so others," he said, "with more potential than I. I'd have to name the two Hungarians, Tabori and Iharos; the two Britons, Ken Wood and Brian Hewson; Gunnar Nielsen of Denmark; the two Australians, Bailey and Lincoln, and your Bobby Seaman of U.C.L.A. They all have greater speed than I, a factor which cannot be developed. I'd even risk saying that Seaman has the best potential for approaching 3:50.

"But I can't see that happening now. No one can do it on the knowledge available to us now, but there may be new and revolutionary theories for dieting and training which may bring the mile record far lower than it is at present. I can visualize a mile in 3:55 but I can't visualize myself running it."

An engaging and articulate bloke is John Landy. He's given much sound thought to the business of bursting past the four-minute barrier and can appraise with detached interest the most remarkable miler to date, John Landy.

A Remarkable Woman

September 30

The team championship at the National Amateur Athletic Union track and field meet in 1932 was won by the Employers Casualty Company of Dallas. Its points were achieved through the winning of five individual championships and the tying for a sixth. The entire "team" consisted of one 18-year-old girl, Babe Didrikson.

Implausible is the adjective which best befits the Babe. As far as sports is concerned she had the golden touch of a Midas. When she was only 16 she was named to the All-America women's basketball team. She once hit thirteen home runs in a softball double-header. Her top bowling score was 237. In the 1932 Olympics she won two events, setting world records in each, and placed second in the third test although again breaking the world record.

But it was as a golfer in her later years that she gained most renown, dominating the distaff side of the divot-digging pastime with awesome efficiency. Best remembered is the rueful flippancy Bob Hope tossed over his shoulder after pairing with her in a charity match.

"I hit the ball like a girl and she hits it like a man," he said.

Hope was at least half-correct. The Babe hit the ball like a man.

But behind that steel-sinewed, square-jawed facade was feminine softness and gushy sentimentality. The first time the Babe ever had any extra money, she took her mother to a department store in her native Beaumont, Texas.

"Momma, pick you out a dress," drawled the Babe pridefully. Momma did.

"Pick you out another one," urged the Babe, glowing with satisfaction at the astonished look on her mother's face. The Babe kept urging until eight dresses were selected.

"Momma," said the Babe triumphantly, "now you got a dress for every day in the week and two for Sunday." Her devotion to her beloved Momma and Poppa was heartwarming.

There was a tender awkwardness to her romance with George Zaharias, the massive wrestler. They were mutually attracted the moment they met and their love story was a rich and rewarding one through courtship, matrimony and beyond.

Babe Didrikson Zaharias made a strange confession in her autobiography *This Life I've Led,* a wonderfully human character exposition that she wrote with the aid of Harry Paxton.

"Before I was even in my teens," she declared, "I knew exactly what I wanted to be when I grew up. My goal was to be the greatest athlete that ever lived."

This was an odd ambition because the best woman athlete in almost any sport is about on a par with a schoolboy champion. Yet the Babe became the greatest of her sex beyond question and her golf frequently attained unbelievable proficiency. It was no accident, no reliance on natural ability alone. She worked at it with the same indomitable ability with which she fought against the cancer that was to take her life.

Before she started out in the first golf tournament of her career, a reporter asked how well she expected to score.

"I think I'll shoot a 77," she said nonchalantly. This was a bit of bombast which she airily characterized as "Texas talk."

So the gal from Texas shot a 77. It was a freak, of course, and she did not linger long in the match play rounds which followed. But this experience impressed on her the need for giving polish to her game. She did it in typical fashion.

The Babe practiced sixteen hours a day each weekend. On weekdays she was on the course at 5:30 A.M. for a three-hour session. Then she went to her regular job. Most of her lunch hour was spent chipping balls onto a leather chair in her boss' office. After work she took lessons for an hour and practiced until dark.

"I'd hit golf balls until my hands were bloody and sore," she once grimly explained. "Then I'd have tape all over my hands and blood all over the tape."

The price for perfection was high but she paid it willingly. The rewards were high, too. Yet there never were any shortcuts for the Babe in anything, either in getting to the top or staying there. Once she was leading a tournament when she discovered that she played the wrong ball out of the rough. She alone knew it.

"That's it," she said resignedly to the officials. "I've been playing the wrong ball and I have to disqualify myself."

"But no one would have known the difference," remarked some unthinking spectator.

"I'd have known the difference," said the Babe sharply, "and I wouldn't have felt right in my mind. You have to play by the rules of golf just as you have to live by the rules of life. There's no other way."

This was no mere muscle girl who died the other day. The greatness of her athletic achievements permeated the entire character of Babe Didrikson Zaharias until the strength and splendor shone through. She was a remarkable personality.

A Remarkable Tribute

November 12

The Touchdown Club of New York is the first organization of its kind in this country. On its membership rolls are some 500 former varsity football players from every Conference in the land, united in their devotion to the gridiron game but undistracted by any stardust in their eyes. They have been too close to the sport to be emotionally moved by anything except the genuine article.

They represent as complete a cross section as can be found and that's what makes tomorrow's affair so remarkable a tribute. The Touchdown Club will hold a "Knute Rockne Memorial Luncheon" at Leone's Restaurant to mark the twenty-fifth anniversary of the death of the great Notre Dame coach in a plane crash.

Perhaps nothing better demonstrates the unique hold that Rock still exerts on the imaginations of football folk everywhere. Coaches such as Pop Warner, Amos Alonzo Stagg, Percy Haughton, Hurry-Up Yost, and Gil Dobie were famous before Rock finished high school. Each still has a coterie of devoted followers but Knute Kenneth Rockne wove such a spell over everyone that his appeal spread far beyond the parochial confines of South Bend. He was a national figure.

Knute Rockne, a symbol and an inspiration.

The President of the United States sent condolences at Rock's death and millions of Americans mourned because the one-time immigrant boy from Norway was more than a football coach. He was a symbol and an inspiration. Nor was this entirely due to the fact that Knute was so astonishingly successful, although it did serve to focus attention on him.

As soon as Rockne entered a room, he dominated it. He

seemed to exude electric sparks that had magnetic qualities. His voice had a sing-song stridency of unforgettable distinction. His eyes flashed and twinkled. He had keen intelligence and sparkling wit.

The Notre Dame coach was one of those rare beings who could outsmart the other fellow and then give him the beguiling talk that would make him like it. Even his fellow coaches admired him immensely. His Notre Dame players worshiped the ground he trod—and still do.

It was a happy accident that took Rock to South Bend. He grew up in Chicago but was so poor that he had to go to work after high school in order to get money for college. He had his mind set somewhat vaguely on the University of Illinois but agreed to accompany a couple of his schoolboy buddies to Notre Dame, even though Rock wasn't a Catholic.

He loved it beneath the golden dome and college was easy for him. His freshman marks averaged 98.3. Then it was 91.3 as a sophomore, 90 as a junior and 92.5 as a senior, including ten perfect marks of 100.

Rock applied that brilliant mind to football and he was always one full season ahead of the rules committee. He'd devise something novel, such as his Notre Dame shift, and the authorities would clamp a restriction on it. So Rock would dream up something else. He was usually one season ahead of the opposition, too.

However, the Swede—as Notre Damers called this Norwegian—was more than just a technical expert. He was a master psychologist, an unerring student of human nature. He knew which player needed praise and which needed a verbal lashing to produce superior effort. He handled each man individually and differently. But he even made a practice a delight. Rock's wit was so bouncy and so sharp that there never was a dull moment on old Cartier Field.

His dressing room orations could rival the one of Spartacus to the gladiators. Or they could be infuriatingly brief. Once Notre Dame was losing to Northwestern, 10 to 0, at the half, the Irish giving a miserable exhibition. Rock merely stuck his head in the dressing room doorway.

"Fighting Irish, bah!" he said. Notre Dame won, 13 to 10.

When Notre Dame beat Army, 7 to 6, in 1930, Rockne went to the West Point dressing room to console Chuck Broshous, the cadet who had missed the extra point.

"Don't let it bother you, son," he said comfortingly. "It's only a game."

But Broshous was inconsolable and Ralph Sasse, the Army coach, was vastly disappointed. It wasn't long thereafter, however, that the news reached West Point of Rockne's death. West Point players sat in a stunned silence.

"Chuck," said Sasse to Broshous. "I'm glad now you missed that extra point. Otherwise Rock wouldn't have won his last Army game."

1957

Between Two Putouts

January 8

In Jackie Robinson's last time at bat in the major leagues, Johnny Kucks struck him out for the final putout of the world series. Yogi Berra was so excited that he fluffed the ball and had to make a forcing throw at first. That happened only a few months ago and yet this reporter had so vague a recollection of it that he had to look it up.

There's considerable significance in that fact because there was no need to check back on Jackie's first at bat in the big time. That episode was imprisoned in memory for keeps and is as clear as if it had been seen only yesterday.

It was opening day of 1947, with the Dodgers facing the Braves at Ebbets Field. The curve-balling Johnny Sain fired one in and Robinson hit the ball sharply on the ground to short. It was one of those bang-bang plays with the ball and the base runner reaching first almost simultaneously, the toughest of all for a base umpire to adjudicate. But Al Barlick, one of the best in the business, never hesitated.

"Y're out," he shouted, jerking his thumb. Immediately he walked away toward right field.

Robbie had raced down the line with that breathless speed

he'd had in his younger days and his momentum carried him far beyond the bag. A look of disbelief spread across his face at the decision. Then he scowled and wheeled toward Barlick.

The Robinson of 1956 would have blistered the umpire. But the Robinson of 1947 had been too well schooled by Branch Rickey to begin his career in troublemaking fashion. He'd taken only one step when he remembered his lessons. Stopping short, he turned and jogged back toward the dugout without making the slightest protest. Up in his royal box, the Mahatma smiled contentedly. Jackie had obeyed orders.

The orders had been given to him in rough and brutal terms. Rickey had hammered home to his hand-picked candidate the burden he was carrying as the first Negro to play in the big leagues. Then the Mahatma suddenly denounced Jackie in language such as the psalm singing Top Branch never used, including racial slurs.

Robinson bristled and the hackles on the back of his neck arose. But he held fast to his temper, an explosive temper.

"Wonderful, my boy," beamed Rickey. "You reacted well. You will hear worse than that before you're through. I was merely testing you and I apologize for it. But you are a pioneer and this entire sociological experiment will depend on you. Never for a moment can you forget it."

Thinking back on the Robinson career, an observer can't help be impressed at the artful way he handled himself and his assignment. His first at bat was a vivid memory, one that was to grow sharper as Jackie let his behavior fall into the more natural pattern of the combative ballplayer he really was. He was careful in everything, even his relations with the press.

If you'll forgive a personal experience, it will be offered as an illustration of Robinson's shrewdness. Midway in Jackie's second season with the Dodgers, this reporter suddenly realized that Robbie had never once addressed him by name, although all conversational exchanges were on a friendly basis.

With that realization came the conviction that Robbie was not quite sure what form of greeting he should use. He didn't want to set himself apart from the other ballplayers by using the clumsy "mister" and yet he wasn't certain whether the first name approach would be too familiar.

Midway in his second season, I asked him an inconsequential question.

"You know the answer as well as I do, Arthur, because you've been around longer than I," he said. He'd smuggled in the first name in the middle of a long sentence and that lifted him over the bump in the road. He never was troubled thereafter.

Maybe it is too insignificant an item to be worth mentioning. But this reporter was tremendously impressed by the incident at the time because it demonstrated how Jackie was to keep advancing in surefooted fashion in the small things as well as in the big ones.

He was up for several years before he was thrown out of his first game by an umpire.

"Aha," said the press box tenants. "Robinson has come of age."

Perhaps he overdid it afterward because he's essentially such a hot-head that the marvel of it was that he stayed so self-controlled so long. Wise indeed had been Rickey in selecting such a trail blazer.

Robinson should be a cinch to make baseball's Hall of Fame after waiting for five years, the probationary period for retired ballplayers. He was great enough a competitor to make it on ability alone. But as the first Negro to play in the big leagues, the fellow who made it so much easier for those who followed, he rates it on that count, too. He was a vivid figure between his first time at bat in the majors and his last.

The Babe Ruth of Hockey

January 27

When Jean Beliveau of the Montreal Canadiens first skated out on the ice, every teen-age girl in the Montreal Forum sighed in the despairing rapture of unrequited love.

"I adore heem," said one. "He ees so beeg and so beautiful."

Beliveau is quite a handsome chunk of manhood, at that. The French-Canadians affectionately call him, "Le Gros Bill," because he is big in size and big in ability.

Physically, he's a wide-shouldered 6 feet 3 inches and a solid 205 pounds. At the age of 25 he hasn't even come close to his potential and yet he's already being acclaimed as the Babe Ruth of hockey. Awed old-timers whisper that Le Gros Bill may become the greatest hockey player of all.

Few athletes have been showered with such unrestrained praise or burdened with such fanatical adulation. However, he dismisses those imposters with a typical Gallic shrug and remains a quiet-spoken, modest youth whose inherent class and decency shine through. Meeting him for the first time the other day, this reporter was more impressed by Jean Marc Beliveau than by any athlete he'd met in ages.

Le Gros Bill speaks with a delightful French accent and has

Jean Beliveau: "He needs no protection."

the charm of a Charles Boyer. A courtly graciousness adds even more to his appeal. In fact, he's so poised in conversation that a fellow can't help but wonder why so much effort was made in the beginning to protect him from interviewers. He needs no protection.

Looking back on the situation, however, an observer must realize that Le Gros Bill was one of the sport's most famous players even before he turned professional. There were a couple of seasons when he just couldn't afford to leave the "amateur" ranks because he was making something like $20,000 a year. He smiled warmly when this was mentioned.

"Everyone was paid in the amateur league," he said, without embarrassment. He shrugged his shoulders. "I don't know why they call it amateur. I was making a good salary and was satisfied. But like any other business I wanted to go to the top. When I got a five-year contract, I signed with the Canadiens." Voilà! He made it sound simple and natural.

However, he didn't bother with the details. Supposedly, he received a $20,000 bonus for signing and $105,000 for the five-year term. That's a fantastic price, by hockey standards. But Beliveau is a fantastic player.

That freshman year was rugged in a couple of ways. In spite of his great natural talents, Le Gros Bill discovered he had so much to learn. He broke an ankle and a cheekbone, impairing his progress. Had the Canadiens overestimated his abilities? All Canada asked that questions with a growing anxiety.

In his second season, though, the big guy moved into his proper place. The Flying Frenchmen tore the league apart. Maurice (The Rocket) Richard led the scorers with 75 points. Another Canadien, Boom-Boom Geoffrion, was second with 74 points, while third place in this sweep went to Le Gros Bill with 73.

There has been no stopping him since. He hammered his way to the scoring championship last year with 88 points and seems sure to win again this season. Folks who know say he'll eventually wind up as the greatest scorer in hockey history.

"It's all done with the wrists," said Jean, demonstrating with a phantom hockey stick. "I shoot for the corner of the cage, whichever one the goalie lets me see the most of." He thought a moment. "Being lucky helps, too," he added.

"I was skating against Detroit," he said, "and I thought I lost the puck. I turned to go back. I looked down and saw the puck between my skates. So I hit it between the legs of Hall, the goalie. That was in the first minute of the game. We won, 1 to 0.

"Another time against Toronto, I was tired and about to go to the bench. So I swung from center ice—it must have been eighty or ninety feet from the goal—and I climbed over the boards without looking back. The crowd hollered. I looked back and discovered I'd scored a goal. It was a blooper that bounced over the goalie."

Beliveau moves on the ice with deceptive grace, almost with the nonchalance of a Nels Stewart. He doesn't seem to skate fast but few can stay with him. He has all the right instincts and all the right shots. And Le Gros Bill is so big and strong that an ordinary body check can't bend him away from a straight line. Unlike his great teammate, the aging Rocket, Beliveau is a two-way player, an asset on defense as well as on offense.

How fast can he make a puck travel?

"The hardest hitter," he said, "is Geoffrion. His shots have been measured at ninety-five miles per hour. Me? About the same."

A remarkable player and remarkable person is Jean Beliveau.

Fastest of Them All

April 21

When the image of Walter Johnson flashed briefly on the television screen during the baseball spectacular a week ago, more than one present-day major leaguer winced instinctively at the sight of the Big Train in action. It was only a glimpse but it was revealing. None of the moderns had ever seen Johnson and to them he was only a legend.

"A side-arm thrower!" exclaimed one with a shudder. "They're tough enough to hit even when they can't throw hard. But they say that Johnson was the fastest pitcher who ever lived. How could anyone hit him?"

The answer is rather simple. Not many did.

The big, raw-boned farm boy from Idaho pitched twenty-one years for the generally forlorn and trailing Washington Senators. Yet he never even bothered to learn how to throw a curve until his last half-dozen seasons. Every batter knew what was coming—a fast ball. But that knowledge was of little help.

Ping Bodie of the Yankees was a good fast-ball hitter. When he faced the Big Train for the first time, he stood frozen at the plate for three strikes.

"You can't hit what you can't see," he said.

Even the umpires had to steel themselves to keep from shutting their eyes when Walter's blazer crossed the plate. The great Billy Evans once made a blind call of a strike on Joe Gedeon. Gedeon questioned the call.

"What did you think it was?" said the umpire, avoiding a direct answer.

"How should I know?" said Gedeon with a shrug. "I'm asking you because I never saw it. I had to close my eyes."

Johnson feared his own speed. He was terrified by the possibility of killing a hitter with an errant pitch. Perhaps that's why he developed such phenomenal control. There even was one unbelievable season when the Big Train walked only thirty-eight men.

And what seasons they were! It took him a little more than two campaigns to orient himself. Starting in 1910, these were the victory totals he fashioned: 25, 23, 32, 36, 28, 27, 25, 23, 23, and 20. Five years later he came back with a twenty-three-game season and then a twenty-gamer. He won 414 games in all and, possibly most remarkable, 113 of them were shutouts.

The Washington ball club came to New York one weekend in 1908 to play the Yankees, then known as the Highlanders. Johnson spun a four-hit shutout on Friday. There were gasps of astonishment the next day when Walter began to warm up again. He pitched a three-hit shutout. There was no game on Sunday because Sunday ball had not been legalized.

On Monday, the Big Train chugged onto the mound again. It may sound like fiction, wildly improbable fiction, but it's in the record book. Johnson pitched a two-hit shutout.

Walter holds the strikeout record of 3,497, a mark that no other pitcher even has approached. His greatest one-inning feat? The Detroit Tigers had filled the bases through errors with none out. Coming to bat were baseball's three most feared hitters—Ty Cobb, Sam Crawford, and Bobby Veach. Johnson fanned them on nine pitches.

The beauty of Walter's greatness was that he was far more than a mere master of his trade. He had a character to match. Although he was a rugged looking, 200-pound six-footer with wide shoulders, long arms and square jaw, he was sweet, gentle and lovable. He never smoked, drank or chased around. He never complained to an umpire. He never "brushed back" a hitter. He was almost too good to be true.

It was because of Johnson that the baseball world rejoiced when the Senators won the 1924 pennant. At long last the Big Train would be in a world series even though he was near the end of his career. But twice the Giants defeated him before Walter came in as relief pitcher in the seventh and deciding game. A freak hit brought him victory in the twelfth inning.

"Don't feel too bad, fellows," said Jack Bentley of the Giants to his downcast teammates. "The good Lord just couldn't let Walter lose again."

There have been other sizzling fireball throwers since Johnson, including Dazzy Vance, Lefty Grove, and Bobby Feller. However, the experts are pretty well agreed that none could match the Big Train.

When Feller broke into the majors, an inquisitive Washington author, Shirley Povich, brought Johnson to a game. As they watched Rapid Robert, Walter repeatedly praised Feller's extraordinary speed.

"Tell me, Walter," said Povich, "is Feller as fast as you were?"

Johnson squirmed as his natural modesty fought a battle with his natural honesty. It hurt him to say so but he had to tell the truth.

"No," said Walter unhappily.

The Mad Hatter's Tea Party

August 21

There is an air of unreality to the fight in Seattle tomorrow night involving Floyd Patterson, the heavyweight champion of the world, and Pete Rademacher, an audacious amateur whose only claim to fame is that he won the Olympic heavyweight crown in Melbourne last December. Nothing about it makes much sense. This is a fantasy which might have been lifted from Alice in Wonderland.

"We're all mad here," said the Cheshire Cat to Alice. "I'm mad. You're mad."

"How do you know I'm mad?" said Alice.

"You must be," said the Cheshire Cat, "or you wouldn't have come here."

The Mad Hatter, of course, is Jack Hurley. He's the utterly delightful con man who is promoting the fight. Being slightly daffy—or extra smart—he's banned television and radio, consenting reluctantly to let a few boxing journalists sit at ringside. By seeming to avoid publicity, Hurley reaped reams of it. This is a deviousness worthy of the Mad Hatter.

Trying to sort out the other characters is not easy. The drowsy-eyed Patterson may be the Dormouse who keeps falling asleep. Cus D'Amato, the champion's proprietor, may qualify as the White Rabbit, who is always in a hurry. Rademacher has to have the same expectations as the Knave who is waiting for the Queen of Hearts to scream, "Off with his head!"

But somewhere in Wonderland at the Mad Hatter's tea party will be those quaint persons who have guaranteed Patterson the spectacular sum of $250,000 to flex his muscles against a rank amateur who is making his professional debut.

All that Patterson will give to Rademacher in exchange will be an awesome beating. There's no other way to figure it. The gulf between the amateur and the professional in sports is as wide as the Gulf of Mexico, a fact of life that leaves the baldish Olympic champion unimpressed and unalarmed.

The production also will leave him unpaid in all probability. Pete the Persuader was able to convince wealthy friends that he not only would be the first amateur ever to fight a professional heavyweight champion but that he would also be the first to dethrone one. So they eagerly anted up the quarter million guarantee to Patterson. Rademacher obviously is wasting his talents in the fight racket.

The zaniest aspect of the affair, perhaps, is that the amateur hardly is likely to take away coffee-and-cake money from the Mad Hatter's party. The explanation is offered that he's doing it in order to advertise an organization in which he's interested. The boys in the gray flannel suits on Madison Avenue, if any stopped to think of it, could advertise it better and less painfully.

This organization is Youth Unlimited, Pete Rademacher, vice-president. However, the fisticuffing veep is no youth and his talents certainly are limited. Although he is bigger than Patterson in physical dimensions, he also is, at 28, six years older. Pete also is better educated, having a college degree. What advantage that will give him deponent knoweth not.

It even brings to mind the story Casey Stengel tells of the low-salaried ballplayer who grumbled at the bonus paid a new teammate, a college graduate.

"Yeah," said the Yankee manager consolingly, "but you was

learnin' your trade and gettin' paid for it while the other feller was wastin' his time in college."

Patterson wasted no time in college. He was out in the world, learning his trade. He even received a course of postgraduate stature from Joey Maxim, the wily old pro who is the only man ever to beat him.

There are no short cuts in the brutal boxing trade. The hard way is the only way. Patterson took that road. Rademacher didn't.

This seems to be an even more one-sided affair than the recent shutout of Hurricane Jackson by the champion. Everyone knew in advance that the Hurricane didn't know how to fight and that he was a slap hitter of feather duster impact. But they also knew that he was tough and that he'd once survived twelve rounds against Patterson. Rademacher, on the other hand, never has fought more than three rounds.

When Mickey Walker was king of the middleweights, he carefully avoided all street fights.

"Professionals," he used to say, "should never fight civilians."

Rademacher is a civilian. That's why this entire production has overtones of fantasy.

"I'll never go there again," said Alice indignantly as she left the Mad Hatter's soiree.

"It's the stupidest tea party I ever was at in all my life."

It's His Own Description

October 14

"If I'm going to be a carpetbagger," said Walter O'Malley with a smile, "I might just as well carry the satchel."

The statement was made a week ago last night and it was made in the spirit of good, clean fun. An engaging person is the president of the Dodgers, a man of charm and amiability. Few men in baseball are as delightful or as likable as he. And none is more clever.

When The O'Malley tossed off his flippancy about being a carpetbagger, he was seated at a table with a few journalistic friends. The switch of the Dodgers from Brooklyn to Los Angeles was so close to consummation that an ordinary operative would have let down his hair ever so slightly and made at least a few guarded admissions. But Walter kept up the pretense to the bitter end.

And a bitter end it was to be for those faithful Brooklyn fans who enabled the Dodgers to amass a profit of $1,800,000 over a five-year span. That's the one ugly and inescapable fact that sets this deal apart from all other franchise transfers. Other teams were forced to move by apathy, or incompetence. The only word that fits the Dodgers is greed.

Admittedly Ebbets Field was a wretchedly outmoded baseball arena, one with hopelessly inadequate parking facilities. But it still could ring a lively tune on the cash register, approximately a third of a million dollars a year. Yet Walter was sincerely looking for a new site in Brooklyn, preferably with assistance from the civic authorities. But once Los Angeles began the siren song The O'Malley was so beguiled that he was lost.

The City of the Angels offered him more than the keys to the city. It gave him the keys to the kingdom. New York balked at twelve acres. Los Angeles enthusiastically proffered 300 acres. This is the biggest haul since the Brink's robbery—except that it's legal.

Baseball is a sport, eh? It may be for Tom Yawkey of the Red Sox, Phil Wrigley of the Cubs, and one or two others. But the crass commercialism of O'Malley and Horace Stoneham of the Giants presents the disillusioning fact that it's big business, just another way to make a buck.

If O'Malley—and Stoneham, for that matter—owned a grocery store or gasoline station, either could move his business to Timbuktu in order to add to his profits without an objection being raised. But baseball is an enterprise that cannot be run with the coldness of an I.B.M. machine. It has to be run with heart and sentiment and emotion, or maybe we've all been worshipping false gods for these many years.

Walter would have everyone believe that he strove with almost superhuman patience to save his franchise for Flatbush. If he didn't kiss the Blarney Stone, it's only because such a smack wasn't necessary. He sounded so convincing the other night. Yet if you permit a man to talk long enough—even a devilishly smart one—he eventually will trip over his words.

The O'Malley frankly proclaimed that Bob Moses' site on the old fair grounds was the best possible place for a new stadium—but not for the Dodgers. Fans in Brooklyn couldn't get there. Later on he declared that his main trouble was that the dyed-in-the-wool Dodger fans had moved from the borough and lived in Long Island. He spoke eloquently of the accessibility of Flushing from any place on the Island or Westchester via the networks of super-highways in bumper-to-bumper crawls.

None of it added up in the final analysis. At least one listener departed with the conviction that O'Malley had his carpetbag all packed. Yet Walter mentioned that four women who could influence him begged him to remain. One was his wife. One was his daughter. The others were Mrs. John Smith and Mrs. James Mulvey, each of whom holds a quarter interest in the ball club. But Walter has the say since he owns a half plus the voting rights for Mrs. Smith.

A day later The O'Malley was on his way to what may be the richest strike since Sutter found gold in California. That was the day when this reporter encountered in a Milwaukee hotel one of the prime movers of the Los Angeles deal, John Olds, the journalist.

"This is the big day," said John cheerfully.

"Sure is," was the answer by a dolt, who misinterpreted his remarks. "But we say the same thing every day during the world series."

"World series?" said John, shocked. "Who cares? This is the day the Los Angeles Council votes in the Dodgers."

He was right, of course. But it took the most adroit maneuvering of the most Artful Dodger to make it possible. This was a coup by The O'Malley that has to rank high among brilliant business sorties and the triumph is exclusively his.

But is it a triumph? The feeling here is that it is not. The feeling here also is one of galling resentment. Perhaps Messrs. O'Malley and Stoneham should be wished good luck and Godspeed in true sporting fashion. But these are not true sporting deals. They go without even a good-bye.

1958

A Ring From Bing

January 7

The phone rang and the operator said that California was calling, just a minute please.

"Hello, Arthur, old boy," said the voice at the other end, "this is Bing Crosby."

The identification was utterly superfluous. There could be no mistaking one of the best-known voices in the world.

"I'm out at Pebble Beach," said Bing. "Since we're about to start our golfing clam-bake here on Thursday, I thought I'd give you a puff. This one is gonna be bigger and better than ever—and all that sort of stuff. Really is."

Der Bingle was discussing—or trying to discuss—the seventeenth annual Bing Crosby pro-amateur invitation tournament, one of the high spots of the winter tour. It's been lengthened this year from the normal fifty-four holes to the championship distance of seventy-two holes; the prize money has been increased to a handsome $50,000 and interest in it will skyrocket the country over because the finish will be nationally televised on Sunday afternoon.

This exercise in divot digging and good fellowship is a charity affair that has raised close to a half million dollars for the communities near Pebble Beach. And it has cost the relaxed Mr. Crosby about half that much to promote it. For most of the years he also competed in his tournament. But not this time.

"I'm gonna be one of the narrators on the TV show," he said casually. "For months C.B.S. has been working on camera angles and we're gonna edit the films of the early rounds to about fifty minutes and then come in live. The joint will be loaded with celebrities and we hope it will be entertaining for the whole family. We're even having my new bride help in a fashion show for the women folks.

"The last time I played in this tournament was with Ben Hogan. We were second into the final day. Then a storm came up and it was pretty grim. It was too much for me and I couldn't help Ben any. So, when we passed my house off the thirteenth fairway, I offered a suggestion.

" 'Let's chuck it,' I said, 'and go inside for a drink, boy.'

"But Ben wouldn't quit. So I couldn't quit, either. Grrrrr. Very rugged. But that house sure looked warm and inviting when we finally made it. Pebble Beach is one of the most awesome courses in the world. When a storm hits, it's impossible.

"We studied the average scores of the pros in the past eleven years and were surprised to find they were 79, a fantastic average. As far as I know, the only guys who ever broke 70 were Cary Middlecoff with a 68 and Lloyd Mangrum with a 69.

"What's my best score? Pardon my blushes—a 71. But that was in the summer when the fairways were baked hard and the elements weren't misbehaving. I once had a 64 on a course that was easy but I find I now do best at Palm Springs, where the desert air is warm and the old bones have a chance to bake out.

"Is Bob Hope in my class as a golfer? Perish the thought! I don't think he is out of the 80s. Seriously, though, he once shot well but has been too busy working and picking up citations. I hate to admit it but he can play pretty good.

"But leave us not waste time on the likes of old Robert. Which reminds me. Whoja think I ran into out here the other day, making more noise than a bull moose? It was Toots Shor. He's waking up things.

"We start out this tournament for the first two days on the Monterey and Cypress Point courses, with 120 of the top pros in the nation and as many amateurs. They play one course one day and the other the next. Then the low-scoring fifty brace themselves to fight Pebble Beach for the next two days.

"The last two holes at Pebble Beach are as wicked a finishing pair as you'll ever find. On the long eighteenth, for instance, you have the ocean on one side, if you hook, and out-of-bounds on the other side, if you fade. I once saw Bobby Locke put two into the drink.

"And No. 9 is tough, long and alongside the ocean. And No. 8 is an uphill drive. Then you have to use a 2 or 3 iron over the ocean. It's a tough hazard, that briny, and the wind is generally blowing in your face. But the ocean is always there, always pounding, always moaning and always awesome.

"I wouldn't want you to underestimate Cypress Point, my boy. The sixteenth is a 220-yard carry over the wild, wild waves. Nothing between tee and green but that wet stuff. This is a hole on which Ed (Porky) Oliver scored a handsome 16.

"I remember the time Henry Ransom hit one short onto the beach with the curling lip of the cliff still protecting that green. He chipped up and the ball hit the lip and rolled back at his feet. He did it again. The third time the ball struck him on the belt buckle. Henry solemnly put the ball in his pocket and started to walk away.

" 'Quitting, Henry?' I asked.

" 'Bing,' he said, 'when they start biting back at you it's time to quit.'

"But it should be a great tournament. If you can't get out here, tune in your magic lantern on Sunday. So long, pal."

Jack the Giant Killer

January 15

"The biggest thrill is the winning of the championship," said Jack Dempsey yesterday. "Everything afterward rates secondary and I suppose that has to include my fight with Luis Angel Firpo."

The old Manassa Mauler smiled almost apologetically when he said it because his historic fight with the Wild Bull of the Pampas must rank as one of the greatest ring spectacles of all. Yet there was nothing dull or lackluster about Dempsey's winning of the championship from Jess Willard, as terrifying a bit of butchery as the sport has known.

The Mauler was back in town yesterday for the Boxing Writers' annual dinner, where he received the James J. Walker trophy for long and meritorious service to the cauliflower trade. Gray though his hair may be getting, Jack still moves with the same cat-like grace he used in stalking prey in the ring. Before he even had a chance to cut up old touches with his pals, he had memories stirring.

Willard was a formidable mountain of a man on that scorching Fourth of July in 1919. He was 6-foot-6 and 259 pounds with an oaken body and with ham-like fists. Dempsey was boyish in comparison, a restless 187-pounder who flitted and struck like a tiger.

Under Willard's battering ram left jab weaved Dempsey, searching for an opening. Then he found it. The Mauler's right exploded like a stick of dynamite in the midriff of the Pottawatomie Giant, bending him in two and bringing that jaw down within range. The Mauler exploded another stick of dynamite, his left. It struck a mite too high for a knockout, though. landing with frightening fury on Willard's cheekbone.

The blow splintered that cheekbone into thirteen pieces.

The giant wavered, but did not fall. The tiger pounced. Another one, two and Willard toppled with the majestic impact of a towering redwood tree, felled by another right to the body and another left to the jaw.

Dempsey could hardly wait for the kill, a tiger who had tasted blood. Referee Ollie Pecord held him off. There was a sickly, startled smile on Willard's face as he staggered uncertainly to his feet at the count of six. He did not remain uncertain long. The Mauler went raging in, fists flailing as Willard backed to the ropes. Dempsey had to stand on his tiptoes to hit him, but hit him he did. Big Jess sagged to the canvas.

Only a sadist could have enjoyed what was happening. Willard's face was a bloody pulp, his right eye closed tightly and features ripped to shreds. All he had left was his courage. Somehow the champion arose. Dempsey knocked him down. Once more Willard arose, phoenix-like. Down he went. It was up and down until there was no movement after the seventh knockdown. Dempsey had won—or had he?

There was confusion over the bell that the amateur timer merely compounded. Doc Kearns, Dempsey's manager, had hustled his tiger out of the ring and it was in the dressing room that they learned Big Jess had been saved by the bell. Back they went with Jack too disappointed and too arm-weary to continue at so frenzied a pace. Willard, a punching-bag by now, survived the second round, but was knocked out in the third.

How much money did Jack get from the fight?

"Nothing," he said with a grin. "At least there was nothing left. Just before the fight Doc came to me.

" 'Can you knock this bum out in the first round?' he asked.

" 'Why?' I said.

" 'You'd better,' he said, 'because I bet $10,000 against $100,000 that you'd flatten him in the first.'

" 'You're nuts,' I said. 'We're only getting $17,500. Don't tell me you've bet $10,000 of it.'

"I never did know whether or not Doc was kidding—you know what a kidder he was—but I do know that expenses ate up the $7,500 that was left. I was the champion of the world and broke.

"But the next week Doc booked me into Cincinnati. It was like a fair grounds with a stage and a big outdoor theatre. I gave boxing exhibitions and for that I was paid $7,500 a week. That wasn't bad, you know, considering the fact that I didn't even have 75 cents in my pocket."

It's now thirty-nine years since that momentous battle and the appeal of Dempsey has diminished little. His popularity is enormous still and only Babe Ruth ever could challenge him as the No. 1 sports colossus.

In fact, there have been only eight million-dollar gates in the entire annals of boxing. Joe Louis was involved in three. But Jack Dempsey was a part of five, including the biggest of all, the $2,658,660 gate for the second fight with Gene Tunney.

The Mauler's ring earnings have been more than $3,000,000, which isn't bad for a fellow who received nothing for winning his championship.

End of the Road?

January 29

The news that Roy Campanella had suffered a broken neck in an auto accident early yesterday morning was a genuine shocker. Round Roy always has been such a delightfully warm and wonderful guy that the report of his crack-up had to be weighed not so much from an impersonal baseball standpoint but from the totally personal standpoint of Campy himself.

Few ballplayers in the major leagues have enjoyed the immense popularity of the jolly Dodger catcher. Everybody likes him, because he always has a cheerful smile and a flippant greeting for everyone. And few men have loved baseball with Campy's intensity.

There was the time, for instance, when Buzzy Bavasi, the Dodger vice president, offered a blank contract to Campy. This is an old front-office trick that has been known to put ballplayers on the defensive, deflate their exorbitant demands, and result in a more modest salary. Campy signed happily and tossed it back, still blank.

"Let's not kid around," said the smiling Round Roy. "You know that I'll play no matter what you give me. I'll play for nothin' if I have to. You can write in the numbers yourself."

Bavasi sighed and gave a higher salary to Campy than had been intended. Whatever he received—and he always was handsomely rewarded—Campy still was underpaid. Three times he was voted the most valuable player in the National League and yet his true value could not always be reflected in his powerful hitting and in his adroit craftsmanship behind the plate. There just was no way of estimating his value to the team from a morale standpoint.

The best way to get a glimpse of the real Campy was to see him at Vero Beach, Florida, during spring training. He never sat alone. Younger ballplayers always clustered around him and a lot of the older ones did, too. Round Roy was like a mother hen with the chicks at his feet as he philosophized and talked baseball hour after hour.

"In order to be a good ballplayer," he was overheard to say one evening, "you gotta have a lotta kid in you. I mean you gotta be like a small boy. I'm still a kid. There ain't gonna be no retiring with me. They'll have to cut the uniform off my back."

Little did he dream that the end would come in a different way, an auto accident. It seems inconceivable that Roy could recover sufficiently to resume an active baseball career, not at the admitted age of 36. Whatever that age may be, Campy has been a professional for most of his life, starting at 14.

"I was big for my age," he said matter-of-factly, "and good enough to play with older boys."

He made it sound reasonable. And never did he give with the wink or indicate that he might be stretching the truth. Furthermore, the man talks with such sincerity that you have to believe him.

Deep was his scorn for the gripers and grousers who complained at some of the fancied discomforts of big league ball.

"Being up in the big leagues is heaven, son," he often would say. "I remember one day when I was catchin' in the Negro leagues. I caught a double-header in Cincinnati one afternoon, hopped a bus to Middletown, Ohio, and caught a double-header that night. And you complain?"

Roy's first year in organized ball was 1946, when he played under Walter Alston, the present Dodger manager, at Nashua, New Hampshire. One day Alston went to him.

"If the umpires ever throw me out, Campy," said Walter, "I want you to run the team."

"Me, skipper?" said Campy, wondering how the eighteen white boys on the squad would react to his leadership.

"Yes, you," said Alston firmly. "The other players have more respect for you than anyone else on the ball club."

Not too many years later Campy was with the Dodgers and the situation hadn't changed any. He still was held in the highest esteem.

Pee Wee Reese, the Kentucky colonel, once autographed a picture for him. It read:

"To Roy Campanella, a wonderful catcher and a wonderful person."

Few men on the Dodger squad were more helpful to the younger men than Campy. He was a good example, too. He didn't drink, and was a sound family man. He did smoke big cigars, though, his only weakness.

Many baseball men have long felt that he was destined to become the first Negro ever to be a big league coach. Not many men have a better way with kids than he. What's more, he talks their language.

"Cheat a little, son," he kept telling John Roseboro last spring.

Campy could have urged his possible successor to inch up behind the batter. But that graphic word, "cheat," told the story much better.

They don't come much nicer than Campy. He always has been one of the best.

Amid Hollywood Hoopla

April 19

Los Angeles, April 18—The first major league team ever to press spikes into the turf of the Memorial Coliseum was not the Dodgers but, ironically, the Giants. The transplanted Brooks were too busy being feted in a parade through town to take first licks in batting practice. So the former Polo Grounds tenants were accorded the dubious honor of drawing bead on the target of the neighborly left-field fence.

This is neighborly to the point of being ridiculous. It's a mere 250 feet down the foul line and the forty-two-foot screen is hardly a challenge.

The Giants emerged from the darkness of the runway under the stands and blinked in the blazing sunlight. Then eyes slipped into focus and every gaze turned toward the left-field barrier.

The ballplayers stopped in their tracks and laughed and laughed and laughed.

"Oh, man!" shouted Willie Mays.

He was convulsed. Then he pointed to the distant right-field barrier.

"They weren't thinkin' of Duke Snider," he said, "when they

built this ball park. Poor Duke. He ain't gonna reach that fence."

"Here goes, fellers," said Ed Bressoud, the first major leaguer to step into the batting cage at O'Malley's Alley. He hit one over the screen.

This was only the start. Before the Giants had finished their target practice, they had clouted twenty-five over the chummy screen. The Dodgers were not quite so productive, hitting only seven. Yet the temptation was so irresistible that Junior Gilliam took his cuts right-handed against a right-handed pitcher. By way of completing the travesty Pee Wee Reese took his last swing left-handed and "singled" to left. Even he was aiming at the barrier.

The boys were having fun and none of the tension that had been evident at the San Francisco opening was apparent.

"Ho, hum," yawned Valmy Thomas when Andre Rodgers cleared the screen.

"Bressoud takes an encore," said Coach Salty Parker. The young infielder thereupon hit another.

"This is a joke," said Whitey Lockman.

"You going for the porch, Willie?" taunted Hank Sauer as Mays was short with a violent cut.

"No, I ain't," said Willie the Wonder.

"Yes, you is," said Sauer as Mays hit one far over the screen. Willie hit six before he finished.

"Here she goes," yelled Sauer before he had even completed a swing that lofted the ball over the barrier. He grinned apologetically at the rubber-neckers. "I just had to try it."

The late-coming Dodgers drifted out of the runway, stared at the fence and laughed, too.

"Gosh," said Rube Walker, shaking his head when he saw the screen. "I better hold onto every pitch. If the ball ever pops out of my glove, it'll go over the fence."

"Hey, Walker," jibed Daryl Spencer. "I hear you're gonna bat right-handed this year."

"Look, Duke," shouted Mays at Snider. Willie pointed at the distant rightfield fences.

"Don't know why they wasted all that money putting up a fence," said the Duke sadly.

"How's the supply of baseballs holding out?" Greg Mulleavy asked Marv Grissom, the custodian of the ball bag.

"Not good," said Grissom.

"Why don't you bat rightly, Duke?" Reese asked Snider as the deposed Duke of Flatbush ripped a couple to his power field.

"I'll get one this way," said the Duke, shifting his feet and aiming at the left-field fence. He hit one deep.

"Did that go over the wall?" asked Reese.

"It sure did," said the Duke. "Mark it down on the score card."

Gil Hodges belted a pair in quick succession.

"You're a cinch to break Babe Ruth's record," said Reese, the ever helpful.

"The only record I'll break is Tommy Brown's," said big Gil. Brown was the young Dodger utility player in the postwar era who kept accurate count of his batting practice "home runs." He made Ruth look like a weakling. He hit 285 into the seats one season.

It wasn't until the game started, however, that one thing became apparent. The Giants were hitting against a background of empty seats. The Dodgers were hitting against partially filled stands that blurred visibility. Once the festivities began even the wondrous Mays was losing sight of fly balls against the white-shirted spectators.

It wasn't a record crowd for major league ball, however. The prediction of 90,000 customers, it seems, was just a Hollywood exaggeration.

Listening at the 19th Hole

June 27

East Norwich, Long Island, June 26—Tommy Bolt strode into the locker room at Pine Hollow today, still wearing the halo of his new, sweet-tempered amiability. It didn't seem to fit too naturally.

"Did you read those terrible things about me in the paper today?" he asked. He spoke with restraint and there was the same hurt in his eyes which would be seen only in the eyes of a collie that had just been kicked by Albert Payson Terhune.

"I was thanked for showing up at Piping Rock," said the new Open champion. He was referring to the one-day tournament in which he quit because of exhaustion after only nine holes. "I could have broken that commitment but I wouldn't. And then they write those lousy articles."

The hackles were starting to rise. The fellow with him put a calming hand on the arm of the explosive Bolt.

"Easy, Tommy," he said hurriedly, then turned to the listener and continued. "Tommy has learned control. I was with him in Italy during the war when he got so mad during a tournament in Florence that he threw his bag into a pond. But it was government issue and he had to wade in to rescue it."

"Watch what you're saying," said Tommy. "You're talking to

a newspaperman." He spat out the words as if they were unclean. Elsewhere in the locker room some of the more pleasant members of the golfing fraternity were gabbing away. Mention was made of the freak shot Bolt fired in the Open, in which the ball lodged inside a man's shirt.

"I once had a dilly in the Hartford open," said the beaming Ed (Porky) Oliver. "It was a par 5 and I belted a beautiful shot with a No. 4 wood. When I got down the fairway, the gallery was gathered around one spot as if a crap game was in progress. I walked up and there I find a lady of about 65. She's on a camp chair on the edge of the fairway and is wearing a full skirt. She has a huge bag in her arms. I'm looking for my ball when she says, 'It's here.' She points to her lap. Then she says, 'What do I do now?' I scratch my head and tell her, 'Just run this way, honey.' "

"I chipped a ball into a doll's lap in the Masters," said cheerful Jimmy Demaret.

"You would," said Claude Harmon.

"All I told her," said the grinning Demaret, "was, 'Stand up, sweetheart.' "

"I once hit a ball into a guy's pocket," said Doug Ford. "He fished it out and dropped it. But Middlecoff had one worse than that in the Palm Beach tournament one year. What was it, Cary?"

The golfing dentist made a wry face.

"That one was expensive," he said. "It cost me a thousand dollars. When I hit the ball into the fellow's pocket he got scared and ran into the woods thirty yards away and then dropped it. He left it behind a tree and in tall grass.

"By all the laws of golf and common sense, I should have been permitted to shoot from where the ball originally stopped. But some official ruled that I had to play it from where he dropped it—behind the tree and in the tall grass. I took a double bogey and finished fifth instead of second.

"Hey, how did you fellows like the greens today?"

"They were better than they were yesterday," cautiously answered young Ken Venturi.

"I got a door mat at home," said Middlecoff sadly, "that provides a better putting surface than these greens."

"I remember one," said Venturi, returning to the original topic. "It was in a play-off at Palm Springs with Demaret two years ago. Remember it, Jim?"

"I was on the other side of the fairway," said Demaret, "but I know what you're going to say."

"I hit a ball into a man's pocket," said Venturi. "He took it out and dropped it. But before he did that he walked behind a tree and dropped it there. Cost me a stroke, too. Actually it didn't make much difference because Jimmy beat me by more than one stroke."

"How about the time Walter Hagen hit one into an empty peanut bag in a trap?" said Harmon. "The officials wouldn't let him remove his ball from the bag as they should have done. But nothing ever bothered the Haig. He lighted a cigarette and then he lighted the bag."

"He couldn't get away with that today," said Demaret. "I'd have to say it's slightly illegal. Like the time Dick McCreavy wanted to burn away some moss in which his ball was buried. No dice, he was told, because it would be improving your lie and that would cost you two strokes."

Most lies are improved in the locker room.

Completely at Sea

September 21

Newport, Rhode Island, September 20—This is no place for a landlubber who can't tell the difference between a barnacle and a binnacle. He hasn't the foggiest notion of what the wild waves are saying. In fact, he's not sure that he likes what the wild waves are doing. They go up and down, up and down. Avast there, mates, it ain't soothing.

But Coast Guard cutters take unwary newspapermen out to sea for a somewhat distant view of the America's Cup races. The cutters go about as far from shore as a garbage scow before jettisoning its cargo. For the scows this isn't far enough. For those yachting experts who don't have sea legs, it's much too far.

"Roll on, thou deep and dark blue ocean, roll!" wrote Lord Byron, presumably in a weak moment. But he was more on the ball when he later wrote "He sinks into thy depths with bubbling groan." That's more like it. Glug! Glug!

Yachting is a sport in which familiarity with the hit-and-run, the T formation, the right uppercut, the service ace, the chip shot and the hand-ride in the stretch are totally valueless. The amphibious gentlemen who sail yachts speak a language all their own. To the uninitiate, it's as unintelligible as Sanskrit or Stengelese.

Once a landlubber consults a nautical dictionary, however, he gets some rude shocks because words never had the same meanings he originally gave them. Here, for example, is a glossary of impressions and actual definitions:

Luff—What makes the world go 'round. (Turning the helm to bring the ship nearer the wind.)

Schooner—A glass of beer. (A vessel with two or more masts.)

Flaw—A defect in a diamond. (A gust of wind.)

Clew—What detectives look for. (The lower corner of square sails and the after corner of fore-and-aft sails.)

Fore—Warning cry used in golf. (Anything forward of amidships.)

Heaver—Any landlubber during a storm at sea. (A short wooden bar, tapering at each end, used as a purchase.)

Purchase—Something you just bought. (A mechanical power which increases the force applied.)

Sleepers—Guys catching forty winks. (The knees that connect the transoms to the after timbers in the ship's quarters.)

Bar—A saloon. (A bank or shoal.)

Skyscraper—A basketball player. (A skysail when it is triangular.)

Pennant—Something Casey Stengel wins every season. (A long narrow piece of bunting, carried at the masthead.)

Gripes—Protests that ballplayers lodge with umpires. (Bars of iron, with lanyards, rings and clews, by which a boat is lashed to the ringboats of the deck.)

Deck—Fifty-two cards except in pinochle. (Planked floor of a vessel resting on the beams.)

French fake—A phony from Paris. (To coil a rope with each coil outside the other, beginning in the middle.)

Heel—A cad. (The after part of the keel.)

Poop—To tire out. (A deck raised over the afterpart of the spar deck.)

Spanker—A parent who doesn't believe he should spare the rod and spoil the child. (The after sail of a ship.)

Waist—It's higher than natural in the new fashions. (The fore part of the upper deck between the quarterdeck and the forecastle.)

Bumpkin—A rube from the country. (Piece of timber projecting from the stern of the vessel.)

Spurs—Those things Eddie Arcaro wears. (Pieces of timber fixed on the bilgeways.)

Snub—To cut a guy dead. (To check a rope suddenly.)

Cat—A feline. (Tackle used to hoist anchor to cat-head.)

Bum boat—A boat with a load of bums in it. (Provisioning boats in a port.)

That should give you an idea of the new language that must be learned by landlubbers here. The experts even must say that they're "going below" when all they mean is that they are going downstairs. When the Coast Guard cutters begin to pitch and roll, many a guy wishes that the America never raced around the Isle of Wight in 1851, thereby setting the America's Cup business in motion. Motion? Please don't mention the word.

Jim Roach, then sports editor of *The Times,* said that this column elicited greater response than any other Arthur did.

1959

A Pyrrhic Victory

January 1

This would seem to be the saddest day in the history of American tennis. The United States has won the Davis Cup—technically. A few more such rousing victories and the prestige of this country in tennis will sink to an embarrassing low.

A sports-minded nation of 171,000,000 persons can't even find three players good enough to wrest the cup from Australia with a population of 9,640,000. So a foreigner is recruited to do the job that this country can't do by itself. Alex Olmedo of Peru won his two key singles matches from the Australians and was a member of the winning doubles team.

Hence the only decent thing to do would be to send the trophy to Peru and hold the next Davis Cup challenge round in Lima. This was a Peruvian triumph, not one for the United States, no matter what the official records say.

The dark-haired descendant of the noble Incas is an estimable young man, charming and popular. He polished his tennis at the University of Southern California. But he is not an American citizen and has no intention of becoming one. If a victory toast was drunk from the Davis Cup, the champagne had to be mixed with an overdose of bitters.

Few tennis experts even dreamed that the United States had much chance of upsetting the gifted young racquet-wielders from Down Under. The Aussies had won every major championship in 1958, often finishing one, two. No American reached the semifinals at Forest Hills and only one, Barry MacKay, got as far as the quarterfinals at Wimbledon.

So there were few raised eyebrows when Olmedo was added casually to the Davis Cup squad. It seemed at the time that this might even be an idealistic gesture toward the furtherance of the Good Neighbor policy. Peru didn't have a team for international play and big-hearted Uncle Sam was generously adopting the nice orphan from next door.

But then Olmedo wins the cup for us and Uncle Sam has egg on his goatee. If the Commissar of Tennis in the Soviet Union had a sense of humor, he promptly would have cabled glowing congratulations to Perry Jones, the nonplaying captain of the United States team, for the clever way he manipulated the reverse lend-lease.

The unwanted triumph has to make American tennis the laughing stock of the rest of the world. MacKay, a native American, lost his two singles matches. Ham Richardson, another native son, helped the Peruvian in the doubles, although reports from Brisbane indicated that Olmedo was the dominating operative in the tandem play. What does that leave for the Land of the Free and the Home of the Brave? One half of one victory at best. It's as impressive as a glass of Volstead beer.

The drafting of Olmedo was legal enough because the Davis Cup rules seem to be strictly catch-as-catch-can. They do things much more properly in the Olympics. An Olympic contender must be a native or a national of the country he represents. And once he makes his choice, he is committed to it forever.

Willie Ritola's naturalization papers as an American citizen had not come through just before the 1924 Olympics and Willie desperately wanted an Olympic championship. Since he couldn't represent the land of his choice, the United States, he represented the land of his birth, Finland. So the carpenter from the Bronx won the 10,000-meter championship for the Finns.

That is far more proper than Olmedo capturing the Davis Cup for the Colossus of the North. Sure, he's an American—a South American.

When the United States defends the trophy in August, it would be well for the selection committee to sign on a Patagonian and an Eskimo as well as the Peruvian. That would embrace more territory and more people. Isn't Australia a continent? Ah, logic!

The adviser to Jones in the intercontinental mishmash was Jack Kramer, the boy promoter. He is such an ardent patriot that he probably doesn't have any regret at the way things worked out.

But Kramer surely wrecked Kramer. The king of professional tennis was about to pluck the two top Aussies, Ashley Cooper and Malcolm Anderson, from the amateur ranks and add them to his troupe of Pancho Gonzales, Lewis Hoad, Ken Rosewall, Frank Sedgman, et al. However, Olmedo beat both Cooper and Anderson and dumped them into a buyer's market. No amount of ballyhoo can make them red-hot draws at the box office now.

The list of United States heroes in Davis Cup play is long and illustrious, presenting such titans as Maurice McLoughlin, Bill Tilden, Don Budge, and Kramer himself. Should Alex Olmedo be added?

The Davis Cup should be enshrined in an Inca museum in Peru so that proud Peruvians can admire it. The old trophy is too tarnished to be admitted through Customs into the United States.

Crossing of the Bar

February 5

The telegraph keys clattered with jarring stridency. Few ever had heard telegraph keys in Madison Square Garden before. But this was not an ordinary occasion. A 17-year-old boy had cast such a spell over 15,000 persons that they were frozen into immobility and bewitched into silence.

John Thomas, a tall and willowy freshman at Boston University, was in the process of making sports history. The roars of the crowd faded. The hubbub of conversation dwindled. Then it seemed as if folks stopped breathing. And across the arena the telegraph keys in the press box cut through the hush.

They were clicking as Thomas rose to his feet in the infield. He inhaled deeply. He tucked in his shirt. He stared at the crosspiece of the high-jump bar, unawed by the fact that it rested 7 feet 1½ inches above the board floor. Then he began his diagonal approach from left to right, four short steps and four big ones.

The crunch of his spikes on the boards resounded in the stillness, every step as sharp and clear as a hammer blow on a tin fence. Then the left foot pounded down and the right leg snapped up, drawing the red-shirted body with it in a graceful, curving ascent. But the exultant shrieks of the crowd turned to whoops of dismay as Thomas barely dislodged the bar. However, the boy was tired and he did not come that close in his final two tries.

Yet he already had achieved something that no man ever had accomplished indoors, the first 7-foot high jump. The entire tingling drama of the affair was extraordinary. Over the past thirty years this reporter has viewed countless track meets from Los Angeles to Berlin and back again. Never did he witness anything quite like the Millrose high jump.

When the ovation for the Thomas 7-footer had spent itself, the kid from the Hub elected—as the announcer, Stan Saplin, expressed it—"to go for broke." He'd take a whirl at a greater height than any man ever had achieved.

By that time the meet itself was over. However, the stands seemed as full as they had been for the Wanamaker Mile more than an hour earlier. No one, it appeared, dared to leave. The other athletes sat in vari-colored pullovers in a giant semicircle on the sprint runway and the runway apron. And a funereal hush settled over the arena until even the silence was oppressive. The lone intrusion was the click of the telegraphers at work in the press coop on the mezzanine ledge.

That Thomas failed at 7 feet 1½ inches really was unimportant. The bigger moment by far was his hitting 7 and raking in the pot. The kid wore no elevator shoes as did the three Russians when they topped 7 feet. He wore the same type regulation shoes as did Charley Dumas of Southern California in his breaking of the 7-foot barrier outdoors just before the 1956 Olympics.

Thomas and Dumas, the latter in his indoor debut, had tied at 6 feet 10 inches when the officials decided on 7 feet as the deadlock destroyer. The uprights weren't high enough. So the ingenious Jim Lyon, chief judge of the field events, placed stacks of heavy cardboard markers under each upright and whipped out his steel tape. The bar was 7 feet high.

Thomas poised on the runway and swooped in. His off-leg sent the bar spinning from its perch, dropping alongside the young jumper on his back on the red mat. He didn't change expression. In dead-pan fashion he walked slowly back to where Charley Stead, the Villanova jumper, and George Dennis, the Shanahan Catholic Club leaper, awaited him. The animated Stead was all gestures.

"When you took off, John," he said, jerking his body in demonstration, "you didn't give it enough snap. Look." He gave with the pantomine.

"That's it," agreed Dennis. "Make that leg do the work."

Thomas nodded appreciatively. He sat down on his red pull-over and rested, hands clasped across upraised knees. He dropped his head and meditated. Finally his head snapped up boldly. He got to his feet and stared at the uprights with calculating eyes.

The kid didn't miss this time. Up he went in a twisting straddle of the bar. About two inches of light showed as he yanked his off-leg over. Down he crashed on the soft, red padding. He held his breath, blinked and broke out into a seraphic smile before dancing to the infield to be mobbed by his fellow athletes.

The gangling freshman will operate in his own back yard at the Boston Athletic Association meet Saturday and then will "go for broke" here at the New York Athletic Club meet on February 14 and the national championships on February 21. By then Dumas will be more experienced on boards and so will a newcomer, Richard Dahl of Sweden, the European champion at 6 feet $11\frac{1}{4}$ inches.

This can't miss being one of the great indoor track seasons of recent years.

1960

Somber Second Thoughts

September 13

Rome, September 12—The party is over. In the cold light of the morning after, too many disquieting thoughts keep intruding. Yet it must be admitted that it was a whale of a shindig while it lasted. Maybe it was the best. It's impossible to visualize or recollect any Olympic Games that could match the ones these noble Romans threw.

The stadiums and arenas were more sumptuous and opulent than those of any predecessor's. Furthermore, the entire production was conducted with totally un-Italian efficiency but with the typical Italian flair for drama and beauty. By way of giving them a distinctive air, the Olympics were staged against the ancient backdrop of the grandeur that was Rome.

In Saturday's climactic marathon race, for instance, the first kilometer skirted the Circus Maximus, where the Roman emperors entertained the populace with chariot races and with bloodletting of Christian martyrs. Not much more than a stone's throw away, across the fragments of what once had been the Forum, was the finish line.

No prosaically located finish line was this. It was at the Arch of Constantine. Directly back of it, in the glow of the floodlights, was that battleground of gladiators—the Colosseum, old and crumbling, but still unutterably majestic.

With the ineffable élan that is their nature, the Italian hosts spanned the centuries. Only Rome could have handled it with such grace. And the show itself was worthy of the setting. Records toppled in profusion. Upsets were a lira a dozen. The form chart turned topsy-turvy. But every upset was achieved on the wings of a stabbingly brilliant performance.

The world is stirring not only politically. It is stirring athletically, too. Nations that weren't in existence at the time of the Melbourne Olympics four years ago competed here with distinction. The United States scares not a soul any more. Once the Americans dominated the show. They don't any more. Nor are they likely to do so again.

The totalitarian powers have the ability to marshal their youth for what they regard, among other things, as part of the propaganda war. They have said so, bluntly and unashamedly. And the Rome Olympics, on that basis, represented a resounding victory for Soviet Russia. The Red brothers beat us in total medals and in unofficial total points.

The disturbing thing about the Russians' success was the masterful way in which they broadened their base of operations. They can't outscore us in men's track and field, the kingpin sport of the Olympics since their inception with a foot race in 776 B.C. The chances are that they will not do so, at least not in the foreseeable future.

But they moved into the somewhat aristocratic sports of yachting, equestrian and fencing. They won gold medals in each. They finally broke into the scoring in swimming and, more surprising, diving. They won in cycling, previously the exclusive domain of the French and Italians. They've come on in water polo and in rowing. They almost swept the decks clean in canoeing with 43 points and in gymnastics they collected a fantastic 233.

They are spread out in so many directions that they can't help but reap the richest of harvests. America pays attention to track and to swimming, sneering at all other sports as "minor league."

But they are not considered minor league throughout the world.

Such weight-lifting countries as Turkey, Iran, Iraq and Egypt have to be impressed by the smashing Soviet victories in the strong-man sport. Italian, French, and Hungarian fencers have to be impressed. And so it goes. Is there a solution?

Once every four years, the United States stirs slightly and discovers that it has to assemble teams in sports it has been ignoring. The Russians are prepared and so is up-and-coming Germany, the most intensely nationalistic nation of any here even though a divided Germany competed under a compromise flag. Worthy of note is the fact that no other group could unite East and West on anything.

"We're never going to win," warns Tip Goes, the boss of America's oarsmen, "as long as our youth is more interested in hot rods, television, and fun. No country can win in international competition that way. The mass athletic programs the Soviet Union and Germany established six years ago have started to pay off."

"No one can win a championship by shadow-boxing," warns Eddie Eagan, former Olympic boxing champion. "Our athletes must be steeled in the same kind of constant international competition that other nations get."

Since the United States never will be able to force its amateur athletes into sports in which they are not interested, there seems to be no way to wrest top honors from countries that have no hesitance in doing so. This may not be a pretty picture, but it's a reasonable accurate one.

A Sad Day for Baseball

October 19

Competence has ceased to be the measuring rod in the Yankee scheme of things. It can be overruled and negated by the date on a man's birth certificate. The Yankees cold-bloodedly jettisoned Charles Dillon Stengel as their manager yesterday, not because his immense skills had become impaired but only because he had passed his seventieth birthday.

This has become an even blacker day for baseball than the resignation of John McGraw as manager of the Giants in 1932. But McGraw was ailing and he resigned voluntarily. However, Stengel still has the vigor that made him the most successful manager in diamond history—the record book proves it—and he did not resign.

"I won't say I'm fired," growled Casey into the microphone at a hushed and historic press conference. "You can say what you want to say. I'm not writin' it." Okay, then. He was fired.

Nervously puffing on a cigarette, Dan Topping, coowner of the Yankees with Del Webb, read a prepared statement. It was full of empty words, as barren of meaning as one of Casey's rhetorical flights into Stengelese. It was written more or less in the past tense and never did say bluntly whether the Ol' Per-

Casey Stengel, left, hears the announcement that he will no longer be manager of the New York Yankees, in October, 1960.

fessor quit of his own accord, was fired, or what. After reading it, Topping faded into the background as if ashamed of himself. He should be.

Stengel was grim and unsmiling for the most part. That old ebullience burst through occasionally, as when he said that he had been required to attend "baseball meetings and, when stuck, the baseball writers' dinner" or when he declared that "Mrs. Stengel is my wife and she would want me to do somethin' somewhere because she thinks I'm a pretty good manager."

Without saying so specifically, Casey indicated that his own preference was to continue. "But," he said, "they have a program which should run into an old-age program and I am positive they are the owners of the ball club. Mr. Webb is of the same opinion as Mr. Topping as regards the age limit and Mr. Topping runs the ball club. I was told that my services no longer were desired."

From the welter of words emerged the definite impression that George Weiss, the general manager of the Yankees, also is on his way out. But the front-office genius will be kicked upstairs. Casey didn't even get that much. He got a word of thanks, the sum of $160,000 from a profit-sharing plan and the back of Topping's hand.

Gigantic organizations such as General Motors and United States Steel have retirement deadlines, but they have sense enough to use them with flexibility. However, a puny organization like the Yankees blindly adheres to the letter of its own law. It's a new law, too. It could have waited for implementation until Casey had decided to quit of his own will.

In twelve years Stengel brought the Bombers the most productive period in their glamorous history, ten pennants and seven world championships. He imparted warmth to a cold organization, giving it a colorful appeal that it couldn't have bought for millions of dollars. He was priceless.

The Yankees never had it so good as they did under Stengel. He won for them in his first season of 1949 and he won for them in his final season of 1960. Significant is the fact that Yogi Berra is the only ballplayer to remain throughout the entire regime.

In other words, Ol' Case demonstrated his genius in spite of constant turnovers in talent.

Stengel avoided the use of Stengelese for most of his rambling discourse. He was so serious that he spoke grammatically, as if he were afraid that his resentment at such cavalier treatment would not seep through. There were only flashes of double-talk.

In a throwaway line he hinted that the axe had been sharpened for him in 1958. But then he engineered the managerial miracle of having his Bombers win the last three games of the world series against the Milwaukee Braves. It checked the fall of the axe.

"A little question in 1958 until the world series is over. A doubt in my mind." That's the way he phrased it, leaving everything to conjecture.

Apparently he was bucking a stone wall this time. Even if he'd won the final game against the Pirates a week ago, it would not have saved him. He gave that idea in round-about language, indicating that he never did get to discussing his future because that renowned reader of tea leaves, Topping, already had determined what that future would be.

From a public relations standpoint the Yankees have done great damage to themselves. They may have done the same from a baseball standpoint, especially if Weiss is to follow Casey into exile. It's a shabby way to treat the man who has not only brought them glory but also has given their dynasty firmer footing than it had ever had. So long, Case. You gave us twelve unforgettable years.

Flattened Ex-Champion

January 5

Shocking is the news that Ezzard Charles is flat broke. The man who earned almost $2,000,000 during a career capped by winning of the heavyweight championship is not only without a kopeck to his name but also is deeply in debt. It would be understandable if he had been a wastrel. He was not. It would be understandable if his managers had robbed him blind. But his comanagers, Jack Mintz and Tommy Tannas, were reputable men with a sincere interest in his well-being.

Yet Ez always was a baffling man, a bit of a paradox. He played the bass fiddle and had the sensitive soul of a musician. Too often he also fought like one. The lowest, crummiest characters in sport populate the slum area of boxing, but Charles was not one of them. He did not swear, smoke or drink. He won the most glamourous title of all and not a shred of glamour rubbed off on him. His reign was colorless and insufferably dull.

Charles contributed little, of course. The day after he'd outpointed Jersey Joe Walcott in the world's dreariest bout for the crown Joe Louis had vacated, the ebullient Mintz was bubbling with excitement when he awakened sports' newest hero.

"Feel any different bein' champeen of the world?" asked Mintz.

"Nope," said Ez.

That was his trouble. Humility is a virtue but there is such a thing as overdoing it—as Dickens' Uriah Heep discovered. The Charles humility was genuine, though. He was totally unimpressed by himself. Yet he was an extremely competent workman, a highly skilled boxer and a punishingly sharp hitter. It was his own fault that he never capitalized fully on his talents.

Pigeons always were escaping from his grasp. He had Louis set up for a knockout when the aging Dark Destroyer attempted to reclaim the title he had vacated. Here was a chance for Charles to give dramatic emphasis to his victory. He didn't take it. The Jolter barely staggered through to the end of the fifteenth round.

Long before a Louis–Charles bout had been contemplated, Ez was questioned as to how he would react to the opportunity of throwing punches at his boyhood idol.

"I got no particular ambition to fight Joe Louis," he said.

"Would they have to put a gun at your head to make you?" he was asked.

"Joe's been a long-time champion," he said. "I'd fight him if they made me. But I never would want to see Joe Louis beaten. He's been too great."

A strange attitude for a fighter to take? Certainly. But Charles never did have the true instincts of a fighter. He worshipped Louis and just couldn't put the crusher on him. The Jolter achieved greatness, however, because he resolutely put sentiment to the side.

John Henry Lewis was Joe's friend. They were matched. So the Bomber did the kindest thing he could do. He did not prolong the agony. He knocked out John Henry in the first round.

There was one clique of highly regarded boxing writers so impressed by the nobility of Charles, the man, that they transferred those same virtues to Charles, the fighter. They insisted that he was one of the most underrated of all heavyweight champions, one of the truly great ones. They were wrong.

When Ez was matched for the third time with Walcott, in July of 1951, few New York newspapers even bothered to send their experts to Pittsburgh. Seemingly, the result was foreordained. Ezzard the Gizzard—an uncomplimentary tag that dogged him to the end—cautiously would box the ears off ancient Jersey Joe. But Walcott unexpectedly tagged him with a sucker punch in the seventh and knocked him out.

A year later the rematch saw Ez box Walcott dizzy in a hit-and-run exhibition in Philadelphia. But Charles fought like a turtle who was forever withdrawing into his shell, continually bypassing opportunities for a finishing blow. The ringside experts made ready to write sob stories about the defeat of a gallant old man, so clear cut was the Charles margin of victory. So they were dumbfounded when the unanimous decision was in favor of Jersey Joe. Charles couldn't even win a championship he had won.

The Timid Tiger was put in the ring with the eat-'em-alive Rocky Marciano in June of 1954. Oddly enough, this was to be the greatest fight of the Charles career. He fought with skill, daring and purpose against the most pulverizing hitter of recent times. The Rockabye Baby hammered Ez to a bloody pulp, but the courageous Ez weathered those blockbusters to the end. Three months later Charles reverted to type and Rocky knocked him out in the eighth.

It was a downhill road after that, losses and knockouts by nonentities. Ill-starred as a champion, Charles was ill-starred as a business man, too. Nothing ever seemed to go right for him. He lost his money as he lost his fights and he had no colorful personality to exploit. Fate had flattened him again. It's a shame.

Unlucky Thirteenth

June 4

It was a sad and dismal afternoon under weeping skies. Carry Back, the equine phenomenon who was beginning to assume the legendary qualities of Pegasus, proved to be mortal. The tough little winner of the Kentucky Derby and the Preakness could not fasten the last golden link to the Triple Crown at Belmont yesterday.

He was thirteenth to try for it and thirteen hardly was his lucky number. By way of compounding the jinx, this also was the thirteenth time that Johnny Sellers rode the colt, hitherto a marvel at cyclonic finishes of high drama. But Carry Back had nothing this gray, drizzly afternoon. He finished seventh, some fifteen struggling lengths behind the 65-to-1 winner, Sherluck.

"He was jostled around and didn't care for it," said the articulate Sellers as he toweled himself off in front of his locker. "We started around Dr. Miller on the last turn. Then Carry Back spit out his bit and said, 'The hell with it' and that was that."

Johnny tried to hide his bitter disappointment under a brave smile. But he couldn't quite make it. He looked up and saw Braulio Baeza, the winning jockey, standing nearby. The gentlemanly Sellers leaped to his feet and extended his hand.

"Congratulations," said Johnny with such enthusiasm that he even was able to crowd sincerity into his words.

"I sorree for you," said the Panamanian sympathetically.

"Oh, well," said Johnny. He shrugged his shoulders unhappily. "Thanks for being so gracious."

All the jocks crowded around a television set to watch the rerun of the Belmont Stakes on video tape.

"Ha, ha," said Bob Ussery who had ridden fourth-place Ambiopoise. Some facet of the racing strategy had amused him but he never bothered to explain it.

Sellers finally turned away. He was wasting his time. Carry Back was so far to the rear for so long that he didn't show up in the film.

"I could give you a lot of excuses," said Johnny, groping vainly for an explanation—and trying to avoid a sour-grapes approach. "But none would amount to much. I guess you might say it was racing luck."

It was odd that he should hit on such a phrase because it was just the other day that Jack Price, the trainer of Carry Back, had made a bold prediction.

"The only thing that can beat my horse is racing luck," he had said. Could Johnny define his own statement?

"We were the horse to beat," said Johnny. "Naturally everyone was watching us and giving us nothing. Along the backstretch we were shut off and I honestly don't know which horse hemmed us in.

"We were jostled and Carry Back didn't care for it. I couldn't very well say, 'Let me out and give me racing room, boys.' When Carry Back gave up, I couldn't very well get off and carry him home. It was a bad race and I never was more disappointed in my life."

So animated was Sellers that he looked far more like the winner than did the phlegmatic Baeza. What instructions had been given to Baeza by Harold Young, the trainer of Sherluck?

"He tell me that I know heem," said Baeza, flashing a gold-toothed smile. "He tell me to stay behind the speed horses and I know the horse wit' the onlee speed she is Globemaster. At half-mile pole, I know I weel beat Globemaster. I see one horse in back—maybe Heeting Away—and I shake my horse to wake heem up. That ees all."

Johnny Longden noticed the dullness that had overcome Carry Back when they were neighbors on the track a half mile from home. The grandpappy guy, aged 54, rode Flutterby, who came in an undistinguished last. The last winner Longden had in the Belmont was the brilliant Count Fleet in 1943. This magnificent colt merely won by twenty-five lengths.

"At the half-mile pole," said the wizard gnome, "I knew I was dead. Then I looked over at Carry Back alongside of me and he didn't look alive either. He just couldn't get hold."

Price was so nervous and jittery before the race that he couldn't sit still, almost as if he had a foreboding of what would happen. After the race he quixotically sent a bottle of champagne to his badly beaten steed.

"You hailed me in victory," he said. "Now drink to me in defeat."

Carry Back didn't even take a sip. He's a teetotaler.

1962

On the Wrong Coast

July 15

From the time he was a small boy in the Bedford-Stuyvesant section of Brooklyn, Tommy Davis had dreamed of playing ball some day for the Dodgers—the Brooklyn Dodgers. Like most kids in the borough he regarded Ebbets Field as a paradise on earth, populated by demigods.

But by the time Tommy had been graduated from Boys High, emotion was being nudged aside by practicality. The Dodgers were loaded with talent all the way to the bottom of their farm system and advancement to the big leagues through so crowded a field might be inordinately slow. So the 17-year-old from Brooklyn listened, first with reluctance and then with increasing interest, to the siren song of the Yankees. They sold him a bill of goods. He decided to sign with the Bombers on a July night of 1956.

That afternoon Davis had a visitor, Al Campanis of the Dodgers. The chief scout had long since been given a post-graduate course in sweet talk and Blarney Stone-kissing by Walter O'Malley. He is a glib salesman without a peer.

"A Brooklyn boy should play in Brooklyn," began the smooth Campanis. "You know how the fans here react. You'll be a bigger hero some day than Jackie Robinson."

Off he went in a spell-binding spiel, putting the Dodgers on the same lofty plane as patriotism and motherhood. When Campanis left, he had the signed contract of the bewitched Davis in his pocket, thereby leaving the Yankees tangled up in the starting gate. A year later O'Malley had cold-bloodedly uprooted the Dodgers from Brooklyn in his personal gold rush to California.

"It broke my heart," said Tommy. He hastily added: "I don't mean I don't like it in Los Angeles. I do. But . . ." He left the rest unspoken.

So Davis never did get to play at Ebbets Field, although he's now a Dodger of virtually limitless potential. At the time of the all-star break he was the leading batter of both major leagues, a starter on the National League team and the clean-up hitter for pennant-bound—perhaps—Los Angeles.

If there is no clear-cut picture of him in the mind of the average fan that is understandable. Confusion has been compounded by duplication. He crashed the big time with Willie Davis, no relation. Each is an outfielder. Each is 6 feet 1½ inches tall although Tommy at 200 pounds is fifteen pounds heavier than his roomie. Willie is faster. Tommy is stronger.

Tommy's speed on the basepaths has been negated to a considerable extent this year because he's been given the spot in the batting order where he's supposed to drive in the gazelles in front of him, specifically Maury Wills, Junior Gilliam, and Willie Davis.

But when Tommy was free to roam while he was playing for Pete Reiser at Kokomo in 1957, he not only led the league in batting with .357 but also in base-stealing with sixty-eight thefts. Crude and inexpert though he was, Tommy still stole with the ease and éclat of a Wills. Reiser still wasn't satisfied.

"Tommy," said his earnest boss, "you're stealing a lot of bases but you don't take a proper lead off the bag. You stand too close to it. You should move down the line farther."

"Mr. Reiser," said the respectful Tommy. "Can I ask you a question?"

"Go ahead," said Pete.

"How far do you want me to steal those bases by?" he asked.

If the blossoming of Tommy to stardom was delayed, it might be because he is a bit too talented for his own good. He showed so much promise in his rookie season of 1960 that the Dodger Brain Trust came up with an idea. The club was surfeited by outfielders but thin in infielders who could hit. So it was decided that Tommy would be converted into a third baseman during the next spring training at Vero Beach.

Young Davis even opened the regular season at third but he never was sure of himself, the expert tutelage of Leo Durocher to the contrary. Eventually the experiment was abandoned when the campaign was a third over and he returned to the outfield. He was batting well over .300 until he injured his back sliding into third on a triple. Then he faded to .278 at the end.

"Tommy is over the hump in the road now," proudly says Reiser, now a Dodger coach. "He's gonna be a real good hitter, the Jackie Robinson type."

Like Robbie, Tommy has the knack of coming through in the clutch. He won a game for Sandy Koufax, 1 to 0, with a home run off Bob Gibson of the Cardinals in the ninth. He hit a two-run homer in the ninth for a 2-1 victory. He hit a three-run homer in the twelfth ("that one caromed off the foul pole," he says with a grin) for a 6-3 victory and won another, 6-2, with a grand-slammer in the tenth.

At present, Tommy Davis is trying to get Willie Davis interested in progressive jazz. Whether he succeeds is of little consequence. The Davis boys are in complete harmony. They have made the Dodgers swing on the upbeat.

Visit With the Champion

August 28

Elgin, Illinois, August 28—With hands clasped contentedly behind his head, Floyd Patterson was relaxing at his hilltop training quarters in the bucolic setting of Marycrest Farm. He was wearing a T-shirt, rumpled brown slacks, heavy walking boots and his ever-present sly little grin. Suddenly his right hand flashed out and captured a buzzing fly.

"Got him," said Floyd.

"Young Griffo used to do it better a half-century ago," he was told. "He won free drinks in saloons by catching flies with just his thumb and forefinger. He'd bet the bartender."

The champion's eyes twinkled and the smile grew wider.

"It merely denotes progress," said Floyd in his precise and careful speech. "It proves that the flies are faster these days."

It is speed, however, that will be his main asset when he defends his world heavyweight championship against Sonny Liston at Comiskey Park in Chicago on September 25.

"Speed should be helpful against Liston," Floyd agreed. "Speed could confuse him, style could confuse him and combinations could confuse him.

"Yet it all could work out vice versa. Let me give you an example. Harold Johnson, Paul Andrews and Broadway Billy Smith fought each other—not at the same time, of course. As I recall it, Andrews knocked out Smith who knocked out Johnson who knocked out Andrews. My style could be made to order for Liston or his for me.

"I saw Liston twice on television and I was tremendously impressed by his ability. I have an image of power, strength, massive punching and all-around skills. It's an image I intend to keep."

Floyd gives the impression he has recaptured the crusading zeal that he had before his second bout with Ingemar Johansson. His dethronement by the handsome Swede crushed his pride, and his sensitive nature was seared by brutal comments. So he whipped himself into an emotional frenzy and was a ruthless destroyer for the first time. He demolished Ingo with one mighty left hook in their return bout. Was that impression correct?

"I suppose you're right," he said hesitantly. "It could be that I believed too much what I read in the papers about Ingemar before our first fight. The writers sneered at him and downgraded him. That defeat was such a blow to my pride that I resolved it wouldn't happen again. I guess you might say that I feel the same way about Liston."

Patterson stabbed at another fly and missed. He shrugged his shoulders to indicate that the faster modern flies were more elusive than in Young Griffo's day.

"After this fight," he said casually, "I want to give charity exhibitions in Sweden and then do the same in Africa. One thing I want understood. The tour is on only if I'm victorious. If I'm not, you can reach me at Highland Mills, New York."

His grin was a wide-range one. Keyed up as Floyd is for the go-around with Liston he is still relaxed and totally without tension.

"I'm still being swamped with mail from Sweden," he said contentedly. "I figured I must have heard from every Swede in the country. The other day was when I knew it was complete. I received a post card wishing me luck. It came from Ingemar.

"I weigh about 190 now and want to come into the ring at that weight. But one rarely knows when he's overtrained and past his peak. I should have rested for a week after the Brian London fight and done only road work before the first fight with Ingemar. But so many people came to see me work that I couldn't disappoint them. I became so sharp that one day I knocked out five sparring partners, each in the first round.

"It was different before the second bout. Only a few townspeople came to watch me at Newtown, Connecticut, until the final week. Then they read that Joe Louis and Jimmy Cagney had visited me. So the neighbors said, 'Hey, this fellow must be important.' So they came out to watch."

"Some of the experts say that a left hook will be best for beating Liston and others say a straight right," Floyd said. "I don't know, but Liston holds his hands high—good for him."

It was hard to tell whether Floyd was being derisive or was letting his wry, bubbling sense of humor sneak in. Once he was a shy and inarticulate mumbler, but now he speaks with fluent and grammatical assurance. Once he slipped and said, "I haven't did it since." Otherwise his conversational footwork was perfect as he hammered home with the high-powered 50-cent words. He even can jest at himself, something he wouldn't have dreamed of doing a few years back. A photographer broke in with a plea for one quick shot.

"All I want is a picture of you shoving your fist into the camera," said the shutterbug operative.

"Can't do it," said Floyd, the half-smile becoming three-quarters.

"Why not?" said the astonished lensman.

"Liston holds the copyright on that pose," said the champion. "Maybe I should shove my chin into the camera so that the people can judge for themselves whether it's made of glass."

He said it defiantly. He shoved his chin into the camera but spoiled the picture by being unable to restrain his laughter.

1963

Marvelous Marv

April 1

Saint Petersburg, Florida, March 31—Marvin Eugene Throneberry became the symbol of the New York Mets last season. Even his initials spelled out Met. Like the rest of his team he was lovably inept, but with a flair for heroics. He'd lose games by his bungling or win them with dramatic last-inning home runs.

A beautiful romance sprung up between him and those hysterically loyal Met fans, the aptly named New Breed. It was to be one of the great love stories of our time. More than half the fan mail that came to Casey Stengel's heroes was directed to Marvelous Marv. Ninety-nine per cent of it pledged undying devotion. One per cent called him a bum.

"A ball club like ours needed a patsy," explained Marvelous Marv with total unconcern, "and I don't mind it. When they were on me, they laid off guys who couldn't take it."

It undoubtedly was Throneberry's monumental good nature that endeared him so much to the New Breed. It also endeared him to the baseball writers who voted him their Good Guy award. The subject was mentioned when Marvelous Marv became involved in a salary hassle with George Weiss, the general manager, and Johnny Murphy, his assistant.

"Don't forget," said the Marvel, "that I brought a lot of people to the ball park."

"Yes," said Murphy, "and you also drove a lot away."

"You are confusing the Good Guy award," said Weiss, "with the Most Valuable Player trophy."

The drawing power of Marvelous Marv was extraordinary. He is the only man in baseball history whose admirers paid two admissions to worship at his shrine. Five slightly obstreperous fans showed up one day. Each wore a T-shirt. One had the letter M on the front. The next had an A and the next two wore R and V. The fifth guy's shirt was adorned with an exclamation mark. When properly lined up, they spelled out "Marv!"

They raised such a commotion that they were thrown out. A few minutes later they reappeared in the bleachers, having purchased another set of tickets.

Nothing, it seems, could destroy the enthusiasm of the Throneberry fans—or of Throneberry. Even his teammates carried out the illusion. A nameplate is above every Met locker in the clubhouse, all trimmed to bare essentials such as Craig, Jackson, Thomas, Hodges and the like. The name of Throneberry is missing. The card above his locker says with simple candor, "Marvelous Marv."

Harvey Haddix of the Pirates hogtied the Mets into the ninth one day, winning 4-1. Typically, the Mets rallied. Richie Ashburn singled, Joe Christopher walked and Felix Mantilla singled in a run. In came Marvelous Marv as a pinch-hitter with two out in the ninth and clouted a 450-foot game-winning homer deep into the stands in right center.

"If you keep this up," said Ashburn afterwards, "you'll lose your fans, Marv."

"Don't worry," said the Marvel, "I can get them all back with one lousy night."

Such an instance came when Throneberry came to bat with the bases full. He sent out a screamer that rolled to the fence. Marvelous Marv pulled up at third with an apparent triple. The enemy first baseman shouted for the ball and stepped on the bag at first.

"Yer out!" bellowed the umpire. Throneberry had neglected to touch the bag when he sped past. Stengel charged from the dugout in protest. The umpire shut him up fast.

"Throneberry didn't touch second either," he said.

Once the Mets unbelievably rocked Don Drysdale of the Dodgers with three runs in the eighth for a 6-3 lead. Up came the Brooks. Maury Wills, jackrabbit, sent a twisting grounder down the first-base line. Throneberry fielded it like Hal Chase and made a great stop and greater toss to Jay Hook, covering the bag. He did the same on the fleet Junior Gilliam.

Then Willie Davis creamed one. In right field Ashburn moaned out loud. "Here we go again," he said. But Throneberry went 10 feet in the air to spear the liner and landed on the flat of his back, the ball still in his glove. The unpredictable Marvel had saved the day.

On Stengel's birthday, the Ol' Perfessor received a birthday cake. Throneberry pretended to be miffed.

"Why didn't they give me a cake on my birthday?" he asked.

"We was afraid you'd drop it," said Stengel.

The Crackdown

April 19

When Commissioner Pete Rozelle lowered the boom on malefactors in the National Football League, he did nothing to cushion the impact. He let it crash. The result was stunning. After a careful investigation of impressive thoroughness, he made public his long-awaited findings. With them came disciplinary action of singular severity.

He indefinitely suspended—this could mean for life—Paul Hornung, the Golden Boy of the Green Bay Packers, and Alex Karras, the great defensive star of the Detroit Lions. He slapped the Detroit Lions with a jolting $4,000 fine and whiplashed five individual Lion players with $2,000 fines each for making $50 bets on one game.

These are harsh penalties. Yet they are justified because the honor of the National Football League is involved. If pro ball does not have integrity, it is worthless. The parties penalized by the strong, young commissioner impugned that integrity by their actions. Rozelle uncovered no evidence of illegality, game fixing, score rigging or hanky-panky. But he didn't like the lesser items his investigators had revealed. He cracked down.

Hornung and Karras were found guilty of betting on football

games—not piddling wagers but substantial ones. Neither bet against his own team. One ironic disclosure was that Karras had bet $100 on his own Lions against the Packers in their first 1962 meeting. Green Bay won, 9 to 7, on three field goals by Hornung, the last coming 33 seconds from the end. Hornung was careless in his associations with sharpshooters and Karras even more careless because he was found to have consorted with known hoodlums.

Wagering of any description or of any dimension (this includes $1 fun bets) is expressly forbidden by league rules. That of itself is sufficient to condemn the two main culprits. But there is a danger inherent in big betting by football players. They expose themselves to being entrapped in a gambling web.

When rumors of an impending scandal broke more than two months ago Rozelle refused to let himself become panicked or stampeded into action. He had the courage and the good sense to ignore the barbed criticism of the hatchet men who had accused him of preparing a whitewash. Instead, he turned loose his squad of former F.B.I. agents for a thorough investigation.

Only three names had been mentioned in the early rumors. They were Karras, Rick Casares of the Chicago Bears and Bob Saint Clair of the San Francisco 49ers. Casares and Saint Clair were exonerated, but the investigation was so painstaking that Hornung, neither mentioned nor suspected hitherto, was uncovered by the commissioner's gumshoes.

That this was no surface job was proved by the surprising details in Rozelle's formal statement. Hornung's actions were traced back to 1956, which antedates his entry into the National Football League. That's when he first became involved with the big-betting businessman who was to lead him along the rosy trail to disaster.

So meticulous was the work of Rozelle's operatives that they revealed the Golden Boy had won $1,500 one year on his football wagers—college and professional. Other than that, the best he could do was break even—which may prove that a little knowledge is a dangerous thing.

The harshness of the commissioner's punitive action was governed by his determination to make an example of the guilty. If he had merely slapped wrists, this would be no deterrent to others in the future. But he hit so hard he broke wrists. Uppermost in his thoughts is the conviction that the National Football League has to be like Calpurnia—she was Caesar's wife—above reproach.

There is no exact precedent for this newest development in pro ball. In 1946, two Giant backs—Frank Filchock and Merle Hapes—were approached by fixers before a Giant-Bear playoff game. They spurned the offer to be a party to a fix. But they failed to report it. For this they were suspended indefinitely by Bert Bell, Rozelle's predecessor as commissioner.

Pete inherited Bert's obsession for eternal vigilance. Unlike other commissioners in other sports who pretended that gambling did not exist, Bell had a pipeline to all odds-making centers. The instant there was suspicious fluctuation in odds, Bert turned loose his bloodhounds to run down the scent. His successor has done the same. Rozelle even had an eye on Hornung a month before the Karras investigation began. There was no outside urging. He did it on his own.

The American Football League and the Canadian Football League deserve credit for honoring the N.F.L. ban, although each could profit by the use of two superstars of such magnitude. That such a ban was deemed necessary is a blow to pro football. Yet it is indeed reassuring to know that Rozelle is so jealous of the good name of his league that he didn't flinch from meting out the most uncompromising penalties at his command. The price of integrity comes high. It is worth every penny.

A Night for the Duke

September 12

For 16 years Edwin (Duke) Snider wore a Dodger uniform and the Flatbush Faithful lovingly looked upon him as one of their own. Oh, they'd snarl at him on occasion, but love has always had strange manifestations in Brooklyn. They even forgave him when he went on the California Gold Rush with Walter O'Malley (whom they never forgave) but he was welcomed back as a prodigal when he returned this year to play with the New York Mets.

The erstwhile Duke of Flatbush, more popular with the local citizenry than ever before, will be signally honored at Duke Snider Night in the gloaming this evening before the farewell game with the Giants. Tribute will be paid to the outfielder who contributed so much to Brooklyn's baseball history and whose booming bat also has made considerable contributions to the still formative Mets, even if the passing years have muffled it a bit.

"This has been a happy year," said the Duke with a flashing smile. "It's been a wonderful experience and I'll never forget it."

There was a boyish eagerness to the Duke as he spoke. In one

Duke Snider: Welcomed back to New York as a prodigal.

respect he seemed pleasantly surprised by the way things had worked out. After long residence in the Dodger mansion he had been dumped into the fallen-down shack on the wrong side of the railroad tracks. But things were nowhere near so dismal as he had expected them to be.

"I've been disappointed in my batting average and production," said the 36-year-old California native, "but I do feel that I helped the ball club and that's the main thing. All in all, this has been a thrilling year. What made it so, I guess, are two factors—Casey Stengel and the fans.

"I've learned more baseball from Casey than I dreamed existed. The other day in Philadelphia he wandered up and down the dugout, talking in analytical fashion about Ryne Duren and various phases of the game as it was being played. Presumably he was talking to everyone, but I felt that he was directing every remark to me, an educational cram course, so to speak.

"As for the fans, they've been an inspiration to me and to every member of the ball club. They never quit on you and that's why we don't dare quit on them. Maybe they just like losers. You have to admit that there are more losers in the country than winners. So they're on our side."

He grinned at his mild witticism and brushed an imaginary speck of dust off his bat.

"It's difficult to adjust to losing so many games," he continued, "and that was something I never had to face with the Dodgers. But the strange thing about it is that we expect to win every time we step on the field. Right now we're playing good baseball again and these kids are starting to come along rather well. It's depressing to a young hitter—also to old ones—to hit tremendous drives down the long Polo Grounds center-field alley and have them caught.

"I'm absolutely positive the change to Shea Stadium next year will pick up the entire ball club. It will give us the equivalent of a uniform playing field. As it is now, every hitter is tempted to pull the ball down the foul lines at the Polo Grounds and then remodel his style all over again when he goes on the road.

"I can remember what it was like when the Dodgers went

into the Coliseum with the short left-field fence. Our right-handed hitters couldn't resist the temptation to pull. It was frustrating. Gil Hodges changed his style and soon he couldn't hit at all. My problem there was different. The right-field fence was so far away that it was almost impossible to reach it. Once I convinced myself of that, I hit straightaway and became a .300 hitter again. Don't forget that at Ebbets Field a guy could belt one out of the park in any direction."

Few did it better than the Duke. Once he got in the groove he had successive home run seasons of 42, 40, 42, 43, 40, and then the plunge to 15 in that maiden season in the horrendous O'Malley's Alley on the Coast. The Duke started to chuckle.

"I hope you realize," he said, "that my first hit as a Met was a home run off Warren Spahn. Sure, he's a lefty but he's not bad to hit against. You can see the ball good. Actually, his screwball makes him far more effective against right-handers than against lefties like me.

"I've often thought about Spahnie. If I were scouting young pitchers and he was an 18-year-old prospect, I'd never sign him. Now they insist on kids with an overpowering fast ball and curve. He has neither. He just gets the ball over exactly where he wants to get it and makes hitters chase balls they don't want to hit.

"Oh, well. It's been a pleasant year with the Mets and I've enjoyed it even though it would have been nicer if we'd won more often. Next season? I'll decide that later on."

Don't be surprised if the Duke returns. He likes it with the Mets.

Jimmy and the Bronk

October 15

It is inevitable now that comparisons will be made between Jimmy Brown and that paragon of fullbacking perfection Bronko Nagurski. Is Brown of the Browns a more devastating operative than the Bear bruiser of a generation ago?

Anyone who has the accurate answer to that query also can solve a few of the other intriguing riddles of sports. Could Joe Louis have beaten Jack Dempsey? Would Bobby Jones have been able to match Arnold Palmer as a golfing shotmaker? Could any modern sprinter, stopwatch evidence to the contrary, have outrun Jesse Owens? How do the hallowed heroes of the past compare with the superstars of today?

The answers are based strictly on opinion and therefore have quite unreliable foundations. Yet the awesome performance of Jimmy Brown against the Giants on Sunday has to make an observer wonder a bit. It's a cinch that the Cleveland powerhouse will some day be installed at the pro football Hall of Fame in Canton, where the Bronk already is enshrined.

When this comes to pass, the Bronk won't be asked to vacate his niche. There is room for both because the only measuring rod is true greatness. No one has to be better than someone who has made it to gain admittance. Comparisons are ignored. However, there is an inherent fascination in evaluating Brown and Nagurski on a vis-à-vis basis—if such an evaluation even be possible.

Perhaps it isn't possible. They hail from two entirely different eras. The Bronk was the line-crunching terror of one-platoon football when scores were low and forward passes were used with judicious restraint. Jimmy is a wizard at two-platoon football when scores are high and the aerial phase of the game opens up the defenses.

They cancel out on size because each weighed about the same, 230 pounds give or take a few. But the Bronk did not have to burrow through the monsters that Jimmy has to penetrate. Few enemy players were bigger than Nagurski but most are bigger than Brown. What muscle there was, however, massed against the Bronk. It is spread out in front of Jimmy.

According to the statistics at the start of this season, Jimmy averaged 5.01 yards per carry and the Bronk averaged 4.62, not too eye-opening a difference. Nagurski was primarily a bore-ahead fullback. But Brown is so inordinately fast and shifty that he really is a halfback in the fullback spot.

In the Cleveland scheme of things all that Jimmy is required to do with the ball is run with it. A Michigan critic of Red Grange once said with lofty disdain, "All that Grange can do is run." Bob Zuppke, the redhead's coach at Illinois, gave an explosive rejoinder:

"All Galli-Curci can do is sing," said Zup.

Jimmy has no reputation as a blocker. The Bronk was a devastating blocker. When Beattie Feathers set his then record total of 1,004 yards in ground gaining in 1934, Nagurski opened the holes for him.

"Beattie always ran with a hand in the middle of my back," the Bronk once said. "So he always could sense which way I was going to block and I could sense which way he wanted me to turn the play."

Nagurski also was the linebacking bulwark of the Chicago Bear defense, a crashing tackler who piled up the plays. He performed for 60 minutes—or the better part of them—in every game. Jimmy operates only with the offensive platoon and is infinitely more effective because of it.

"Tacklers to the Bronk," once said Steve Owen of the Giants, "were like flies on the flank of a horse—a nuisance but not serious."

The Giant system of halting Nagurski was to have the first tackler slow him down, the second spill him and the third pin him.

"We find we lose fewer men that way," said Owen.

Jimmy doesn't try to bulldoze tacklers if he can avoid them. But when he has to splinter a line, he has the ferocious drive and enormous strength to carry half a ton of flesh with him. That's when he most resembles the Bronk.

But even when Jimmy doesn't carry the ball he puts extraordinary pressures on the defense. His mere presence on the field has transformed Ernie Green from a run-of-the-mill halfback into a good one. Defenders rush impetuously into action when Brown as much as blinks his eyes. They commit themselves and Green pierces weakened defenses. Or else Frank Ryan spins clever little passes to open receivers.

A magnificent football player is Jimmy Brown, the finest fullback of this era. But is he superior to Bronko Nagurski, an immortal from another era? No one knows the answer. Perhaps it isn't even too important that such an answer be found.

A Day of Mourning

November 26

This is a time when the heart is heavy and tears come unbidden to the eyes. Only the mind can see and it still carries the image of a buoyant, laughing, and vibrantly alive John Fitzgerald Kennedy in attendance at baseball games and football games. It brings back pictures of him as a golfer, a swimmer, a sailor, a lover of all sports.

The world of athletics felt a kinship with him such as it had never had with any predecessor in the White House. He was no dilettante assuming a pose. He had been an athlete himself and that was the difference. He spoke our language so that meeting him was not freighted with formality. It was a relaxed period of bright interchange, as casual as a conversation with the guy next door.

The sharpest memory, perhaps, was the occasion of the opening game of the 1961 baseball season, the first time he threw out the first ball. Washington was playing Chicago at old Griffith Stadium. An incident before the ceremonies delighted the late President when he heard about it afterward. It was the kind of thing that appealed to his sparkling sense of humor.

Al Lopez, the White Sox manager, was chatting with sports writers while waiting for the President to arrive.

"What do I do when I'm introduced to the President?" asked Lopez, a man with an occasional wayward wit. "Do I curtsy?"

"No," said a Washington expert on protocol. "You just shake his hand because you're older than he is."

It was the youth of the President that made him seem so accessible and easy to talk to for those members of the sports world who were privileged to meet him. At an All-Star game in Washington he asked that Stan Musial be brought over for a hello. They had as friendly an exchange as if they had been a couple of college buddies.

He asked to meet Casey Stengel and Ol' Case, ordinarily a nonstop conversationalist, surprised everyone by acting a trifle awed. He tossed in a few quips and then offered an excuse.

"I'm only a coach today, Mr. President," he said, "and I gotta get back and help Freddie Hutchinson which is managin' the team."

There is a remembrance of him ducking away from a foul ball and laughing at his aide, Dave Powers, for muffing a catch even though Dave was wearing a fielder's mitt for just such occasions.

Recollections come, too, of the President at the Army-Navy football game, usually scorning an overcoat while everyone around him was well bundled. A parenthetical note is appropriate here for the authorities in the Pentagon. At this moment there seems to be doubt whether the service classic should go on as usual this Saturday at the Municipal Stadium in Philadelphia. There should be no hesitancy. The game should be played because the President would have wanted it that way. As Joe Williams adroitly phrased it, this game could be turned into a massive memorial for the late Commander in Chief. It would indeed be fitting.

One year in Philadelphia an event of frightening implications took place. A drunk burst through the cordon of cadets and midshipmen and approached the President as he crossed the field. Secret Service men subdued the drunk quickly. In the light of the most recent tragedy, this incident also could have had tragic consequences. It made people shudder.

The President's love of football was manifest by his constant attendance at the Orange Bowl game in Miami. He'd usually drive down from Palm Beach with Powers, Ken O'Donnell, Larry O'Brien, Lemoyne Billings, and other friends for an afternoon in the sun. He usually sat in shirtsleeves, wearing sunglasses and smoking little cigars. He was a fan enjoying a respite from his heavy burdens.

The President's prowess as a swimmer made him a war hero after his torpedo boat was cut in two by a Japanese craft in the Pacific. He swam for miles, towing a wounded member of his crew, and later swam many miles in seeking the assistance he eventually obtained.

He was quite a man, even when viewed from the circumscribed world of sports. Another sports term kept flickering to mind during television's remarkable portrayal of the events of the last few days. The word is: Thoroughbred. It can be applied in its most majestic connotations to his widow. Class always will tell. John Fitzgerald Kennedy had it, too.

1964

A Boy on a Man's Errand

February 23

Miami Beach, February 22—At the moment Cassius Marcellus Clay may very well be—to borrow his own florid description of himself—the "prettiest and greatest" of all heavyweight fighters. Before Tuesday midnight, however, the situation could very well undergo a rather violent metamorphosis.

On that evening the loud mouth from Louisville is likely to have a lot of vainglorious boasts jammed down his throat by a ham-like fist belonging to Sonny Liston, the malefic destroyer who is the champion of the world. The irritatingly confident Cassius enters this bout with one trifling handicap. He can't fight as well as he can talk.

If words were punches, Liston would be so cut and bleeding that he'd be begging for mercy. That childhood jingle of yesteryear has lost none of its validity: Sticks and stones may break my bones but names will never hurt me. It would seem that yond Cassius doth waste his breath.

After his final sparring session in the seedy old Fifth Street Gymnasium the other day—he was to shift a day later to the more antiseptic auditorium—Cassius sat on a chair inside the ring ropes and talked and talked. He kept jiggling two circular

Cassius Clay shows how he will crawl to Sonny Liston's corner if he loses. He won the fight to make him heavyweight champion.

metal weights in his hands while he yackety-yacked in somewhat self-conscious amusement. The weights clicked as he flicked them from hand to hand and up from nowhere popped a rather haunting memory.

It was the image of Captain Queeg clicking steel balls during the Caine Mutiny court martial. And Queeg was slowly going nuts at the onrush of something he dreaded. On the surface, though, Cassius shows no awareness of the imminence of disaster.

He's light-hearted and breezy and has just enough twinkle in his eyes to take most of the obnoxiousness from the wild words he utters. When they are imprisoned in print, however, the twinkle is never captured and Cassius just becomes nauseous.

"I've been fightin' since I was 12 years old," he says with an engaging grin, "and I learned how to protect my beautiful face. Now you take Floyd Patterson. He was too dumb to back up but I'm so fast that not even slow-motion pictures can catch me. I promise you this . . ."

With that he leaped up and dropped to all fours. Then he started to crawl across the ring to a corner, throwing words over his shoulder as he moved.

"If that big, ugly bear should knock me out," he said, "I'll crawl like this and kiss his feet." He kissed the ring corner, jumped up and salaamed. " 'You are the greatest,' I'll say to him—and I'll leave the country."

Clay was wearing a blue denim zipper jacket with red lettered script across the back. It said, "Bear Huntin'." Earlier he had worn a fire-engine red robe with white border and white letters across the shoulders, proclaiming "Cassius Clay the greatest."

He surprisingly admitted that he didn't expect to slay the big ugly bear with one punch.

"No," he said, "one punch won't do it. It will be steady taps like drops of water and that's been known to drive a man crazy. When I hit like that somethin' gotta give. I have not revealed half my ability in this gymnasium."

If he is to be taken at his word, he still doesn't have much. He's as fast as he says he is, perhaps even faster. He's bigger than Liston at 218 pounds but woefully younger at an inexperienced 22. Virtually all of his competitive background came from the amateur ranks and he still fights alarmingly like an amateur.

The Louisville lip holds his hands too low and he has a rather fatal habit of jerking back his chin to avoid a punch. It should not be forgotten that Liston has a longer reach than most. Nor should it be forgotten that any well-schooled fighter has the knowhow to take advantage of this amateurish maneuver, even including the stubby-armed Rocky Marciano.

Harry (Kid) Mathews was a swift-moving fancy Dan of a boxer when he met the Brockton Blockbuster. Then he jerked back his head when the Rock came at him. A left hook came whistling after the retreating chin and Mathews abruptly hit the deck with the seat of his breeches. And Liston's left hook is his best punch.

Clay looked dreadful in his next to last boxing session. He didn't show a good jab, a good hook, a good cross, a good combination or a good anything. One sparring partner, Cody Jones, hooked in at will to jaw and body. If Cassius was studying defensive encounters by permitting this, he sure waited until the last minute to do it.

There was one thing, though, that Cassius did with consummate skill. It was when he was shadow-boxing in front of a mirror. The mirror gave him an exquisite opportunity to admire himself. He took full advantage of it.

Another Surprise

February 27

Miami Beach, February 26—There is just no end to the astonishing surprises that are constantly being produced by Cassius Marcellus Clay, the new heavyweight champion of the world. This was the day when he really was entitled to shout in rhapsodic glee. This was the day when no one could have gainsaid him if he preened and strutted and bragged.

But when Cassius wore his invisible crown into his first news conference this morning, he also wore a discernible cloak of humility. No longer did he rave and rant with his superlatives and outlandish claims. He spoke with such quiet modesty that those not close to the platform had to call out, "Speak louder, Cassius. We can't hear you." In the past no one had to give him that sort of urging.

It had to seem that Cassius had achieved a public relations coup of enormous magnitude, a total abandonment of his phony role as a distasteful braggart, now that he had gained his objective. If he sticks to this pose, he also can win a vast amount of popularity. I still can remember him as a delightful young man of infinite charm at our first meeting four years ago in the Olympic Village in Rome.

"I'm through talking," he said today. Then he cast a sad and pitying smile at the experts who had almost unanimously picked Sonny Liston to slaughter him.

"I'm not mad at the experts," he said. "They made me fight better. My mouth overshadowed my ability."

It sure did. Cassius was a stunning revelation in this strange and quite preposterous fight. Not only did he destroy the myth of Liston's fearsome invincibility, but he also exposed Sonny as a crude, lumbering oaf who needs a sitting-duck target like Floyd Patterson to be effective. Come to think of it, few of the ringsiders ever saw Liston except for four fleeting minutes against a somewhat terrified foe who was made to order for him.

Liston was wild and ineffective against the swift-moving Clay. Maybe he did throw out his left shoulder in the first round, as he claimed. The injury, he says, grew in severity until he had to surrender without leaving his corner at the start of the seventh round.

But he still flung punches with the left in the fifth round when Clay was blinded by some searing foreign substance that had entered his eyes. Cassius could fend off Liston only with his glove in that session while he strove to keep out of range of the floundering bear. Clay never even jabbed, much less threw a real punch.

When a fight ends in the fashion this one did, with the unbeatable monster remaining in his corner, suspicions of larceny are immediately aroused. They are not helped by the fact that Liston, an ex-convict, was sponsored by mobsters at the start of his career.

For the larceny theory to be valid, however, there would have to be an overwhelming reason for it. The prospects of a betting coup can be dismissed because the 8-to-1 odds in Liston's favor never varied more than a point. If there had been a rush of smart money on the underdog, the odds would have plummeted. This is an unfailing barometer of hanky-panky.

What would Liston have gained by throwing the fight? The heavyweight championship is the most valuable commodity in the world of sports and not even a man of Liston's criminal background would willingly toss it away. It also brought him an aura of respectability such as he never had known before.

In a rematch he can get only a minor fraction of the loot as challenger instead of the major share that the champion automatically commands. Clay had fought so amazingly well in the six rounds the bout lasted that even if he had been knocked out later, a return bout would have had tremendous appeal at the gate—most of which would go to Liston, by the way.

Perhaps the rematch will have even more appeal since the original had such an ending. On the other hand, though, Clay may be taken into the Army for a year or two. By the time the second fight is held, Liston will be an even older man than he showed himself to be last night. And he surely looked old. No, suspicions of skulduggery have to seem ill-founded mainly because they cannot be based on logic.

When Patterson fought Liston, he moved straight into him as if he were a man who realized the inevitability of his destruction. But Cassius followed the instructions implicit in the chant he used to sing during training: "Float like a butterfly, sting like a bee." First and foremost he wasn't afraid. He maneuvered smartly, moving away from the Liston hook and staying out of the corners as he boxed at long range.

He bothered the slow-thinking Sonny with his tactics. Furthermore, Liston either couldn't or didn't hammer away with his murderous body punching. The cobra stare that immobilized Patterson had no effect on Cassius and the fleet younger man displayed both skills and class he never had demonstrated in training, a highly improbable sequence of events. No fighter ever behaved that way before.

The ending was just as implausible as everything else connected with this fantastic production. It's still almost impossible to believe, but Cassius Marcellus Clay is the heavyweight champion of the world.

Fastest Man in the World

October 16

Tokyo, October 15—"When Bob Hayes comes off the starting blocks," said Jesse Owens, "he looks like a guy catching a ball behind the line of scrimmage and dodging people."

The winner of four gold medals at the 1936 Olympics was seated in the press box today and was offering his appraisal of the heavyweight sprinter who had just reasserted claim to a title Jesse himself had once held—the world's fastest human.

The analogy was uncannily accurate. Owens floated. Hayes lumbers. His arms flail out at rather grotesque angles, and his feet misbehave with pigeon-toed inelegance, but the 21-year-old from Florida A. and M. is a 190-pound thunderbolt with more power than grace, more speed than form.

Hayes careened down the red-clay track in the Olympic 100-meter final with a burst of such unbridled fury that he had his championship all locked up in the first couple of strides, then he won, going away, by daylight light in 10 seconds, equaling the world record.

That Hayes should turn the century into a romp was a rather unexpected development. But his victory surprised no one, least of all Bullet Bob himself.

"I'm confident of winning," he said with flat finality a few days ago. "I'll be facing good opponents, but I don't believe they'll beat me."

None had a chance especially when Hayes, not a particularly good starter, came roaring off his blocks with jet burners blazing. That he was able to equal the world record virtually was foreordained. Earlier, there had been gasps of disbelief from the crowd when his time in the semifinal had been announced at 9.9 seconds. But this had been a wind-blown job and was disallowed because he had had a junior-sized gale at his back. For the final there wasn't enough breeze to ruffle a feather.

The only thing about Hayes's victory that caused any doubt was whether he'd hold together for the Olympics. When he won the national championship in late June, he tore a hamstring muscle in his left thigh just after crossing the finish line.

He was unable to compete for an Olympic berth in the first trials the next week, but the Olympic Track and Field Committee wisely gave him a pass to the secondary trials 10 weeks later. That's when he qualified. It's lucky for the United States that he was given a rain check because both of the other 100-meter men—Trenton Jackson and Mel Pender—broke down in Tokyo.

The burly Hayes is now so sound of limb that he can hardly wait to get back to college and rejoin his football teammates for the last half of the season. They'll have a head start on him, but he travels so fast these days that he should be able to catch up.

Hayes was not the only American winner today who baffled the medical profession. At least he had time to heal. Al Oerter, the huge discus thrower, had no time at all. This two-time Olympic champion was rounding into form when he ripped cartilages off his rib cage while making a near-record practice throw last Friday. There was little hope that he'd be able to compete at all.

But he came out, encased in an ice pack, and achieved what amounted to the impossible. The Olympic physicians—Harry McPhee and Dan Hanley—thought the injury was so severe it would require a month and a half of slow healing. The big fellow from West Babylon, Long Island, couldn't wait that long. He climbed off his hospital bed and won his third straight Olympic championship.

"Don't play this up like I'm a hero," he said afterward with light-hearted modesty. "But I really gutted this one out. Nervousness bothered me in the other two Olympics. Soreness bothered me this time."

When Ludvik Danek of Czechoslovakia, who recently took the world record from Oerter with a toss of more than 211 feet, was short with his last throw, big Al walked slowly and painfully toward the circle for his own final effort. Then he flipped the platter aside as a sudden thought entered his mind.

"The hell with it," he said. "I don't have to torture myself again. I've got this Olympic championship already won." So he declined his last throw. It was a remarkable demonstration of the indomitability of man—this man, anyway. Billy Mills, in the 10,000 meters yesterday, and now Oerter today were unbelievable.

Not even the impossible is out of the reach of these Olympians.

1965

Clay and His Pigeon

May 28

Primo Carnera stabbed out with an ordinary left jab and Ernie Schaaf went down. He stayed down while the crowd in Madison Square Garden screamed "Fake." It did look like a palpable dive and the cynics in the press rows even risked laws against libel to hint as much. After all, the Preem was mobster-controlled and this appeared part of the build-up to maneuver the Italian giant into a shot at the world heavyweight championship.

Schaaf was taken on a stretcher to Polyclinic Hospital across the street and there he died. It later developed that a fearful beating he had taken from Maxie Baer a few months earlier had driven him so close to the borderline that an innocuous jab had been sufficient to send him the rest of the way.

Kinetics is a branch of physics dealing with the effects of forces. There is absolutely no method, however, of applying kinetics to boxing so that the force of a punch can be measured.

How hard did Cassius Clay hit Sonny Liston when he knocked out the big Bear to end their pantomime quiz in Lewiston, Maine, the other night? The punch certainly did not seem to be a crusher. Yet Jim Braddock, a man of unquestionable probity, raised a provocative point during breakfast the morning after the fiasco.

"That guy, Clay, is a pretty fair fighter," said the old heavyweight champion. "I have a feeling that he's a lot better than any of us gave him credit for being. It isn't the knockout punch that sticks in my mind as much as a punch he let go a few moments earlier. It was a right to Liston's jaw and it was a beauty. It shook Liston to his shoetops.

"For all we know, it could have been the one that set up the knockout. You might call it delayed action. When anyone is as old as Liston must be, he's liable to fall apart without warning."

The closest anyone has come to a verification of Liston's true age is on file at the Missouri State Prison. It indicates that he now would be 33, but the old jailbird undoubtedly used the birthdate of a younger brother. He must be close to 40 at least and the disintegration he showed in his Miami surrender to Clay 15 months earlier merely continued with even more marked celerity during the Maine fandango.

In all his training workouts except the last, Liston looked awful. This eyewitness watched the final impressive session and had pointed out afterward that Sonny had sparred only with Amos Lincoln, his slowest sparring partner, avoiding the fast-moving ones who had made him look so leaden-footed and ineffectual.

A postfight report from Boston offered an intriguing theory. It said Liston and his camp followers had been so discouraged by the departure of his skills that one brain truster had hit on an idea. He approached Lincoln and rigged up a secret deal with him.

The Lincoln assignment in that final workout was to make Liston look good and he was paid an extra $100. There's nothing illegal or improper about this. It merely was a morale booster. As such it worked. Sonny perked up after he had given Lincoln a pretty good thumping, but his camp followers were not misled. They knew in their hearts that the old man didn't have it any more.

It's quite possible that Clay knew it, too. He must have had scouts at the Liston workouts and they hardly could have mistaken the evidence before their eyes. Sonny was the proverbial hollow shell. No one can be a harmless tabby cat in training and a raging tiger in real action because the habits of one are carried into the other.

"Sonny sure has slipped badly since I fought him," said the sad-eyed Floyd Patterson. "It's hard to believe that a man could go back so far so fast."

Hardly had the bell sounded than Cassius fetched Liston a clout on the kisser. In spite of expert opinion to the contrary, the champion was going for a one-round knockout. It would have been recklessly foolhardy for anyone not forewarned as to Liston's unmistakable decline. Cassius had a sitting duck and he just flicked him off the fence post.

Was it a fix? This ringsider does not think so. A fix would have been more artfully arranged. This was so bad that it had to be believed, including the chicken-with-his-head-off antics of Jersey Joe Walcott, the miscast referee.

But for small favors, let us be thankful. At least the boxing racket is completely rid of the deflated ogre, the unsavory Sonny Liston. That alone makes the Lewiston charade worthwhile.

Out in the Open

June 17

Saint Louis, June 16—The slim little guy in the white linen cap looked wilted and worn. In the blistering heat at the Congressional Country Club in Washington a year ago, he walked with the leaden steps of an old man, the strength sapped from him He had virtually collapsed after the morning round and a physician accompanied him on the final tour of the course, watching with constant anxiety.

Some inner force kept driving Ken Venturi onward until he had reached his date with destiny. He won the United States Open golf championship because he had the ingredients of skill, fortitude, and determination to such an extent that he gained the unstinting admiration of those who could appreciate his battle against almost insuperable odds.

Yet life for Venturi has invariably been against almost insuperable odds and this was one of the few times he conquered them. Before his Open triumph a back ailment that led to the disintegration of his beautifully stylish game had kept him off the victory trail for three years. Then before he could capitalize on his Open success, disaster struck him from another quarter.

Circulatory trouble in his hands has kept him so sidelined

this year that it was doubtful for the longest while that he'd be able to defend his championship at the Bellerive Country Club in the tournament that starts tomorrow.

He has kept insisting that he will take a fling at it before submitting himself to tests at Mayo Clinic. His chances of winning again, therefore, are considered virtually nonexistent.

If nothing else, though, he will go out with one distinction. He will be the last of the champions who won his title over the grueling and exhausting 36-hole route on the final day. Beginning this year the Open will be a four-day tournament, just as is the Azalea open or the Bing Crosby clambake or any whistle stop on the winter tour. Once it was an awesome test of skill and stamina. The stamina has been removed. Only the skill remains.

Yet it is inaccurate to disparage the Open into "just another tournament." It never can be that. It carries its own built-in recognition as the supreme event in golf throughout the world even if the Masters does crowd it a lot more than was the case in the past.

The Masters is played on the same course every year and the top-ranking stars finally reach such a point that they get to know every blade of grass at Augusta by its first name. They're aware of the quirks and foibles, the safe stretches and the treacheries. The challenges still are there, but they are not accompanied by a dread of the unknown.

However, the Open keeps leapfrogging from place to place as a constant surprise package of sorts. It has been played on long courses and short ones, on flat courses and on ones better suited to mountain goats. Regardless of topography, though, it always is the most wicked challenge that this ancient game of cow pasture pool can offer.

Joe Dey and his fellow spoilsports in the United States Golf Association narrow the fairways by letting the rough grow. They add traps and give the links extra muscle by various other devices.

A year ago the layout at Congressional had the pros moaning. It was more than 7,000 yards in length, the longest ever. But this year's setup at Bellerive is even more of a blockbuster because it is almost 7,200 yards. The natural assumption is that it is geared for a power hitter like Jack Nicklaus.

Yet it must be remembered that Venturi, a medium hitter, conquered the other monster last June while Big Nick got nowhere. Never should it be forgotten that golf has the same elements of uncertainty that mark horse racing.

In spite of it all, however, Nicklaus will go into tomorrow's show as the favorite. His record scoring in the Masters last April makes the 25-year-old strong boy from Ohio the solid choice over Arnold Palmer, Tony Lema and the rest of a crack field. But on the beautiful course here, one artfully designed by Robert Trent Jones, Big Jack won't be able to reach some greens with a driver and wedge as is his normal wont.

Although the premium will be on distance off the tee, accuracy will be equally necessary. The narrow fairways have extra psychological guardians in out-of-bounds, creeks and walls of trees. Since one bad shot or penalty stroke can undo an awful lot of good ones, disaster is never far away. This Open has to be a suspense story all the way to the end.

In yesteryear the climax of this drama was compressed into the final day, the two rounds on Saturday. For the first time it will be spread out into an extra day, Sunday. But it still should carry the same emotional wallop.

This is the only column Arthur Daley had mounted and framed to display in his den.

On Losing a Friend

July 1

This will have to be personal. There's no other way I can write it. When Jack Mara, president of the New York Football Giants, died on Tuesday, the sports world lost one of its best-liked and most admirable executives. He was my closest friend —a friend for more than 30 years.

When the association began, Jack and I were a couple of young fellows trying to get ahead in different but allied branches of the sports business. Back in the early 1930s the Giants were still struggling for survival. In fact, they never became outstandingly successful until the perceptive Jack recognized the dangers of remaining in the obsolescent Polo Grounds and switched the field of play to the Yankee Stadium.

Although the Giants changed during the years from a faltering enterprise to a multi-million-dollar business, Jack never changed. His tastes stayed simple and he lived the same unostentatious way he always had. To the very end he was a delight and a comfort to be with.

A little more than two months ago the Maras dropped in on the Daleys. Jack and I watched a ball game on television. I didn't notice that he seemed unusually quiet. When we rejoined

Jack Mara: "He was my closest friend."

the others, he revealed that doctors had discovered a small tumor and he had to undergo an operation.

"I've straightened out my financial affairs," he said, "and I'm at peace with my God. There's nothing more I can do but resign myself to whatever God wishes."

His religion was his strength. He was a good man, kind, generous and thoughtful. He had all the virtues. On top of that he had a glowing personality, a quick smile and a ready quip that drew people to him, high and low. Everyone liked Jack Mara.

Over the years Giant esprit de corps was generally rated as perhaps the highest of any sports organization. It came from the top; fierce loyalties there led to other loyalties in the ranks. The Maras never forgot their own. No Giant or former Giant in need stayed that way long.

Years after lesser owners would have replaced Steve Owen as coach, the reluctant decision was reached to pension the man who had served the team so well. Jack told me about it in advance.

"I want you to be the first to know," he said. "We're making a coaching change."

"Oh, Jack," I said. "That makes me sick at heart."

"How do you think I feel?" he said.

He looked miserable. Even a necessary change tore at his sensitive, sympathetic heart. The warmth of his character spread through the organization and gave it a one-big-happy-family relationship that is unusual in sports. Perhaps Charlie Conerly, the valiant quarterback of yesteryear, expressed it best.

"I never thought of Jack as my boss," he said. "He was my friend. I haven't cried often in my life. But I cried when I heard of his death." He was not alone. Other Giants and former Giants shed tears unashamedly.

At the Giant rookie camp on the Fordham campus a few days ago, Emlen Tunnell, the defensive backfield coach, was let in on the news that Jack had cancer and that death was imminent. He sat on the steps, head buried in his arms, crying. A priest walked by.

"Would it be all right, Father," he said, "if I went in the

chapel and lit a candle for Jack Mara?"

Jack was the finest man I ever met. As I left his room in Memorial Hospital for the last time, I kept thinking of the farewell that Horatio uttered at the death of his cherished friend, Hamlet.

"Now cracks a noble heart. Good-night, sweet prince, and flights of angels sing thee to thy rest!"

1966

A Visit With Brian London

August 5

Blackpool, England, August 4—In a somewhat improbable setting, a somewhat improbable challenger for the world heavyweight championship goes through the motions of training for a goal that is virtually unattainable. Brian London, a journeyman fighter of such little distinction that he isn't even ranked among the top 10 by *Ring Magazine,* will attempt on Saturday to dislodge the crown from its secure perch on Cassius Clay's noggin.

Far from the maddening tumult of London (the city) London (the fighter) plods away at his preparations without having to submit to the inquiring gaze of too many curious experts. He has made it much too inconvenient for them because he elected to set up his training base in his home town of Blackpool, Britain's biggest and most popular summer resort. It's almost a five-hour train trip from London (that's the city again) and it nestles alongside the Irish Sea.

When a clammy rain drips down, as it did yesterday, Blackpool has all the delightful appeal of Coney Island in November. No wonder the British are so indomitable. Not only has Brian picked this spot but also his quarters are pitched in the sprawling expanse of Holiday Camp, a far from elaborate series of boxlike, motel-type rooms.

There also are shopping centers, bazaars, and one horse-betting parlor to supply an extra creature comfort to the thousand or so temporary residents. It's much too drab and plebian to rank as even a lower-class Grossinger's.

However, it does have the advantage of inaccessibility and that keeps Brian safe from the prying eyes of most experts. It's just as well. He hardly is likely to convince any that he has much of a chance against Clay. British boxing writers must get most of their news of him by osmosis because there isn't even a publicity agent at hand to tell them lies.

The most truthful man on the premises clearly is Danny Vary, the gray-thatched cockney who trains London. He was talking barely translatable English during the staging of a "Glamorous Grandma Contest" shortly before Brian appeared for his final brisk workout.

"My man might be a bum but he's a good bum," said Danny, making a hairline distinction. "He's tough and he's fit. He'll be throwing punches all the time and if luck comes our way . . ." His voice trailed off, leaving the sentence unfinished. Only a lucky punch, it would seem, can save this London bridge from falling down.

Brian himself is just as realistic. He's a flat-nosed, prognathous-jawed husky of 32 who has invested his ring earnings so wisely that he has become the richest British heavyweight. He speaks with a heavy accent that's a cross between Lancashire and Northumbria.

"The way I see the fight meself," he said, not sparing the clichés, "is that I have everything to gain and nothing to lose. If I'm beaten, I'm a rich fella. If I win, I'm richer."

Brian's share of the loot will be at least £35,000, a shade under $100,000. Never would he turn his back on a windfall like that any more than he could refuse to meet Floyd Patterson for this same championship at Indianapolis seven years ago despite the refusal of the British Board of Boxing Control to certify him.

"I'd be daft if I didn't take it," he said then. In effect, he's saying the same thing now. Brian needs no sanity tests when it comes to money.

Although others have scored knockouts over him without—strangely enough—actually knocking him off his feet, Patterson is the only man who has toppled him to the deck. It took 11 rounds, too.

"I wasn't fit for that fight," said Brian, grimacing at the memory. "I'd just been beaten by Henry Cooper and wasn't certified for a title fight. In order to get it, Cus D'Amato demanded that I sign on his man, Nick Baffi, as my manager. He gave me one sparring partner, Dusty Rhodes, who had been discarded by Patterson.

"Before that he kept me locked in a lawyer's office for two days, somewhere in old New York down where the big skyscrapers are. I lived on sandwiches and coffee for two days and never trained until I got to Indianapolis."

"A bloody tomb it was," said Jack London, Brian's brother, speaking of the cement block cells in which they had to live.

"They led me to believe that they'd let me go the distance," continued Brian. "When Patterson tried to knock me out in the first 40 seconds, I said to meself, 'You bloody bum. I won't let you knock me out.' By the 11th round I was just too tired to continue. I never got marked but he cut me up terrible in the kidneys and I couldn't breathe."

If Brian has improved in the intervening years, it was not visible to the naked eye yesterday in his final sparring session. He seemed slow, sluggish and somewhat ponderous. He threw single punches for the most part and few combinations. He did not impress. So maybe it's just as well that the British experts have stayed away from Blackpool. London, the city, has to be a lot more exciting and interesting than London, the fighter.

Lord of the Manor

August 29

Cashel, Ireland—Vincent O'Brien, an elegant and aristocratic man in an elegant and aristocratic setting, swung down the path from the manse at his Ballydoyle estate. Impeccably dressed and with wavy gray hair giving him an added look of distinction, he might have been the lord of some baronial fief. But two things betrayed the fact that he was in Tipperary. He was carrying a blackthorn cane and he had a warm smile of Irish welcome.

Vincent is a horse trainer. He's not an ordinary one mind you. He and Paddy Prendegast outrank all others of their ilk in Ireland and rate among the most famous in the world. Yet it is to be doubted that any trainer anywhere has an establishment that can match this magnificent layout, not far from the rock on which Brian Boru was crowned king of all Ireland almost a thousand years ago.

"It's quite sizable," modestly conceded Vincent in utter defiance of the characteristic Irish tendency toward overenthusiasm.

Sizable? Faith, man, even the most backward tourist can see that it's enormous, almost 500 acres of rolling Irish countryside. Kentucky has its blue grass, but the Emerald Isle has the greenest green grass that mortal man ever did see. And the Celts have a love for the horse and a way with the horse that's proverbial.

"There's a big advantage, there is," said Vincent in his soft, lilting voice, "in having your own private set-up. You're the master of the situation. At public training establishments a man can work only on the particular ground assigned him, even though it may be unfavorable. Here we have everything."

He sure has. A spotless and handsomely designed barn area, fireproof throughout, easily handles 60 horses and borders a training field unlike anything seen in the States. It stretches over a five-furlong straightaway and is 100 yards or more wide.

Along the inner border is a black lane of finely ground ashes that is similar in texture to American dirt tracks. Then come lane after lane of green turf, marked by white pegs and each accommodating a half dozen horses at racing speed. In another field he has a half-circle of a track. When the chute is used, the track stretches for a mile. When two bends are used, the layout represents a mile and a quarter.

"All our racing is on turf," explained Vincent. "And our horses become lost on dirt. They don't have the experience to handle it. Another thing is that we run our races clockwise instead of counterclockwise as you do in the States.

"It must come as a bit of a surprise to one of our horses to go to America and discover that he has to run left-handed instead of right-handed. They learn quickly, however, even though there always will be some who do it better one way than the other."

By this time Vincent had driven a white station wagon with four-wheel drive around much of the park-like enchantment of Ballydoyle. Mares with foals at their sides played within fenced enclosures, all in the proper picture-book style.

"See that one?" said Vincent, pointing toward a gray. "She's Courbette, the daughter of the greatest mare in the United States, Gallorette, and she's by Native Dancer."

Handsome is his collection and half of his stock is owned by Americans. Larkspur, owned by Raymond Guest, now the

United States Ambassador to Ireland, gave him his first training victory in the English Derby at Epsom Downs a few years ago. As a matter of fact, Vincent has won every important stake in Europe "except for the 2,000 Guineas." The Irish Derby he has won thrice. Yet, as everyone knows, training horses is a somewhat inexact science. With a wry smile Vincent offered an illustration.

"Last year," he said, "I was about to send James Cox Brady's Long Look after the English Oaks. It was to be held on a Friday. I had worked her here on Monday and vanned her to the Dublin airport on Tuesday for shipment to Britain. Suddenly everything closed down tight. It was one of those lightning strikes we get here occasionally—wildcat strikes, I think you call them.

"With all planes grounded it seemed as if there was no chance to get her across the Channel. But I finally got an English company to send a plane for her the day before the race. All she did while waiting was hang around the Phoenix Park track. For the better part of the week she did little more than walk about. Really. That was all. And she won the Oaks."

Horsemen continually live on hope. Recently Vincent went to Saratoga for the yearling sales and came away with two top prospects for Charles Engelhard, the American industrialist. One is a half-brother of Kauai King, the winner of the Kentucky Derby, and the other is a son of the great Ribot. Hope comes easier to an Irishman, however, especially if he is a Vincent O'Brien who operates in the relaxed atmosphere and sumptuous setting of his equine empire at Ballydoyle.

The Honest Wrestler

September 6

No professional wrestler who has the slightest respect for his intelligence will ever watch a wrestling match. He knows that it's a barney with the outcome prearranged and he wouldn't be found dead as a spectator. But on one wintry night in 1933 a troupe of matmen dreadfully shortchanged the customers at the Broadway Arena in Brooklyn. In their haste they saw to it that every bout ended in nothing flat.

The rasslers were so carried away by impatience and eagerness that they refused to prolong their acts. They rushed through their assignments, piled into taxicabs and hastened to Madison Square Garden where Strangler Lewis was about to meet Ray Steele in what the boys in the trade call "a shooting match." This was something they had to see, an honest match that was shorn of hippodroming and where skills instead of the booking agent would determine the winner.

In enraptured delight the wrestlers were glued to their seats while the ordinary spectators stamped their feet for action. To inexpert eyes this was utter boredom. But to expert eyes the masterly moves of the Strangler were things of beauty. Lewis was old and fat. He outweighed Steele by 30 pounds, but still maneuvered with the catlike grace of a jungle beast, wise to the ways of combat.

Steele was an exceptionally fine wrestler even by the high standards of that era. However, Lewis knew every trick, had every counter and had a hold for every opening. After only 20 minutes of helplessness and frustration, the younger man lost his temper and was disqualified.

The next day Herman Hickman, later a Yale football coach but then a practicing wrestler, encountered Lewis whose stature had grown greatly in Herman's estimation.

"What did you think of Steele?" said the awed Hickman.

"A good little man," said the Strangler, flicking the ashes nonchalantly from his cigar. "A good little man."

Perhaps that match was the last of the honest professional wrestling bouts and the death of the Strangler not long ago brought it back to mind. They had real rasslers in the old days and not the vaudeville tumblers they have today.

In fact, the Strangler may have inadvertently precipitated—in a left-handed sort of way—the trend toward staged productions. When he was world champion, he met Wayne Munn, an oversized Nebraska football player who couldn't tell the difference between a hammer lock and a leg scissors. But brute strength compensated for blind ignorance and Munn merely pitched Lewis out of the ring and became the new champion.

Eventually the Strangler won back the title but yielded it later to another former football lineman, Gus Sonnenberg of Dartmouth. Gus was the inventor of a billygoat tactic known as "the flying tackle." He butted Lewis out of the ring.

"Do you call that wrestling?" snorted the Strangler in disgust afterward.

He was entitled to his disgust. The mat game soon became flooded with other gimmicks and the more fanciful they were the more a deluded public went for them. Wrestling stopped being wrestling and became a new art form, a total burlesque of a once-noble sport.

One of the first recorded matches was that between Ulysses and Ajax, reported by the Grantland Rice of his day, a guy named Homer. Most bouts in the ensuing centuries were what the present generation of rasslers knows as "shooting matches." Some of the more cynical brothers, however, claim that the last honest bout was the one between Frank Gotch and George Hackenschmidt in 1910. But the Lewis–Steele match was on the level in 1933 and the match between the Strangler and Joe Stecher in 1916 had to be honest. No one could have had the fix in. For the first hour neither of these clever artisans even went to the mat. They tugged and hauled, maneuvering for position. The Strangler was seeking the headlock that gave him his nickname. Stecher was trying to clamp on his famous leg scissors.

They started at 4 o'clock in the afternoon at the Omaha Fair Grounds. A hot sun beat down on them mercilessly. They toiled for hour after hour. Soon darkness came and automobiles, not too plentiful then, were driven to ringside so that the headlights could enable the weary gladiators to carry on. At 9 P.M. the referee called a halt—and a draw.

They had wrestled for five hours, automatic certification of the on-the-level qualities of the match. A couple of years earlier they had grappled two hours to a draw and a couple of years later they went another two hours before reaching their third deadlock. This was honest wrestling in its most exaggerated form.

Only the amateurs remain to carry on the standards of honest wrestling that Strangler Lewis and the great professional craftsmen of another generation once upheld.

Barney's Toughest Foe

November 30

There will be a boxing show at Sunnyside Garden tonight, an event of little intrinsic importance. What lifts it out of the ordinary, though, is that 100 ringside seats have been set aside at $100 apiece as this low-brow and cold-blooded sport yields to a rare gush of sentiment to lend a helping hand to one of its more admirable characters.

A slew of great champions from yesteryear will make appearances at Sunnyside and the $10,000 raised will go to Barney Ross, onetime lightweight and welterweight king, who is currently fighting his most formidable foe, throat cancer. Treatments are expensive and Barney, always a fast man with a dollar bill, needs the financial assistance.

In any ranking of the great ones Barney is always placed in the upper echelon and deservedly so. He beat Tony Canzoneri for the lightweight title and Tony was one of the best. He beat Jimmy McLarnin for the welterweight crown and Jimmy was one of the deadliest knockout artists the division ever had.

But his most notable victory was to come long after the bludgeoning fists of Henry Armstrong had retired him from the ring. When the war broke out, Barney enlisted in the Marines

Barney Ross, right, and Henry Armstrong as they squared off for cameras at weigh-in for big bout in 1938.

and was cited for heroism after he had stood guard in a foxhole over wounded comrades in the face of withering machine gun fire at Guadalcanal.

Barney was wounded and the medicos shot him so full of morphine to ease his pain that he contracted the drug habit. But he licked that, too. Unashamedly he presented himself to the Federal hospital at Lexington, Kentucky, and emerged a free man.

It figured, though. That's the kind of guy Barney always had been. He walked unafraid. He did what he had to do. This was demonstrated when Mike Jacobs was trying to match Ross with McLarnin for the welterweight championship. But Sam Pian, Ross's co-manager with Art Winch, balked. He wanted no part of a thunderous hitter like McLarnin. Into the room strolled Ross.

"What's going on here?" said Barney.

"They're trying to talk me into a fight with McLarnin," said Pian, "and I won't go for it."

"Listen, Sam," said Barney, "sign up. I'll take care of the rest."

That's exactly what he did. He outpointed the feared McLarnin and was the welterweight champion of the world. Four months later he lost the title back to the Vancouver Irishman, but he regained it the next year.

Barney was not quite 29 years old when he retired from the ring. Perhaps it would be more accurate to say that Armstrong drove him into retirement. Hammerin' Henry was then at his peak and had won 29 of 30 bouts by knockouts while Ross was definitely on his way downhill with only his flaming spirit unimpaired.

Yet they fought furiously and evenly for the first two rounds. For just one brief spurt in the third Barney looked like the Ross of old. One of the fastest of all ringmen, he never was faster than he was in that first minute, swarming over Armstrong and looking as though he would slash him to ribbons as the crowd roared in anticipation.

But Henry never took a backward step. With startling suddenness he gained command of the fight. A tireless, windmill type, he punched ceaselessly and hurt with every punch. He beat down Barney's guard, smashed him in the face and hammered away at the body. No matter how much Ross twisted and turned to escape from his tormentor by artful use of his great skills as a boxer, there was no avoidance of the rain of crashing punches.

After that the rounds were repetitious, brutally and savagely repetitious. The crowd had lapsed into silence and then the roar grew louder again as the fans pleaded with Arthur Donovan, the referee, to halt the slaughter. By the tenth round Donovan begged Ross to let him stop it.

"No," said Barney through tattered lips, "let me alone. I'm the champion. He'll have to beat me in the ring, not sitting on a stool in the corner."

"Please let me stop it, Barney," said Pian.

"If you do, Sam," said Barney, "I'll never talk to you again."

So Barney went out for more punishment. In the last two rounds Armstrong didn't even try for a knockout. He was too filled with admiration for a gallant foe to humiliate him further by a knockout. So Barney lost his championship by decision and called it a career.

He's still fighting, though.

1967

Registering a Kick

April 26

Once upon a time the only guys who kicked footballs in top level competition were genuine football players who also blocked, tackled and performed all the normal gridiron chores. Usually they were 60-minute operatives with the toughness and skills to function on offense and defense. But nowadays the kicker doesn't have to be a real football player at all. He can be a specialist.

This was emphasized last week when the Dallas Cowboys concluded a 10,000-mile Kick Karavan in a countrywide search for undiscovered phenomenons with a rare talent for applying foot to ball. No professional team has to go to such extremes for assembling the musclemen who fill out the roster and do the work. They are handpicked after exhaustive scrutiny and then ruthless attrition weeds out all but the best.

No longer does the kicker have to be a heavy duty performer, who is part of the team. He can be a man apart and the only time he experiences rude contact is just before a roughing-the-kicker penalty. If you want a for instance, you merely need take a quick glimpse at the case histories of two men who scored 18 points in a game, Garo Yepremian and Jim Thorpe.

Who is Garo Yepremian? It's a good question and not many football fans could supply the answer. He is a multilingual Armenian who was born on the Mediterranean island of Cyprus and played some soccer there without distinction. After living in England for a half dozen years, he came to the United States last June and walked into Tiger Stadium on October 12 during a practice session of the Detroit Lions. So impressive was he in a kicking exhibition that the Lions signed him that day despite the fact that he is 5 feet 5 inches tall and weighs only 155 pounds.

The first live action he ever saw was his own left foot kicking a ball in the opening play of a National Football League game. He was somewhat short of sensational. But a month later against the Minnesota Vikings he put on a show that bordered on the fantastic. He kicked field goals of 33, 26, 15, 20, 28, and 33 yards. If you count 'em up, they add to six, displacing the one-game record of five set by the mighty Ernie Nevers in 1926 and later matched by Bob Waterfield, Roger Leclere, and Jim Bakken. Furthermore, the Lions defeated the Vikings, 32 to 31.

"What are you going to do about Yepremian?" an interviewer asked Norm Van Brocklin, the Minnesota coach.

"I'm thinking of having him deported as an undesirable alien," said Van, joking amid his tears.

And who was Jim Thorpe? No alien was he. His ancestors were here before Columbus because he was a Sac and Fox Indian. Not only was the noble redman acclaimed in a poll as the greatest football player of the first half century but he was probably the greatest all-round athlete America ever produced—a wondrous football player, a big league baseball outfielder, the winner of the Olympic decathlon championship in 1912 (later disqualified), a 70 golfer, a 200 bowler—well, you name the sport. The big Indian could outperform anyone. He was the fictional Frank Merriwell come to life.

There was nothing he couldn't do on a gridiron. In a game against Lafayette, for example, his shortest punt measured 70 yards. But it was the Harvard game of 1911 that provided the stage and the scenario for his most incredible heroics. Proud

Harvard had won the national championship the year before and was loaded again, three-deep in manpower, when the Crimson faced the Carlisle Indians. The redmen brought only 16 players to Cambridge. But one was Thorpe. It was enough.

The Crimson horde swept easily for a touchdown. Then Jim began to slash off tackle and pound the middle. Thrice he carried the ball into scoring range and kicked field goals of 23, 45, 37 yards. To the vast astonishment and dismay of the Harvards, the little Indian school led at the half, 9 to 6. The indignant Cantabs stormed back for a touchdown and a field goal for a 15-9 lead. At the next kickoff Thorpe walked over to his quarterback, Gus Welch.

"Gimme the ball," said big Jim.

They gave him the ball for nine straight plays. On the ninth he rocketed over the goal line for a touchdown. The score was tied. Harvard knew it had the tiger by the tail and was ready to settle for the tie. Thorpe was not. He led a one-man assault but ground was yielded more grudgingly. It was fourth down on the 43.

"Set the ball up," growled Thorpe. "I'll kick a field goal."

"From midfield?" asked Welch.

"Yes, from midfield," snarled Jim.

So he kicked a 50-yarder to win the game, 18 to 15, in one of football's most stunning and memorable upsets. The big Indian scored every point, 18 in all. But Yepremian also had an 18-point day. Is there any comparison between them as football players? Don't even waste your breath in answering.

Day of Decision

April 28

This is the day when Cassius Clay is confronted by the most important and fateful decision of his young life. Will it be induction or imprisonment? The heavyweight champion of the world has indicated that he will take jail rather than be drafted into the Army. Military service, he claims, is contrary to his religious beliefs.

It would appear that he doesn't think the United States is worth fighting for. Yet a couple of memories keep intruding on that jarring supposition, flashbacks to the Olympic Games at Rome in 1960. It's always an emotional moment when an Olympic champion stands on the topmost part of the three-part pedestal and the flag of his country rises on the center staff while the band plays his national anthem.

At the magnificent Palazzo della Sport, a cathedral to muscle, the Roman band played a truncated version of the "Star Spangled Banner" and ended somewhere in the middle, such as "the perilous night."

But the exuberant Italians had produced such a dazzling show that their impetuosity could be forgiven. Yet of all the champions to be crowned, none stood at attention with more obvious pride than Cassius Marcellus Clay, the light-heavyweight winner. Nor has the sharp recollection of those vivid moments faded over the years.

Sure, he had won for himself but he also had won for his country. Even when he returned to the States, he went wandering around Times Square in New York in his pullover uniform with the U.S.A. lettered across his chest. He was proud to wear it and show it off.

People change in seven years and few have changed more than Clay. The delightful boy of 1960 has become a mixed-up man. If there was skepticism about the sincerity of his motives when he first fell under the sway of the Black Muslims, it exists no longer. He has been so thoroughly brainwashed that he now believes what he says even if the words are put into his mouth by the Muslims.

This reporter was captivated by Cassius the first time he met him at the Villaggio Olimpico in Rome. Not even the intermediate developments have completely broken that hold, even though such an admission might be a rebuke to intelligence. But it just can't be helped.

That's why there's a tragic feeling here at what is about to happen to Cassius. Actually it's merely a minuscule offshoot of the greater tragedy of Vietnam. But because he's the heavyweight champion and therefore the world's best fighter, his refusal to fight for his country gets disproportionate emphasis and may produce ensuing ground swells of unpredictable potency.

The Muslims, who direct his every move, have lost their meal ticket and gained a martyr. The shrewd men at the head of the movement must think that sacrificing him is worth the price.

Some legal beagles think that more delaying action is possible, perhaps as much as a year, to ward off the jail sentence that confronts him if he refuses induction into the Army today. Yet it's inconceivable that he still could ply his boxing trade profitably during that period.

So perhaps Cassius has fought his last ring fight. He now is 25 years old. The normal sentence for those refusing induction is five years. If he were to try to resume his career after he has passed his thirtieth birthday, time will have eroded his skills, even if he could stay in sharp physical condition in the jug, an unlikely possibility.

Clay's strength as a boxer has been his blinding speed. He does a lot of wrong things but he is so unbelievably fast that his errors in technique are covered up by his swiftness of hand, foot and brain. Wise boxing men have acknowledged as much.

"No one is gonna beat Clay," they have repeated over and over, "until the years slow him down. Then he won't be able to pull back his head the way he does now. When he's a fraction of a second slower in his reactions, some young guy is gonna tag him on the chin. But it will be an awful long wait."

There will be elimination contests to produce a new champion just as there were after the retirements of Jim Jeffries, Gene Tunney, Joe Louis, and Rocky Marciano. Both Jeffries and Louis later assayed comebacks, only to be beaten by holders of the once vacated title. Cassius has defeated almost everyone in the division except young Joe Frazier, who still may be a year or two away from top rank, although he may be able to advance faster with Clay no longer a roadblock. It is not an enticing prospect.

As a fistfighter Cassius might very well have become the greatest. But we'll never know. Instead, he seems fated to bring about his own destruction.

1968

For Auld Lang Syne

February 11

When nostalgia descends on the Madison Square Garden hockey rink this afternoon, there will be enough warmth in it to melt the ice. The New York Rangers will bid farewell to their ancient battleground with a game against the Detroit Red Wings and the arena will be awash with sentiment. The stars from the past will materialize in the old Garden for a salute to the glories of yesteryear, stirring up rich memories by their very presence.

The first Ranger team ever to play in the old Garden will skate on to the ice in a ceremonial obeisance of sorts to the last Ranger team ever to play there, the same group that will introduce the new Garden to hockey a week later.

From four decades of All-Star teams will appear fabled heroes who left their imprint on hockey history, ageless performers such as Eddie Shore, King Clancy, Maurice (The Rocket) Richard, Aurel Joliat, Dit Clapper, Milt Schmidt, Black Jack Stewart, Bill Durnan, Syl Apps, Turk Broda, Ted Lindsay, and so many more. Not to be overlooked is Lorne Carr of the old New York Americans, who beat the Rangers in the longest game in Garden annals with a goal in the fourth overtime period at 1:25 in the morning—the next morning, that is.

But most of the plaudits deservedly will center on that first Ranger team, symbolizing the dynasty that Lester Patrick built and setting in motion the hockey mania that has gripped our village ever since. In 1926 he assembled a marvelous group, all work horses. They didn't play in quick bursts the way the moderns do, constantly shifting personnel. The original Broadway Blues got on the ice and stayed there.

Their primary line consisted of Frank Boucher and the Cook brothers, Bill and Bun. The goalie was Davey Kerr. The defensemen were the late Taffy Abel and the unforgettable Ching Johnson. The gallery gods worshipped the bald-headed Ching, the popularity kid they called the Chinaman.

Only the super stars of today are on the ice as much as half a game. But Boucher and the Cook brothers were in the thick of the action for at least two of the three periods. In the Stanley Cup year of 1928 the only rest Ching got was when he was in the penalty box. Otherwise he was on the ice for the full 60 minutes. In the season when the Chinaman broke a collarbone, Taffy took over the 60-minute stint.

The first Ranger game was against the Montreal Maroons, now defunct, but then the Stanley Cup champions. It was billed as a match between the best team of the world and the worst. The Rangers won, 1-0. Boucher and the Cook brothers were highly skilled professionals, but Johnson and Abel were little more than semipros of limited experience. Yet when the game ended, Bill Cook patted each on the back.

"You fellows will do," he said.

This was praise from Caesar and the two neophytes from the sticks swelled with pride. Such confidence would not be misplaced, they vowed. It never was.

The Chinaman had to be one of the most remarkable of all hockey players. Long after he retired he conceded that he had faked his age when the Rangers sought his services.

"I told them I was 28," he said, "but I was almost two years older. I even demanded a three-year contract because I wasn't sure I could last that long. But I lasted 12 years."

Early in the Johnson career, he was knocked cold and was still on Queer Street when he returned to the ice. He didn't know where he was or what he was doing. But suddenly he found himself in front of the enemy cage and taking a beautiful pass from Bill Cook for a goal.

"As pretty a play as I ever saw," said the delighted Bill.

"What are you talking about?" said Ching, not even knowing he had scored.

This group represented the first Ranger dynasty. The second came just before the war with such youthful stars as Neil and Mac Colville, Alex Shibicky, Lynn and Muzz Patrick, Babe Pratt, and Art Coulter. They left their best years in the service, though, and the Broadway Blues have been trying to establish another dynasty ever since. Perhaps it is now in the process of formation. If so, it will be the new Garden that will get it.

Today's slambang hockey game will mark the last display of muscle in the old Garden, a final flourish with nostalgic overtones. The windup event, though, will be the dog show. It seems ironic—maybe it even is proper—that the old Garden will literally go to the dogs.

Compounding a Felony

June 12

How can one man measure another man's grief? It is something beyond measure and that's why the action of the Houston Astros in fining Rusty Staub and Bob Aspromonte a day's pay is reprehensible. Out of respect for the memory of Senator Robert F. Kennedy and moved by a deep sorrow that no front office could possibly estimate, these players refused to perform for their team on Sunday, a day of national mourning.

For this act of decency they were penalized and baseball reeled under another staggering blow. Joe Brown, the general manager of the Pittsburgh Pirates, handled a similar situation more smartly. One of his players, Maury Wills, also refused to play that day but whatever action Brown took—if any—was kept secret.

"I talked to Maury yesterday," said Joe over the phone from San Francisco. "We had a meeting of minds and whatever happened will remain between him and me. He had a personal obligation to himself and another obligation to his employer. There is much to be said for both sides even though I just can't go into chapter and verse on what was involved."

The Pirate executive was pleasant but so guarded that even

his tone of voice revealed nothing. However, he has been at his trade a long time and knows his way round.

Houston was all blunder. Spec Richardson is a rookie general manager serving under the dictatorial Judge Roy Hofheinz, the owner of the Astros. They alienated a lot of people by taking economic sanctions against Staub and Aspromonte, compounding the felony by making it public.

Insubordination on the part of a player is a violation of his contract and lays him open to penalty. But these were unusual circumstances. They almost would seem to call for the same understanding that would normally be forthcoming if it had been the death of a close relation. Millions regarded Bobby Kennedy in exactly that light.

What can be done about this cold-hearted assessment? According to baseball law, any appeal of such disciplinary action can only be initiated by the men so disciplined. There are four stages for such an appeal: 1. the ball club; 2. John Gaherin, labor-management adviser for the owners; 3. the league; 4. the commissioner, where the matter will be settled under binding arbitration. But the players must initiate it. This cannot be ordered from the top.

An observer has to believe that the Astros never did think the matter through clearly. They took the wrong time to take what would ordinarily be deemed proper action. No ball club—or any other organization, for that matter—can be subject to the whims of an employee, particularly one who has contracted his services.

That's why Joe Brown made a point of mentioning that if Wills had a personal obligation he also had one to his ball club. If the Pirate front-office chief declined to disclose how he disposed of it, he at least showed an awareness of its existence.

What places the sport in such an unfavorable position is that emotions are so inescapably intertwined with the whole miserable, hit-or-miss lost weekend. An indignant Milt Pappas resigned as player representative of the Cincinnati Reds when his teammates bowed to club pressure and went ahead with a game they didn't want to play. He was traded to Atlanta yesterday.

Also yesterday a telegram reached him from Frank Mankiewicz, the press aide and close friend of the murdered Senator. It said:

"Please accept my personal admiration for your actions. Senator Kennedy indeed enjoyed competitive sports but I doubt that he would have put box-office receipts ahead of national mourning under any circumstances." Similar telegrams also went to Staub, Aspromonte, Wills, and Gil Hodges.

That's a scathing indictment of the baseball establishment and the unhappy diamond moguls have to feel that too many fans agree with it. What makes their position so untenable is that they had had warning enough of public reaction to national tragedy. Less than two months earlier they went through a similar shock, the assassination of Martin Luther King, Jr.

It came just before opening day and postponements were forced on the owners by rebellious players. This latest one came just before a big money weekend, "Bat Day." For some teams it was on Saturday and others on Sunday, which is why there was no orderly single day of mourning.

Many insiders feel that William Dole Eckert, the commissioner, has become the scapegoat of this episode, taking a bum rap for not exerting powers he actually doesn't have. Only Judge Landis could snap the whip and make the club owners do his bidding. No other commissioner has been so privileged.

The two leagues are fighting between themselves over expansion, schedules, subdivision of leagues and everything else. They can't agree on anything. Meanwhile they have permitted their image to get tarnished. Some sage wrote wise words many years ago, so wise that they can bear repeating.

"Baseball has to be the world's greatest game," he wrote. "Otherwise it never could survive the men who run it."

Forever Is a Long Time

September 4

Satchel Paige was already a legend before he reached the big leagues in 1948. The ageless wonder more or less admitted that he then was 42 years old. Satch has always been a mite vague about his birthdate. A few years ago he wrote a book, *Maybe I'll Pitch Forever*. It begins to look as if he's out to prove it because he signed on recently with the Atlanta Braves in the slightly amorphous role of pitcher and pitching coach.

Since it is exactly two decades since Satch was 42—more or less—he now is somewhat older even though Satch doesn't necessarily use the same brand of arithmetic that ordinary people do. Presumably he has been restored to the fold in a noble gesture by baseball as a whole to work him into the player pension plan because he needed 148 days to qualify for the five-year minimum. But Satch bristles at the thought.

"I didn't sign for a pension," he said yesterday. "I know there are things I can do if I never throw a ball. I can help the young pitchers now and pitch a few innings myself. I gotta get ungreased 'cause I been away from the game since last season. When I get on the field and field with the regulars the manager, he says, 'What the hell goes on here? How can anyone your age jump around the way you do?' I'm not sure I know more about pitching than anyone else but no one ever pitched more'n me."

No one will argue with Satch on that. He figures he's pitched in more than 2,500 games—he started in 1924—and was on the hill for as many as 162 games a season with as many as 100 no-hitters over his career. Virtually all of it was in the Negro leagues or in winter ball. Baseball was a year-round occupation with him and big leaguers who faced him on barnstorming tours were quick to say that he was as good or better than any in the majors.

But Satch was a victim of his times because the color line kept him out of the big leagues until he was far beyond his prime. Bill Veeck brought him up to the Cleveland Indians in 1948 and Satch contributed mightily toward the pennant drive—even if he was 42 years old. Yet he almost missed out on attaining his fondest dream, pitching in the World Series.

"I shoulda started the opening game," he said, not belligerently but matter-of-factly. "I won the pennant for them. If you want me to tell you the truth, I was hot as fire and won 6 of my last 7. There wasn't nuthin' else left but pick me. But I was the last one to get in, the third of three relief pitchers in the fifth game. I stopped 'em."

Experts of about 40 years ago were unanimously agreed that two can't-miss performers in the Negro leagues were Satchel Paige, the rubber-armed pitcher, and Josh Gibson, the brawny, power-hitting catcher. They also would have starred in the bigs. In fact, they might have been Hall of Fame material. Josh never made it. The remarkable Satch made it but a trifle late.

"The two greatest hitters I ever threw against," said Satch, "were Ted Williams and Josh Gibson. They had no weaknesses. I found it easier to pitch against Joe DiMaggio than against Ted. I remember one day when Joe hit a homer off Bobby Feller but when I came on in relief I struck him out. Williams I pitched to on the outside and would rather walk than come on inside. He got hits off me but never a home run."

Among the many remarkable things about Satch was his pinpoint control. When Veeck, owner of the Indians, was trying to sell Satch to Lou Boudreau, his manager, a tryout of sorts was held. Boudreau put on a catcher's mitt and Satch fired in 50 pitches, 46 of them strikes.

Perhaps the most memorable game of Satch's abbreviated major league career was against Detroit in 1952. Satch went into the 12th inning of a scoreless tie and won it himself with his third single. He had allowed only six hits, had walked only two and fanned nine—and he was 46 years old, more or less, of course.

The Browns were pretty dreadful and finished last. But one of Satch's pupils, Ned Garver, was a 20-game winner anyway.

"I was always talking to Garver and had something new for him every day," said Satch with a half-smile. "Like the time I told him about the triple play I made in relief. The bases were full and there was a 3-2 count on the batter when I went in. I picked up an extra ball in the dugout. Then I threw those two balls at the same time, one to first and one to third. I picked off both runners and my motion was so good that the batter fanned. That was three outs. Ned wouldn't talk to me for a whole day after that."

It isn't easy to get Satch to reminisce. After all, his fundamental principle of life is this: Don't look back. Something might be gaining on you.

Amid Matchless Pageantry

October 13

Mexico City, October 12—The opening ceremony of the Olympic Games is more than just an exquisite spectacle. It is an emotional experience as well. Nothing else in the world of sports even can come close to it. It dazzles the eye and stuns the senses, a gorgeous pageant presented in living color, no less. It is the ultimate in stagecraft, soul-stirring in its magnificence.

None can remain unmoved by it. Even those who have witnessed other opening ceremonies find themselves responding to the heart-clutching impact of the glorious show. Mists come to the eyes, throats choke, and guys who thought themselves cynical, yield unashamedly to the majestic sweep of the panorama unfolding before them.

The Mexican spectators left the Estadio Olimpico utterly drained emotionally. They constantly screamed "Mexico" with the throaty roar emerging as "May-hee-co." They made the chant sound like a love song, and a love song it truly was. They waxed rhapsodic time and time again in ecstasies of constant delight.

It was pomp and circumstance all the way with nothing going wrong until 10,000 pigeons were released near the end. One parked on the long-jump strip and called it a day. He didn't even jump. One fluttered into the press box and was tossed in the air. He flapped his way to the Ethiopian delegation in the infield and was still waddling around unconcernedly when the athletes streamed out.

The parade of athletes into the arena is always a spectacular event and this appeared even more eye-catching than in the past. Yet there was peculiar significance to one occurrence. When the Czechoslovaks marched proudly down the entrance ramp, a rumble of applause rippled throughout the stadium. It became a moving wave until it reached the proportions of a standing ovation. Not even the Mexicans in their smart parade uniforms drew the affectionate approbation that the Czechs did.

It was a colorful display from start (Greece, the originator of the Olympic Games) to the finish (Mexico, the host nation) . In between they marched in all sizes, shapes and colors, a record 7,886 athletes from a record 108 nations.

The Australian girls in smashing yellow wore the shortest miniskirts. Fortunately, they had the nifty legs for it. The West German gals wore red while the East German gals, presumably red-oriented, wore yellow. Bermudians appeared, natch, in Bermuda shorts. Traditional robes were worn by the Cameroons, yellow, and by the Nigerians, green.

All flags dipped before the Tribune of Honor where El Presidente, Gustavo Diaz Ordaz, reviewed the parade. The British overdid it by dragging their flag in the dust, but the American flag, carried by a woman for the first time, remained undipped as Mrs. Janice Lee Romary, a six-time Olympian, faithfully observed a practice that began at London during the 1908 Olympics.

The backbone of the United States team that year was supplied by the brawny weightmen from the Irish-American Athletic Club of New York, all with deep roots in the Ould Sod. They took a firm stand and issued explicit orders to the flagbearer.

"Ye won't bow the American flag to a British king," bellowed Martin Sheridan, the discus champion. It didn't bow then, and it has not bowed since.

The tug at heart-strings was constant but the supreme wrench always comes with the arrival of the Olympic Flame. It was lit about two months ago in an elaborate ceremony at the sacred grove of Zeus in Olympia in Greece. Then it was carried by land, sea and air in endless relays with a pause at San Salvador where Christopher Columbus first touched foot in the Western Hemisphere. It ended its journey in the Olympic Stadium, symbolically enough, on Columbus Day.

For the first time in Olympic history, the honor of lighting the flame in the stadium was bestowed upon a woman, the 20-year-old Norma Enriqueta Basilio. She raced gracefully once around the track, pattered up the 90 steps to the ramparts—no mean feat at this altitude—and stood there with the torch triumphantly aloft in her right hand. Then she plunged it into the huge saucer and it came alive with fire.

Anyone with acutely sensitive ears could then hear a spectral sound. It would have been the ancient Greeks spinning madly in their crumbling mausoleums. They never permitted a woman to come near their Olympic Games but had summary punishment for every female intruder detected. She was promptly tossed off a seaside cliff onto the rocks below.

And here was a woman in a focal role a couple of thousand years later. She handled it well. In fact, everything about the opening ceremony was handled beautifully. If those few lazy pigeons had followed the script and accompanied their feathered friends into the sky, it would have been absolutely perfect.

1969

The Prince and the Peasant

May 4

Louisville, Kentucky, May 3—Winsome Willie Hartack outdid himself today. Shortly after he had achieved his fifth Kentucky Derby victory with a superb ride aboard Majestic Prince, he stepped out of character to charm a television audience and then returned to character the moment he entered the jockey room. He set a Derby record for rudeness.

As soon as he sighted his fancied enemies from the press, his lips pressed together tightly and a glowering look spread over his face. With unseeing eyes he stalked to his locker and with unhearing ears he let questions bounce harmlessly to the floor, unanswered. Quickly he peeled to the buff and strode to the shower room.

A yellow towel was around his waist when he returned and a green towel was around his neck. He glared at the encircling reporters as if daring one to ask a question. Finally one did, a flip query.

"Who won?" the journalist said.

"Who knows?" said Winsome Willie, breaking his silence.

"Majestic Prince must be a good horse," Manuel Ycaza, the rider of Top Knight, had said.

"A tough fellow. He can run," Braulio Baeza, the rider of Arts and Letters, had said.

"I think he's a great horse," Jorge Velasquez, the rider of Dike, had said with rare lack of restraint.

Hartack had an unexcelled opportunity to join in the chorus and give unstinting praise to Majestic Prince. But he preferred to act the churl. He dressed swiftly and the questions, once fired so swiftly, dwindled away. Reporters stared at him with amused contempt.

They remembered him from five years ago, when he won on Northern Dancer. He used an exquisite form of torture then, standing outside the jockey room and signing autographs as he kept everyone waiting. Then he delivered his classic injunction.

"I won't answer no stupid questions," he had said.

This time he didn't even give his inquisitors an opportunity to ask stupid questions. He flung down the gauntlet, a trick he probably learned from the Prince.

But Winsome Willie doesn't even have enough class to fling a gauntlet properly.

"I think the press has been unfair to me," he snapped. "I refuse to be interviewed."

Standing at a nearby locker, Ycaza smilingly shook his head at the unmannerly behavior of his fellow jockey. The other jocks have little use for him. His unpopularity is understandable.

A reporter Hartack didn't know asked a question.

"Call me at my hotel tomorrow," said the boy charmer brusquely, "and if I can fit you in for an interview, I will."

A reporter Hartack did know asked a question.

"No interviews," said Hartack, jabbing a finger in his direction, "especially you."

In sharp contrast, the other jockeys had been obliging earlier. Ycaza, a disappointing fifth on the second choice, Top Knight, showed Hartack how it should be done, presuming that anyone ever could show the hardheaded Hartack anything.

"Let me towel myself off first, fellows," said bright little Manny, "then I'll talk. I wish I could talk to Top Knight right now."

He sounded as if he had been betrayed. Then he picked up the conversational thread as he toweled his sweating face.

"He was laying in comfortably," he said. "He just got tired. He ran a good mile, but the last quarter, ah. I wish it had been a mile track."

"My horse ran beautiful," said Velasquez, who had been aboard the fast-closing Dike. "He tried hard and was strong to the end. At the head of the stretch, I thought I might win, but Majestic Prince never came back to us. I think he's a great horse. I just hope I can catch him in the Belmont. The longer the race, the better Dike should be."

"Arts and Letters handled beautifully," said Baeza. "I got inside Top Knight and had to make an earlier move than I intended. Otherwise, I would have been trapped. I went at Majestic Prince three times, but he kept running and taking off. We were in the position we wanted."

Not at the end, though. The Prince won by an aristocratic neck and Winsome Willie was given a matchless opportunity to act like a commoner.

Trip Through Wonderland

October 19

Strange things kept happening to Alice during her trip through Wonderland. As she nibbled on magic cakes and sipped from magic vials, her size kept changing, transmogrifications that she could only describe as being "curiouser and curiouser." She was sitting next to the Dormouse when she could feel herself starting to get bigger.

"I wish you wouldn't squeeze so," said the Dormouse.

"I can't help it," said Alice very meekly. "I'm growing."

"You've no right to grow here," said the Dormouse.

"Don't talk such nonsense," said Alice more boldly. "You know you're growing, too."

"Yes, but I grow at a reasonable pace," said the Dormouse, "not in that ridiculous fashion."

This was a baseball season when the New York Mets grew in a quite ridiculous fashion. If they had grown at a reasonable pace, like the Dormouse, they might have sprouted from ninth place to maybe third. But they grew like Alice, spurting upward so fast they were eventually towering over the Cubs for Eastern Division honors, over the Braves for the National League pennant, and finally over the Baltimore Orioles for the baseball championship of the blinking universe.

Casey Stengel and Gil Hodges in the locker room after the Mets won the 1969 World Series.

How does anyone explain this miracle? Like all miracles, this incredible burgeoning of the Mets from laughing stock to respectability cannot be explained simply—if at all. There are too many tangibles and intangibles. Sometimes a guy wonders if the Mets have not distorted a mathematical principle by having the sums of their parts add to greater than the whole. But nothing about the Mets makes sense.

They had started to grow and mature a year ago during their first season under the unflappable Gil Hodges as manager. Few noticed. From force of habit they remained the target of every television comedian because Met jokes were sure-fire laugh-getters. But they had ceased to be a laughing matter.

It took an awfully long while, however, for the public to accept the new image and that's why it was such a shattering surprise to most when the Amazing Ones continued to advance in stature. That's why the rise of the Mets from buffoons to champions of the world triggered such an emotional reaction. It turned supposedly blasé New York into a city of hysteria. The impossible dream had become reality, one of the great sports stories of the ages.

Over the last two months those dreadful bunglers of yesteryear could hardly make a mistake. When they knocked off the Cubs, Braves and Orioles in step-by-step progression, the belief kept increasing that somebody up there liked them.

"God is a Met fan," was a favorite gag line. No irreverence was intended. It almost was an acknowledgement of the fact that some supernatural hand was guiding them.

Lucky? They were lucky to a fantastic extreme. Yet it is important to affix firmly in proper perspective a penetrating observation once made by Branch Rickey, one of baseball's most brilliant minds and the game's most pungent phrasemaker.

"Luck is the residue of design," boomed the Mahatma.

The design for greatness already was there. Because he seemed to have psychic powers, Hodges used them for all he was worth. In spring training he unerringly sorted out the best rookies. Then he platooned his troops with remarkable skill, squeezing the ultimate out of all 25 men on his roster and thereby keeping everyone happy.

By the time the postseason adventures against the Braves and Orioles had arrived, that island of serenity and calm, Hodges, could not make a wrong move. It was as if he also was directed by the Little People who once had whispered advice to Marse Joe McCarthy of the Yankees.

"Unlike Marse Joe," said the droll Gil, "my ancestry is only half-Irish. But I got the message 100 percent."

There were fantastic catches by Tommie Agee and Ron Swoboda, saving games that might have been lost. There was gorgeous fielding by almost everyone. There was gorgeous pitching by those strong young arms. There was timely hitting. And providence always seemed to intervene when needed.

When Jerry Grote lifted a routine fly to left with the score tied in the 10th inning of the fourth game, fate directed that Don Buford, the left fielder, should be blinded by the sun. The ball dropped for a double and Rod Gaspar, who ran for Grote, scored because J. C. Martin was hit on the wrist by a throw after a perfect sacrifice bunt.

The swift growth of Alice in Wonderland was fantasy. The swift growth of the Mets in their version of Wonderland was fact.

Memories of a Decade

December 28

In December of 1961, I was in Toronto for a fight between Floyd Patterson and Tom McNeeley. The phone rang. The White House was calling. Dave Powers of President Kennedy's staff shocked me into a numbed silence by telling me that the President would like me to join him at the Hotel Carlyle the next night and go with him to the Football Hall of Fame dinner at which he was to receive the Gold Medal Award. Meanwhile, Dave said, the President would like me to line up some funny football stories he could use.

I met Dave as well as Kenny O'Donnell, another of the so-called Irish Mafia, in their suite. Then we stepped in the elevator to be whisked to the penthouse apartment. The door opened and there was John Fitzgerald Kennedy, halfway out of a coat jacket.

"Hello, Arthur," he said, giving the name the broad "A" inflection of all proper Bostonians. "I'll be with you in a minute, as soon as I change my clothes."

He was with me in nothing flat, the most electrifying personality I ever met. While we chatted, he finished off an oyster stew to sustain him until the late dinner began. When we stepped out of the apartment, Secret Service men seemed to emerge from the woodwork. Down we went to the waiting auto cavalcade with escorting motorcycle policemen revving their motors.

Park Avenue had been cleared of all traffic. Police barricades lined the curbs and the peasants jammed the sidewalks behind them. I never rode anywhere in such style before. In fact, that Hall of Fame dinner has not been the same for me since.

What delighted me most about the next incident was that it represented the most outrageous bit of name dropping I ever did. The climax of the 1967 baseball season came at Fenway Park in Boston where the Red Sox and Twins met in the final two games to determine the pennant winner. At hand were Senator Ted Kennedy, a Red Sox fan, and Vice-President Hubert H. Humphrey, a Minnesota rooter.

In the press room I was talking to Senator Kennedy when the Vice-President strolled over. The Senator introduced me.

"Mr. Vice-President," I said, "there's no reason why you should remember the occasion but I've already met you."

"Where?" he said, puzzled.

"I was introduced to you in the White House," I said, enjoying my own lack of modesty, "by a fellow named Lyndon B. Johnson."

A pre-Olympic high spot at Rome was the Papal audience granted to the Olympic athletes in front of Saint Peter's. All the Olympians were there, including the Russians, and about 100,000 persons. The square was so jammed that I couldn't reach my assigned seat. Neither could Avery Brundage, president of the International Olympic Committee. But I knew Avery would make it and I tagged behind while he was led toward the Papal throne. Soon I started to panic as I got ever closer to the throne. Then I ducked behind a long row of Cardinals and found a better seat than I was entitled to.

The benign Pope John XXIII appeared. He sat in profile to me, perhaps 30 feet away. There seemed something vaguely familiar in that Roman nose and jutting chin. There was a tap on my shoulder. I turned and John Carmichael of the *Chicago Daily News* was the tapper.

"I don't want to sound sacrilegious," he whispered, "but doesn't he look like Casey Stengel?" Damned if he didn't.

In the slightly circuitous route to Tokyo with my long-time comrade-in-arms, Jesse Abramson, we not only stopped in Greece, the cradle of the Olympic games, but drove from Athens to Olympia, where it all began. It was there that two broken-down old track writers jogged along the same straightaway where Coroebus of Elis had run in 776 B.C. to become the first Olympic champion.

Sure, that was a thrill. But what may have been the biggest emotional wallop of my lifetime came a week later in Israel, a marvelous and inspiring country. On the way from Beersheba to Jerusalem our guide had been telling us what a remarkably accurate historical document the Bible was because the land is so tiny that everything described can be pinpointed. He drove into a valley, stopped the car, and bade us get out.

"The Israelites were on that hill and the Philistines were on that other one over there," he said. And then casually swept his hand around the area where we were standing before adding, "And this is the place where David slew Goliath."

David and Goliath! I could feel chills running up and down my spine as 3,000 years of history seemed to tumble about me.

For years, I've been having a name problem with Cassius Clay. I'm too stubborn to address him as Muhammad and yet I never wanted him to freeze up on me by calling him Cassius. The morning after his last fight, the one with Zora Folley, we came face to face.

"Well, well," I said, "if it isn't the heavyweight champion."

Cassius saw through the subterfuge instantly. His eyes twinkled. If I wouldn't address him by name, he would pay me back in kind.

"Hello, big shot," he said.

1970

Ultimate in Brotherhood

April 12

The gallant heart of Maurice Stokes was stilled last week. For 12 long years he had fought a heroic and agonizing battle of rehabilitation, slowly freeing his giant body from the total paralysis that imprisoned him a few days after his head had crashed against the floor while playing basketball for the Cincinnati Royals. He was only 24 years old when his career abruptly ended, a three-time All Star and one of the most promising young performers in the sport.

It is a tragic story and yet it has a sub plot that was marked by nobility and grandeur. It's a modern version of the Biblical parable of the Good Samaritan and it graphically demonstrates the brotherhood of man to the purest degree. What gives it a quality of extra warmth is the pigmentation of the two principals. Stokes was black, Jack Twyman, his teammate on the Royals, is white.

Mighty Mo had just entered the hospital and was still in the coma that was to last for a frightening six months when Twyman dropped in for a visit. Mo's mother was there, emotionally torn by so many things. Not the least of them were the skyrocketing hospital costs that his intensive care condition made necessary. Twyman, a practical man, asked her about money.

"He has some in a bank somewhere," she said. "But I don't know where."

"Don't worry," he reassured her. "I'll take care of it—somehow."

Jack was to take care of it for 12 long years. He toured one Cincinnati bank after another until he finally found the one carrying Mo's account. But how to get at it with the depositer in a coma? Being resourceful, Twyman went to court and had himself appointed Stokes's legal guardian.

Then he checked with examining physicians and learned that the original diagnosis of encephalitis, a disease of virus origin, was incorrect. No virus had been found. The new diagnosis characterized it as post-traumatic encephalopathy that resulted from brain damage caused by the crash to the basketball floor. That's all Twyman needed to know.

Immediately he filed application with the state for workmen's compensation because the injury had been sustained in the course of employment. This lifted the financial burden tremendously as the state took over the heaviest payments, the hospital, nursing and therapeutic care.

The pro basketball people had little awareness of Stokes's plight until Twyman went before the Board of Governors of the National Basketball Association and enlisted their aid. An exhibition doubleheader was arranged for Cincinnati as an out-and-out benefit for the stricken Stokes. Even the contestants paid to get in. More than $10,000 was raised but the fringe benefits were enormous. The publicity triggered a flood of donations.

They ranged from pennies to the $1,000 check that was sent to Milt Gross of the *New York Post,* along with a note to be forwarded to Twyman. The note read:

"Where but in this country would I, a Jew, be sending money to you, a Catholic, to help a Negro?"

An annual charity basketball game began operating at Kutsher's in the Catskills with all proceeds going to Stokes. The greatest players in the world gathered at their own expense to help their friend. Incidentally, the only time Lew Alcindor ever played against Wilt Chamberlain was in one of these games.

But Twyman did more than just raise money for his friend. He visited him, sometimes daily, in the hospital and helped in his rehabilitation. Mo's first communication with the outside world was spelled to Twyman. As Jack recited the alphabet, he watched Mo's eyes for the flutter designating the letter.

Therapy was sheer torture for Mo but he persevered and regained movement and muscle. When the Royals tossed a "Jack Twyman Night" shortly before his retirement as an active player after the 1966 season, the sharpshooting marvel was showered with gifts. Watching from a wheelchair with a smile of intense satisfaction was Stokes on a rare leave from the hospital.

"They couldn't give that man enough," his lips seemed to say. Incidentally, Twyman scored 39 points that night.

When Stokes had progressed to a stage where he had regained some use of his fingers, Twyman bought him an electric typewriter. The first words typed on it were these:

"Dear Jack: How can I ever thank you?"

Perhaps there was something symbolic about the fact that Stokes died in Cincinnati's Good Samaritan Hospital. After all, it was a good Samaritan who sustained him there.

Without Prejudice?

November 29

These observations are being offered by a fellow whose legal training is so limited that the sum total of his knowledge of law is only what he learned from watching the skillful court maneuvers of that invincible television barrister, Perry Mason. It's enough, however, to make a layman suspicious of juridical procedure as he wonders how much reliance he can place on something as fundamental as common sense.

For some time now I have been mulling over the puzzling dramatic offering, *The Case of the Reluctant Ballplayer.* It is supposed to be a morality play of sorts. The main character is Curt Flood, an outfielder who toiled for a miserable $90,000 a year on a Saint Louis plantation. His cruel master, Gussie Busch, sold him down the river to Bob Carpenter of Philadelphia, who is about to starve him to death at $100,000 a season.

What thickened the plot was that Flood refused to report to the Philadelphia work-house as required by the reserve clause in his contract. He then challenged the legality of the reserve clause, characterizing it as a form of slavery because it turned players into chattels that could be passed from one to the other indiscriminately. So Flood sued the baseball establishment for $1-million.

By way of establishing his sincerity, Flood spurned baseball's filthy money and refused to play ball, sitting out an entire season. Although a lower court decided against Flood, this case is going to the Supreme Court anyway. That's what adds so much intrigue to new twists in the plot.

Instead of a carefree existence during his sabbatical from baseball the little outfielder discovered that they threw curve balls in business as well as on the diamond. He wasn't batting too well in the financial league and those twice-a-month checks from solvent ball clubs soon started to lose their slavish appearance.

In some mysterious fashion—Perry Mason has yet to explain it—Flood caught up with Bob Short, the owner of the Washington Senators, just before the World Series. They represented two young men with mounting troubles, most of them being financial. Short still was staggering from the lambasting he took for giving away too much of his ball club in the lopsided deal that brought him Denny McLain, the problem child.

As a diversionary tactic he reached out for Flood, another problem child. A couple of baseball rules were fractured in order to work out this odd transaction but everyone looked the other way fortunately so that it could be swung. Token payment was made by Washington to Philadelphia and Flood signed with the Senators for $110,000 a year.

Because Bowie Kuhn, the commissioner, shrewdly refused to permit any omission of the reserve clause from the standard contract that Flood signed, the outfielder again wrapped around him the same chains of slavery from which he had shaken free last December. When Flood first became a prisoner of the oppressive baseball system in 1956, he was only an 18-year-old boy. Perhaps he didn't know any better.

But he is a mature and wiser man of 32 at the signing with Washington and knows so much about the reserve clause that he has a continuing law suit to prove it. Supposedly he signed "without prejudice" to that law suit. I don't believe it.

No matter how the legal beagles stress that "without prejudice" ploy, I'm positive that if I were a judge or a juror I could never erase from my mind certain inherent contradictions within the phrase.

Flood sued baseball in violent protest against the reserve clause. Yet he again placed himself under the reserve clause of his own free will so that he can enjoy eating regularly and other niceties.

Trained only by Perry Mason, I must conclude that Flood prejudices his case. Admittedly, though, I'm one of those guys who can watch a courtroom drama and sneer at the judge who advises the jurors to disregard testimony they've already heard even if it emerged because a lawyer pulled a fast one. I couldn't erase it from my memory if I thought it germane to the opinion I was forming.

Since judges also are human, the belief persists that Flood's resumption of his career has to have subliminal effect at least on every juror assigned to the case. Even if baseball eventually wins, though, one thing is clear.

If the baseball overlords had any sense—which they don't—they would modify the reserve clause immediately to ease the timelessness of its restrictions to an acceptable degree. It also will head off future law suits and bring a quick curtain to *The Case of the Reluctant Ballplayer*, featuring Curt Flood.

1971

Epic Worth the Price

March 9

The multimillion dollar fight in Madison Square Garden last night was worth every glorious heartbreaking penny. Rarely does anything so expensive live up to advance billing or exceed expectations. But the wildly exciting exhibition of primitive savagery that Joe Frazier and Muhammad Ali put on over 15 exhausting rounds was an epic that fit the price tag.

Frazier won a decision because he punched himself out so completely that he just didn't have that extra little zing to put into the one wallop that would have finished it by a knockout earlier. And Ali was still vertical at the end because he was just too proud a man, too magnificent an athlete and too gutsy a warrior to let himself stay down.

He had been toppled in the 15th round by one of those uncountable Frazier left hooks that disarranged and puffed up the right side of the Ali face until it looked as though the former Cassius Clay had been stricken by a bad case of the mumps. But Frazier was no bargain at the final bell. His right eye was almost closed and his profile was a mass of welts.

The margin of superiority was reasonably clear-cut with Frazier ahead on the cards of all three ring officials. Nor did the

Arthur Daley interviews Muhammad Ali—much before his first fight with Joe Frazier.

crowd react in angry disapproval as is normally the case when the spectators let wishful thinking misdirect their emotions. Everyone sensed that Ali had failed.

He failed gloriously, though, in a strange sort of bout where he neither floated like a butterfly nor stung like a bee, supposedly his normal method of operations. His dancing speed fled early.

He was hit more often by Frazier in 15 rounds than he had been hit by all his other opponents together in a hitherto unbeaten career.

In the 11th round, the relentless Frazier—he attacks with the ceaseless whirr of a buzzsaw—began to take Ali cruelly apart with those ferocious left hooks. He exploded one and Ali went wobbling all over the ring, staggering woozily at the end of the round as Frazier's flailing left kept missing the finisher.

He was still missing it through the 12th and 13th when he had an inviting target in front of him, an Ali whose defenses were feeble and whose own punching fires were hardly embers. But in the 14th, Ali unexpectedly came back from the dead, pounded the startled Frazier and detoured his trip to oblivion. He almost went out again in the last round, but survived in some miraculous fashion.

Wait a minute. It wasn't a miracle. Frazier was just too tired to complete a job that had begun to look easy. As the hands of the clock advanced toward the finish of the fight, Frazier pinned Ali in a corner and leaned against him, his face a mask of weariness and his grin a bloodly smirk.

If everything about this fight was not in accordance with the original ideas that had been plotted for it by the experts, it took on a new and appealing character of its own. There were times when Ali looked absolutely helpless. He flicked feeble little teasers at the never-stop foe. The man who had danced out of harm's way for all his fistic life stopped stepping even though there were two at hand to tango.

He let Frazier corner him and pin him against the ropes. At times he even stood there snarling, sneering and offering taunts. Frazier merely thought an old boyhood thought: "Sticks and stones can break my bones, but names will never hurt me." Maybe it was a quirk in the Ali defense mechanism, brought on by the unexpectedness of something that never had happened to him before.

How much his entire mental attitude was warped by the way his jaw was flailed by the Frazier hooks is beyond conjecture. This also was a new experience, and a trip to the hospital afterwards for X rays and diagnosis was proof positive that it was a physical handicap of unquestionable severity.

It was a thriller all the way, jam-packed with suspense and tingling from start to finish with the special brand of drama inherent in all heavyweight championship bouts. Not until the last third of the fight—if it is proper to partition it that way—did Frazier's thumping hooks carry him definitely into the lead.

So breathless was the pace that awed ringsiders sometimes were wondering near the end how either of them could still reach deeply within for a galvanic outburst that provided another electric shock of excitement. Thanks to the last-round knockdown, it was to stay exciting to the end.

Frazier left the ring with undisputed possession of the heavyweight championship of the world, a claim that always had rested in the shadow of his unfrocked predecessor, Muhammad Ali. The cash customers undoubtedly had to feel that they got their money's worth in a magnificent bout that was prize fighting at its best.

Report on Life in the Geriatric Set

May 5

Ernie Banks was 40 years old last January; Willie Mays will be 40 tomorrow; Henry Aaron just turned 37. This somewhat superannuated trio forms the homer-hitting aristocracy among big league ballplayers because they hold the three top positions among all active swingers for distance.

On the over-all list, though, Banks is ninth and should move up a few places before he quits, while Mays and Aaron, both over the 600 mark, are bearing down on Babe Ruth's supposedly unapproachable record of 714. As of yesterday morning these were their totals: Mays, 633; Aaron, 603, and Banks a more modest 509.

At least his remoteness from the excitement up front gives Ernie a chance to appraise the situation as a neutral expert. The effervescent Ernie was in town with the Chicago Cubs yesterday, springing cheerfulness all round him and captivating everyone anew with the warmth of his personality.

"What a great day for a ball game!" he began.

It wasn't a great day for anything, especially a ball game. It was dark and bleak and miserable. But Ernie rejoices merely in living and baseball is a marvelous extra that makes his existence so much more pleasurable. However, he soon settled down to discussing the current state of affairs.

"During my early days with the Cubs," said the smiling Ernie, who had five 40-plus homer years in his youth, "there were a lot of strike-out pitchers in the league. Now you will have a Tom Seaver or Bob Gibson who can throw that ball by you, but most of the moderns pitch more scientifically. They use finesse—up-and-down, in-and-out, changing speeds. They're tougher to hit and a man has to stay lucky to get a record.

"Last year I came up with knee problems, calcium deposits in my knees. That's what happens when you get older. You get slowed down by things that never bothered you before. Colds and flu come quicker and stay longer. I was sorry to read in today's paper that Willie will have to sit out the next few games with tendonitis in his shoulder.

"Willie always stays in shape and has a great physique. But he isn't in as good a ball park for hitting home runs. He was in the beginning, back in the days when the Giants played at the Polo Grounds in New York. Almost all the ball parks in our league were small then and the fence was within reach. A great place was Ebbets Field in Brooklyn. And the fence was in reach.

"I always felt that my own park, Wrigley Field in Chicago, was ideal for my style of hitting. And it has no lights, giving us the blessing of daytime ball only. People used to kid me that I kept bankers' hours, checking in at the park at 10 A.M. and leaving maybe at 3 P.M. when we'd have those fast games we used to have in the nineteen fifties.

"The Giants are playing more day games at Candlestick Park this season and the wind blows in more in the daytime than at night. That makes it tougher on Willie. We played the Giants this year. Willie McCovey was injured and Mays played first base.

" 'This is great,' he said to me, 'I wish I could stay here all year.'

"But he can't. The Giants need McCovey's bat and Willie also needs McCovey behind him in the batting order to force the pitchers to pitch to him. I might say that Willie played first very well. But what else would you expect?

"Just as Willie needs McCovey following him in the batting order, so Henry needs Orlando Cepeda to keep the pitchers honest. Boy, does the ball jump in that Atlanta ball park! I must say, though, that when Hank hits it, the ball jumps any way and anywhere.

"The conditions being as they are, I'd say Henry will come on real strong and has a better chance of reaching Babe Ruth's record. Age doesn't matter with him. He's consistently quick and he has the wrist action to give the ball a ride. I now have a feeling that he's already conditioned himself to think in terms of the home run record.

"I remember talking to Hank about five years ago. 'I'm not going for homers this year,' he said to me. 'I'm going for a high average.' A year later he said to me, 'This season I'm going for the big one.' I liked the way he could change his tempo."

Ernie's smiling countenance was aglow with cheerfulness and light. He probably is the only man in baseball whose liking for people is such that he will be able to root simultaneously for Mays to break Ruth's record, for Aaron to break Ruth's record and for the Babe to hold fast to his record, balking both challengers.

1972

A Fond Farewell to Gil Hodges

April 4

There is a fundamental difficulty in writing about Gil Hodges. Voices in the background keep screaming for restraint and yet every instinct is to succumb to temptation and spill forth the superlatives. Today would have been his 48th birthday. He didn't make it. A massive heart attack felled him on Easter Sunday just after he had completed 27 holes of golf, and death came with stunning swiftness.

He was such a noble character in so many respects that I believe Gil to have been one of the finest men I met in sports or out of it. As tributes poured in from all over the country that same estimate was echoed and re-echoed. As one who knew him for a quarter of a century I never wavered in my admiration for the man. He had all the virtues and the only vice I discovered was that he smoked too much.

Few fans were more knowledgeable than the passionately devoted adherents of the Brooklyn Dodgers, whose players were jealously acclaimed as the Beloved Bums. No player was more beloved than Gil. At times the fans would spill out frustrations by booing some of their pets. But the large and muscular Hodges was a creature apart from the common herd. Not once was he booed during his dozen years at Ebbets Field.

Gil went hitless in the 1952 World Series and no true Dodger fan even grumbled at him. He continued into a horrendous slump in the spring of 1953 and still there was no mutiny. That produced the classic incident of the priest dispensing with a Sunday sermon, merely asking his parishioners to keep the Commandments and say a prayer for Gil Hodges. They must have prayed hard. Gil hit .302 that season.

His place in baseball history is secure because he performed the managerial miracle of leading the New York Mets to the championship of the world in 1969. Scoffers had been saying for years that the Mets wouldn't win a pennant until man walked on the moon, then presumed to be an utter impossibility. Both impossibilities happened in swift succession.

Gil also carved another niche in baseball history for himself. In a game during the 1950 season the big first baseman swung freely in his first three times at bat and was pleasantly surprised to see the ball land in the seats for home runs. Each was more or less an accident. Suddenly overeager in the his next time at bat, Gil swung from his heels and produced a dribbling ground ball. He thought that ended his hopes but the Dodgers kept hitting and he got another turn at bat. This time he connected for a fourth homer, the first man to do so since Lou Gehrig 18 years earlier.

"As far as I can see," needled his pal, Pee Wee Reese, "all you did was prolong the game."

"That I did," said Gil blissfully.

By that time the experts were beginning to compare the powerfully-built Hodges with that other model of durability, strength and greatness, Gehrig.

"I appreciate the compliment," said Gil in his sly little fashion, "but Gehrig had one advantage over me."

"What was that?" he was asked.

"He was a better ballplayer," said Gil, ever the realist.

Yet Gil was a marvelously deft practictioner at first base. It was odd in a way because Branch Rickey, the all-seeing and all-knowing one, had detected a flaw in the Hodges throwing style when he first saw him as a shortstop. So he suggested Gil switch to catching. It was done. During the 1948 season the Brooks opened with Preston Ward at first base.

"Preston Ward can run like a frightened fawn," wrote Bill Roeder one day. "His trouble now is that he's starting to hit like one."

That's when Manager Leo Durocher barked a suggestion at Gil.

"Son," said the always paternalistic Leo, "if I were you I'd buy myself a first baseman's glove and start working out there."

In no time at all Gil was a regular. Roy Campanella was brought up from Saint Paul to do the catching. Bruce Edwards was switched from catching to third base and Hodges from catching to first base. The Dodgers were beginning to settle into the pattern that was to produce "the Boys of Summer," the exceptional team that now has been graphically captured in Roger Kahn's extraordinary book of the same name.

Hodges was the solid anchorman around whom the others revolved. He lent class and dignity and respect to his team and to his profession. As has been written—and rightly so—he had all the attributes of an Eagle Scout. This was quite a man.

Ironically he was able to play golf on Sunday because the strike of the players had caused cancellation of the exhibition baseball game. Normally he would have been in the dugout instead of on the golf course. But who knows? Death doesn't have to go looking for people. Sometimes there's an appointment in Samarra.

Auf Wiedersehen

September 12

Munich, West Germany, September 11—It was raining when Closing Day dawned and the day was to remain damp, dark and dolorous. It is difficult to envision a more appropriate setting for these unhappiest of Olympic Games than the gray, funereal blackdrop that the weatherman provided. The usual parting-is-such-sweet-sorrow motif was missing and these Olympics dragged their way into history with their honest achievements shunted aside by the mishaps and controversies that kept demanding attention.

The tragic assassination of the Israeli athletes by Arab terrorists plunged everything else into relative insignificance, but there were enough blunders, snafus and misadventures by athletes and officials to supply Olympic critics with sufficient material to last a lifetime. Except for Mark Spitz and the other swimmers, the United States had its least productive Olympics. American athletes were both subpar and disappointing while American officials displayed incompetence and arrogance.

Incompetence and arrogance were not confined to the United States, however. These games were riddled by both, especially in events where judgment is involved, because prejudice too often flavors judgment. The basketball final between the Soviet Union and the United States is a case in point. Up till the final palpitating seconds, the Russians demonstrated the shooting skill of Americans like Jerry West or Walt Frazier while the Americans shot like the Bloomer Girls on a bad night.

But when Doug Collins dropped in the second of two foul shots with three seconds to go, it seemed that the United States had won the game by a point. However, the forces of darkness or something entered the proceedings. It began to look as if the officials would give the Russians an extra three seconds for as often as it took them to shoot the winning field goal. This was achieved when a Soviet basket-hanger knocked down an American defender in front of the Bulgarian referee before dropping in the winning basket. No foul was called for the flagrant violation.

Disgusted by such grand larceny, the Americans voted unanimously to refuse the silver medal for second place. It doesn't seem too sporting a gesture but it has to appear justified in this instance.

As a matter of fact, a couple of things have happened in the last week or so that should be sufficient to shake the entire North American continent. The Soviet Union beat the United States in basketball, a game invented by an American, Dr. James Naismith. Meanwhile, in Canada a hockey team of Russian amateurs—if you will pardon the expression—leads the series against an all-star team of the finest professionals in the National Hockey League, two games to one with one tied. And hockey is Canada's national game. These twin occurrences defy all logic and explanation.

Although the planned gaiety of today's closing was toned down by circumstances, the natural buoyancy of the youthful athletes gave it an unscheduled verve. They danced and cavorted to lend a genuine sparkle to the affair, adding the necessary touch of spontaniety to the ceremony. The Germans had arranged an imaginative program and enough of it remained to show that this closing might have rated as one of the best if too much unhappiness had not preceeded it.

There was one final fluff, though. The electric scoreboard tried to say, "Thank You, Avery Brundage." The last name was misspelled, emerging as "Brandage." This had to set an Olympic record for unfortunate gaffes.

The richest of all closing day memories, however, revolve around Rome in 1960. Being masters of stagecraft the Italians even had their marathon traverse the Appian Way where the Roman legions once trod, finishing the race at the Arch of Constantine alongside the crumbling but still imposing ruins of the Colosseum. For the closing they waited until dusk was settling over the Studio Olimpico.

The flame of the torch and the brazier seemed to grow brighter as the backdrop of the sky turned from blue to purple and then into the blackness of the Italian night. Trumpeters in medieval costumes offered a last fanfare and the flames sank in the darkened stadium while emotional Italians wept hysterically.

Suddenly one of them lit a rolled-up newspaper, then thousands and thousands more did the same until it almost seemed as if 100,000 fireflies were lighting up the night and trying to roll back both the darkness and the end of the Olympics. It couldn't be done. The electric scoreboard blazed forth "Arriverderci Roma." No closing could have been more tender.

Tokyo also had a farewell word that said it all, "Sayonara," in another memorable closing. Mexico City had the most exuberant of all finales, and this fiesta carried on almost until dawn as revelers in the downtown streets tooted their auto horns and screamed a joyous "May-hee-co." The happy-go-lucky Mexicans had exceeded all expectations and produced a magnificent set of Olympic Games.

Munich also will be remembered by Olympic historians but for all the wrong reasons.

1973

An Abrupt End to the Frazier Reign

January 23

Kingston, Jamaica, January 22—It was unbelievable. In little more than $4\frac{1}{2}$ minutes, George Foreman destroyed Joe Frazier tonight, and the man who supposedly couldn't lose never had even one ghost of a chance for victory. So there is a new heavyweight champion of the world and he won it with authority in an explosive demonstration of overpowering punching skills.

Six times Frazier was knocked down. He never threw even one effective punch as Foreman handled him with such ridiculous ease that ringsiders were blinking in incredulity. It ended with Frazier on his feet, but also on queer street. Referee Art Mercante, imported from New York for the occasion, took one look into Joe's glazed, unseeing eyes and said, "No more." The reign of Joe Frazier had come to an abrupt and totally unexpected end.

Long Island commuters have long been hearing the phrase "Change at Jamaica." It was Foreman, though, who precipitated the most moumental change of all at Jamaica. Frazier had been a lopsided favorite, a confident champion. But Foreman came at him with an aggressive assurance from the very start. He forced his action and handled the champion with muscular skill.

A right hand to the jaw achieved the first knock-down and Frazier never seemed to regain any sort of mastery again. It was as if the controls had slipped from his fingers and there was no way he could pick them up again. Foreman forced him against the ropes and kept him there. Foreman dropped him with a right uppercut and another right dumped him for the third time in the first round.

Somewhere out in the sticks, Muhammad Ali must have watched the proceedings with sinking heart. On a television show last week, Ali made a fervent plea.

"Don't let nuthin' happen to Joe Frazier," he said.

Plenty happened to Joe Frazier. He was knocked out of his championship, and both he and Ali were knocked out of their multi-million dollar return match, a financial windfall that may have drawn as much as $20-million. The Ali investment in Frazier went unprotected.

From the bout, the unbeaten Foreman emerged as an impressive fighter. Once he had been a wide swinger. But he was a straight-forward puncher tonight, a rather startling transformation in style.

There was good reason for it, of course. When Joe Louis was offering an expert analysis the other day, he repeatedly came back to the fundamental principle that Frazier was easy to hit. It's a cinch that he convinced Foreman at least.

Big George went at the champion from a tight formation at the opening bell, firing a left and right combination. He fired from the inside out and kept covered up. Frazier was unable to get at this big, stand-up guy, although many ringsiders thought the devastating Frazier left hook would overcome this. It just didn't.

"I completely underestimated him," said the dethroned champion afterwards. "I couldn't get underneath and fight him inside the way I planned."

He could fight him neither inside nor outside. Joe was meeting the first really strong fighter he had met since Oscar Bonavena and the Argentinian had twice knocked him down. Maybe the experts were careless in not reading significance into the relation between strength and Frazier knockdowns. Although Ali outweighed Frazier in their superspectacular, he has always been more of a finesse guy than a muscle man.

When Frazier was reeling around the ring on rubber legs in the first round, it seemed fleetingly that he might recover if he could deliver just one solid punch to stay the progress of the powerfully built 24-four-year old who was man-handling him so outrageously. He couldn't throw it.

That first round ended with Frazier on his back.

Frantic applications of smelling salts between rounds couldn't restore the total man. He was easier to hit and easier to knock down. In fact the knockdowns were coming faster, the first three in three minutes and the next three in half that time.

Thus did Foreman complete the cycle. He succeeded Frazier as Olympic heavyweight champion and now he has succeeded him as world heavyweight champion. The final change came, properly enough, at Jamaica.

With a Fast Finish

May 6

Louisville, May 5—When Colonel Edward Riley Bradley was a dominating force in the Kentucky Derby four and five decades ago, he was fond of saying, "If you give me a horse who can run the last quarter mile in 24 seconds, I'll give you a Derby winner." He never had a colt that fast but still took four of the bourbon belt classics. The colonel's eyes would have popped if he had been around for the 99th running of America's premier racing event at sunshine-drenched Churchill Downs today. Secretariat, a big handsome red-coated powerhouse, came charging down the homestretch with such blistering speed that he set a record of 0:23 1/5 for the final quarter on his way to a record of 1:59 2/5 for the total distance. Riding him spectacularly was Ron Turcotte, who had been accused of giving him a rather inferior ride in his disastrous defeat in the Wood. That setback removed the tag of "superhorse" from the Meadow Stable standard bearer. In all probability, the Kentucky Derby restored every last superlative.

Yet Turcotte showed little emotion when he reached the jockey room after the presentation ceremonies were over. In fact, there was little emotion on display. The son of Bold Ruler and Somethingroyal had done such a smashing job that there wasn't much the other little men could say.

"Hey, Ron, congratulations," shouted Laffit Pincay, the jockey of the runner-up, Sham.

"Thanks," said Turcotte, and before he could add another word he spotted a writer who had questioned Secretariat's blood lines in print. The rider's attention swerved and he got in one good but smiling dig. "Bold Rulers won't go a mile and quarter, eh?" he said.

"I wasn't worried about coming out of the gate last," he said. "Being in an outside post position, I was lucky in not even having moved into the gate when there was that delay. So it didn't bother us any."

"Was this his best race?" someone asked. "I can't knock any of his races," said Turcotte warily, "except the one he ran in the Wood."

With that he picked up a towel and headed for the shower room. If he did leave abruptly, he did it pleasantly and there wasn't any of the nastiness that winsome Willie Hartack once used in snubbing the press.

Hartack hasn't changed any. He was in and out of the shower room so fast that it took a studied search by a prospective interviewer (meaning me) to find him. Oh, yeah. Willie had finished dead last on Warbucks, an item not calculated to improve his disposition. With a pink towel around his middle, he was seated on the floor of the recreation room while watching television replays.

"Did your horse disappoint you?" he was asked. This query undoubtedly violated Hartack's long-standing orders to the flower of American journalism. It is: "Don't ask no stupid questions." Winsome Willie withered me with a baleful glance. I am desolated.

Pincay, rider of Sham, really offered no excuses. "The next time he will run better." He said, "I moved too soon."

The delay at the gate was a strange happenstance. Don Brumfield, the rider of third-place Our Native, was one of those involved, although he didn't pretend to think that it would have brought him closer to Secretariat at the wire.

"Twice A Prince reared up," he said, "and his foot came down in Navajo's stall. The other foot came through on my side and he hit my saddle. The mark is still on it. All three jockeys had to dismount and my horse was taken out of the gate from the front in order to get clear.

"I have to feel that it bothered him and got him on edge. It's as if you're waiting for a red light to turn green. Then you spring out for the start. But this time the light turned yellow and Our Native just didn't know what to make of it.

"As for Secretariat, I ain't saying he's not a good horse. He is. But if he keeps running enough, he'll get beat. They all do."

That has long been a fundamental rule of horse racing. That's why there have been so few invincibles on the turf, and the scattered handful who made it achieved their distinction by quitting while ahead.

If Secretariat looks to be the superhorse that his trainer, Lucien Laurin, claims he is, he'll still have a chance to prove it. Just ahead are the Preakness and the Belmont Stakes for the Triple Crown. They will tell.

Farewell to Willie

September 23

Not long ago Joe Pignatano, the Met coach, conversed briefly with someone behind the dugout and then spoke to Willie Mays.

"Hey, Willie," said Piggy, "there's a guy here who wants to say hello to you. He says he played with you in Minneapolis. He's standing in the aisle near the end of the dugout." Willie peeked out cautiously, not wanting to be trapped by a stranger. He ducked back and tossed a scornful glance at Pignatano, "You gotta be kiddin', Piggy," he said. "That fellow couldn't have been on the Minneapolis ball club with me. He's a little old man with gray hair."

"Just a minute, Willie," said Piggy with a softness that was almost tender, "you come pretty close yourself to being a little old man with gray hair."

Willie the Wonder took a more searching look at himself or the calendar or both last week and reluctantly announced his retirement. For 22 years he has been carrying on a love affair with baseball and had become a living legend. Yet he had reached athletic old age. Once he was the most exuberant and exciting player of his generation, one of the most extraordi-

Willie Mays with his wife Mae, just prior to his retirement in October, 1973.

narily gifted ballplayers ever to step on a diamond. But those skills had faded beyond recognition until the vast army of Mays admirers found themselves trying to blot out the present with memories of the glorious past.

Once he could do everything and he could do it better than anyone else with joyous grace. It hurt to see him floundering like an ordinary ballplayer in his final years with the Mets. In a way he overstayed his welcome, although New York fans smothered him with an idolatry that wasn't even diminished during his exile to San Francisco. He felt the same way about them, too. In his valedictory announcement he even said the

New Yorkers kept him in action longer, whereas he would have quit earlier if he had remained on the Coast.

"Coming back to New York is coming back to paradise," he said jubilantly when the Mets ransomed him from the Giants almost two years ago.

He never had won the acceptance or the adulation in San Francisco that had been his during his stay at the Polo Grounds. Californians resented him as a New Yorker and, strangely enough, most of his heroics and most spectacular achievements came on the road. One such was his four homers in one game.

So they concentrated their affection and acclaim on Orlando Cepeda, who never had played at the Polo Grounds. To San Franciscans Cepeda was No. 1, even gaining that peculiar status known in baseball circles as "the big man." This designation normally is bestowed on the superstar—Babe Ruth, Joe DiMaggio, Ted Williams, Stan Musial, and the like.

Finally the Giants returned to the Polo Grounds for the first time since they had lammed West. With them was Garry Schumacher, a reformed baseball writer from Brooklyn and then the Giant's public relations director. He had never been happy about the cavalier treatment accorded Willie in the Golden Gate area. As Garry and I were chatting near the batting cage, Willie suddenly appeared on the clubhouse steps. The thunderous roar of the crowd even rattled the windows in the Yankee Stadium on the other side of the river. Garry beamed in delight and nodded in the direction of the startled Cepeda.

"The big man just discovered who the big man really is," he said.

Willie always was the big man and made the big plays, the big hits. I was pleased to have him pick the Billy Cox throw as a particular gem in his glittering collection. I saw it and still consider it the best throw I ever witnessed, mainly because there were extra factors involved.

In the first place, the Wonder was then a 20-year-old kid, a greenhorn. Yet his unerring instincts directed him to shun the orthodox way of making the play because it could have resulted only in failure.

When Carl Furillo sliced a line drive to right-center, Cox tagged up at third. Willie speared the ball with outstretched glove. If he had followed normal procedure, he would have jammed on the brakes, stopped, turned and thrown home far too late to catch a swiftie like the Dodger runner. Instead, the Wonder wheeled counterclockwise in one fluid motion and fired in the strike to Wes Westrum, the catcher. Cox was out by 10 feet.

"It was the most perfectest throw I ever made," said Willie rapturously.

The description still fits. But he made so many exquisite plays over the years and was so complete a ballplayer. One season he was heading for the home run championship when Leo Durocher, the father figure who managed him, said he wanted Willie to go for quantity instead of quality. So Mays won the batting championship instead. A year later he took the home run title.

I met Willie the first day he arrived at the Polo Grounds, a scared kid of 20 and he won me to him instantly. Nothing has changed in 22 years. He has remained my favorite. Reluctantly he announced his retirement. Reluctantly I bid him farewell. So long, Willie.

Twilight of the Gods

November 4

There is no need to use the somber sounds of the Gotterdammerung, but melancholy marks the realization that the twilight of the gods is enveloping far too many of the Titans who once bestrode the sports firmament with heroic grandeur. Reaching out for them is the inexorable sequence of going, going, gone. However, the only one definitely gone is Willie Mays.

Having formally announced his retirement, Willie the Wonder has completed his active role in baseball. None of the others, though, has announced anything. They are in the going stage and just don't want to admit it to themselves or anyone else. Who are the they? Superstars who must be included in such a category are Johnny Unitas, Arnold Palmer and Muhammad Ali, even though each undoubtedly would resent such inclusion. There are others, but these will do for starters.

Football never had a better passer than Unitas and he holds most of the records. A year ago he was cruelly brushed aside by Joe Thomas during a disruptive housecleaning of the Baltimore Colts, even though Johnny U. was to finish as the fourth-ranking passer in his conference. Then came his shift to the San Diego Chargers, where the 40-year-old sharpshooter has been riding the bench while a 22-year-old rookie, Dan Fouts, tries to lift the Chargers from the depths. Unitas may not be gone yet, but you sure gotta believe he's going.

Around the turn of the century the fable was generally accepted that "golf is an old man's game." It had a sedentary, leisurely look to it and seemed ideally designed for retired aristocrats who were too enfeebled to run but had sufficient stamina to walk over green grass while tapping a little white ball ahead of them.

It took a while for the American public to discover what a marvelous game golf can be, and that's when original misconceptions were scornfully dismissed. If one of golf's earliest images was the picture of John D. Rockefeller taking daily links exercises after he was 90 years of age, along came an electrifying personality like Bobby Jones to propel golf to gaudy new heights while he was still in his twenties.

The youth kick had taken over. It has not changed since. With television helping reflect his charisma all over the civilized globe, Palmer was golfdom's dominating force for the longest while. Even when Jack Nicklaus became a more frequent winner, Arnie was still the darling of the galleries. Arnie's Army won all the battles, even if their commander-in-chief didn't.

Arnie now is a 44-year-old millionaire. The fires still burn within him, but not as fiercely as they once did. He can show flashes of his former greatness, but he cannot sustain them as he once did. He rarely wins tournaments any more because determination alone isn't sufficient to compensate for the loss of his putting touch, the curse of all aging golfers. It even comes as something of a shock to discover that he hasn't captured a major championship since 1964. Nor is he likely to win another. The Palmer popularity may never wane, but he is easing into the twilight zone.

Muhammad Ali is more of a puzzle. He's not quite 32 years old, but twilight is coming early for him. In his prime he had blinding speed to shield him from all harm and cover up every chink in his armament. He has swiftness no longer. The government drained away a major part of it while keeping him in cold storage after he had refused to be drafted. More was drained away by Joe Frazier a few years ago during their magnificent multi-million-dollar brawl of unbridled ferocity.

Each may have pulled the cork on the other, because neither has had that old look of invincibility since. Don't forget that both landed in hospitals afterward. Besides that, Ali may even have lost some of his irresistible appeal. A projected bout in Hong Kong during his recent tour of the Pacific was canceled when only 110 tickets were sold and the remainder of the schedule in the Far East was washed out. He still is good enough to get more big paydays, but he never again will be the whirlwind he once was.

It's sad to see old heroes depart just because they are old. It's sadder still to see them outstay their welcome. Willie Mays did, maybe by as much as two years.

"I saw you make your first hit," said his old friend and former teammate, Monte Irvin, "and I've seen you make your last one. Confidentially, Willie, the last one was easier to follow."

It was a splash up the middle for a run-scoring single in the World Series. The first was a titanic blast over the Polo Grounds roof off the great Warren Spahn 22 years earlier.

Babe Ruth missed his exit cue when he slammed three home runs a few days before he quit on a sour note of frustration. But Ted Williams had a keenly attuned sense of the dramatic when he crashed a game-winning homer into the center-field bleachers in his last game at Fenway Park.

"That's the end," said Ted sadly. "There's nothing more I can do."

There wasn't, either. Too few of them, however, recognize the end when it comes. They are always trying to stretch out the twilight.

Not Just for Kicks

November 18

Week after week the evidence keeps mounting that the field goal has assumed such a position of dominance in the National Football League that old values and old scoring concepts have been kicked lopsided. If the change were for the better, there would be no complaints. But the fans grumble at the overuse of the placement 3-pointer. They regard it as an unwelcome surrender to conservative tactics, robbing them of the more spectacular go-for-broke touchdown thrusts.

Over the last weekend 49 field goals were booted. If this isn't a record, that is because the statisticians have not been true to their trust. They have yet to invent a record for most field goals in a weekend. When Jan Stenerud kicked his fourth last Monday to give Kansas City a 12-0 lead over the Chicago Bears, Frank Gifford offered the unenthusiastic air-wave comment: "This is a fine game—if you like field goals."

The accuracy quotient for these kicking specialists has now risen to 64 per cent and something had better be done soon to crimp their style before football's once ideal attacking balance is totally destroyed. Mention was made in this space a week ago that a discussion was in order for the study of remedies. There is one simple one that would not necessarily be a cure-all, but would serve as a solid starting point for sending the patient along the road to recovery. Relocate the goalposts behind the end zones.

Forty years ago, George Preston Marshall of the Redskins, football's supreme showman, offered his fellow owners a ringing Declaration of Independence as he urged them to break free from the shackles that had enslaved them to the intercollegiate rulesmakers. "When in the course of human events," he was saying in effect, "it becomes necessary for one people to dissolve the political bonds which have connected them with another . . ." Oh, well. Here's what he actually said at a historic league meeting:

"Gentlemen, it's about time that we realized that we're not only in the football business. We're also in the entertainment business. If the colleges want to louse up their game with bad rules, let 'em. We don't have to follow suit. The hell with the colleges. We should do what's best for us. I say we should adopt rules that will give the pros a spectacular individuality and national significance."

When the colleges had placed the goal posts behind the end zone a few years earlier, the professionals obediently had followed suit. Marshall had the posts returned to the goal line and sponsored other changes that gave the league attractive distinctions. No longer do the pros need that 10-yard edge, however. They are now so far ahead of the collegians that they can do as they please. They are so good that they can—and should—put the posts in the back of the end zone instead of in front of it.

If nothing else, it would slow down the field-goal production rate. The 40-yard placement becomes a 50-yarder in actual distance and the 45-yarder is a 55-yarder. Since the chances of completion shrink with every added yard, the repositioned goal posts would make everyone pause. Even the short ones now described as "chippies" will cease to be the chip shots they had once appeared to be. This change doesn't cost a cent and is so harmless that no damage would be done if it were tried and found wanting.

The grandstand quarterbacks never run out of ideas, of course. One group would set up a graded point system for field goals based on distance. Placements inside the 20, for instance, might count 2 points; between the 20 and the 40 the value would be 3 points and beyond the 40-yard line it would be four points. I am strongly opposed to this or variations of same. Once anyone begins tinkering with the basic value structure, he is inviting trouble. The scoring tables become a distortion too hideous to contemplate.

Another group of armchair experts has a proposal that has gained considerable support. It has to do with missed field goals. Any failures from inside the 20-yard line would be returned to the other team's possession at the 20 just as is done at present. But fluffed kicks from farther out would not be placed down automatically on the 20 as of now. Instead, the ball would be handed over to the opposition at the point where the play originated. Suppose the snapback came from the 45 for a 52-yard field-goal attempt that skittered harmlessly into the end zone. The enemy would take over on the 45 and not at the 20.

This would make long-range kicks of desperation such bad risks that few coaches would dare order them. Instead, they would order punts. Is that bad? Many sideline observers think that a punt is as deadly and as soporific to the spectator as is a placement. Maybe even more so, because the punt cannot be converted into points unless some clown fumbles away the ball.

I'm willing to accept the idea of penalizing missed fieldgoals from beyond the 20 by returning the ball to its point of origin at the line of scrimmage. Most of all, though, I stanchly advocate moving the goal posts from the front of the end zone to the rear. This merely gives a reverse twist to the Declaration of Independence that George Preston Marshall formulated four decades ago. This one isn't even revolutionary.

This was Arthur Daley's last column.

1974

Making a Pitch for Pitchers

January 3

The voting habits of the baseball writers in the annual election for the Hall of Fame are not especially predictable. Researchers have found it much easier to chart the mating patterns of the goony bird. Some of the brighter minds have even studied the election returns and reached the conclusion that the first appearance of a superstar on the lists means that he commands so much attention as to brush aside lesser mortals.

By way of proving the theory, they point to Warren Spahn last year and to Ted Williams some seven years earlier. They advanced to Cooperstown as solitary choices of the press box tenants. Two other first-year men, Bobby Feller and Jackie Robinson, fuzz up the picture slightly because they were enshrined the same year. But no others made it in that election.

On the other hand, though, both Stan Musial and Sandy Koufax had company when they were advanced to baseball's holy of holies. Named at the same time as Musial was Roy Campanella, while Koufax drew Yogi Berra and Early Wynn as companions. One of the new eligibles on this year's ballot is Mickey Mantle. The assumption is that he will make it on the first bounce despite the unreliability of forecasting baseball writer election returns. Will the Mick knock everyone else out of the box?

There is no reason why he should. There is plenty of room on each ballot. That's why some vote tabulations defy comprehension. Each listing has spaces for 10 names and the order of placing is of no consequence. Any outsider therefore would have to believe that all obvious choices would rate inclusion somewhere among the 10 slots on the ballot.

But it doesn't always happen that way. Spahn's name was omitted last year on 64 of the 380 ballots cast. Here was a man who won more games than any left-handed pitcher and yet an embarrassingly large number of lodge brothers were either too blind or too ignorant to have given him the homage he deserved.

'Twas ever thus, though. If a guy thumbs through the pages of Hall of Fame history, he finds himself in a state of shock in reviewing the election for the charter members in 1936. All five should have made it unanimously. But Ty Cobb was omitted from four ballots, Babe Ruth from 11, Honus Wagner from 11, Christy Mathewson from 21, and Walter Johnson from 37.

The important thing in the current election for the voters to remember is that there are 10 spaces. Sound judgment should be used to fill any or all of those places and I find it imperative to urge the brothers to consider my three favorite candidates. All are pitchers and each was a superb craftsman with solid credentials for making it to Cooperstown.

They are Robin Roberts, Whitey Ford, and Bob Lemon. That probably should be their order of ranking, too. Yet Ford was second in last year's election behind Spahn. Then came Ralph Kiner and Gil Hodges before our other two heroes arrived on the scene, Roberts in fifth place and Lemon in sixth. Robbie in particular deserves a much better fate. He was the winning pitcher in more games—286—than any pitcher not yet enshrined at Cooperstown. However, he never did fulfill his one overwhelming ambition, to become a 300-game winner. Election to Cooperstown would soften the disappointment.

In a way he had only himself to blame and this was surprising for a man with his high intelligence. He had graduated from Michigan State, but let himself become trapped by his own mental block after he reached the big leagues. The big, good-looking right-hander threw with such an easy motion that he caught batters unaware by the explosiveness of his fastball. For six years in a row the fastball made him a 20-game winner—once he went as high as 28 victories—but he stubbornly refused to develop new pitches and began to slip.

"Robbie can't throw his fastball past my Aunt Matilda," caustically said Manager Gene Mauch, who didn't even have an Aunt Matilda. "He's defending an idea."

But Robbie was a great one who rates a spot in the Hall of Fame. So does Bob Lemon, a reformed third baseman-outfielder who threw a natural sinker. He was a 20-game winner seven times and one of the best in his day.

Whitey Ford was a money pitcher, a clutch performer beyond compare. Oddly enough, he had only two 20-game years, because Casey Stengel was quick with the hook. But they were big ones, 25 victories in 1961 and 24 in 1963. It was in 1961, the year Roger Maris slammed 61 home runs, that Whitey erased from the books the one record Babe Ruth cherished above all others, his feat of pitching 29⅔ scoreless innings in the World Series. When he was chided for being unkind to a sports idol, the flippant Whitey looked over at Maris and grinned.

"It's been a bad season for the Babe," he said.

Afterword: Arthur Daley, My Father

by Robert Daley

The day I was born my father covered a fencing match in Brooklyn. He wasn't the illustrious Arthur Daley then. He was twenty-five years old and earning $75 a week. I was his first born, and three weeks later when he was in Boston covering some other event he wrote me a letter, the first of hundreds. It was really a love letter to my mother, of course. I don't think I ever saw it until she showed it to me after he died. In it he promised that he would teach me to play ball when I was big enough. But when I was twelve he started writing "Sports of *The Times*." He had to turn in seven columns a week. He had to write one every day. God! He didn't have time to play much ball during the remaining years when I lived at home. Later, when I became a *Times* foreign correspondent myself, I felt guilty about filing only three stories a week and offered to send more. Only three were wanted, I was told. Three. I had grown up thinking seven was the norm.

I was the only one of his four children who followed in his footsteps. I fought against him and competed against him every day of my life and, especially when I was little, he could have crushed me easily, but he never did. I would never have accepted an ordinary job on the sports staff of *The Times* in New York. I was determined to make a career that would somehow be different and more exotic than his. My father was the first *Times* sportswriter ever sent over to report from Europe—he covered the 1936 Olympic Games from Berlin; in 1959 I became the first ever stationed permanently in Europe. I was rather proud of myself and thought I had outdone my father, but given the world changes in the intervening years I don't suppose I had. It was about even, except that he had had to start from much farther back. He was the son of a rope dealer, whereas I was the son of Arthur Daley.

In my first two years abroad I was what is called a stringer. *The Times* would pay me $50 an article for any articles they used. I was in Europe with a wife and two tiny kids and no savings and there were days when I felt vulnerable and scared. My father wrote every week to tell me how well I was doing, and he clipped and sent every single article I wrote, about 1,000 of them over six years. Every single word of praise he picked up around the office he sent, too, except one. One day Harrison Salisbury, then an assistant managing editor, pointed to a piece I had filed and said to my father: "Arthur, you've outbred yourself." Plenty of kings down through history had had their sons murdered for less, but my father was delighted. He went around repeating that comment to everybody—except me; my mother told me the story only after he died. He never really told me he was proud of me at all. He just gave that incredible support during those years I needed it most.

I went on to write novels he didn't approve of, and he would not have them on his bookshelf. After two of them, for periods of several weeks he wouldn't even talk to me. I had left *The New York Times.* I had given up writing about sports. I belonged to a different world than the one he had brought me up in, and we never talked about any of this. I had once supposed that fathers and sons would be able to talk to each other, and so had he when I was born, but it isn't so. We never even talked professionally except towards the end, when he would sometimes ask my advice. To the very end I always felt presumptuous to tell him a particular column was especially good. After all, he was my father and he was also Arthur Daley. But sometimes I would do it, and he would nod. Later my mother would tell me how pleased he had been: "It must have been a good column if Bob liked it."

I guess he loved me. After he died, I found a whole drawer full of news clippings about me and aspects of my career that he had saved, clippings I had never bothered to save myself.

Somewhere along the line I conceived the notion that I wanted to write "Sports of *The Times*" one day, and one day only. I wanted to write about my father in that space on the day that he would die.

Then the day came when he did die, suddenly, and long before any of his children were ready for it. It was January 3, 1974, and he was to retire on his seventieth birthday the following July 31, and on his desk calendar for the day of his death he had scribbled: "Only 89 more columns."

There weren't 89 more for him. There weren't any more for him at all, but there was one to go for me, or so I thought in my grief. After rushing over to hold my mother tight, I left my sister with her and came back to make the calls that had to be made. One went to A. M. Rosenthal, Managing Editor of *The Times*. I told him I wanted to write "Sports of *The Times*" for tomorrow, and then I began to bawl.

There went any chance of being allowed to write the column. Rosenthal soothed me. Later he gave Jim Tuite, editor of this book, the delicate job of calling back to say that obviously I had enough jobs to do that day, they couldn't ask me to write "Sports of *The Times*," too. Someone else would do it.

I wrote it anyway. I wrote it all that afternoon between friends calling to offer sympathy, and my brother calling from New York about arrangements for Arthur Daley's funeral. I wrote it because somehow that afternoon, for the first time in my life, I felt one with my father. He and I were the same. I wrote it as if, by writing it, I could tell him before it was too late that I was glad to have been his son. It would never appear as "Sports of *The Times*." I wrote it anyway. I wrote it to hold grief off. I wrote it because I had to write it, and two days later

Father John Conolly, who had taught both my brother and me at Fordham Prep so many years ago, read it from the pulpit of Saint Patrick's Cathedral during Arthur Daley's funeral. Here is that eulogy:

What a boyhood it was. My dad was a sportswriter on *The New York Times.* He used to take us to the Polo Grounds, Yankee Stadium, and Ebbets Field. He used to take us in under his arm. We would sit in a corner of the press box, or even sometimes on the bench. He would bring us home used baseballs. My brother and I had a used (brand-new to us) Giants' football every season to kick around the streets of New York until the tips peeled back.

When I was about seven my dad introduced me to Mel Ott. The home run hitter gave me a baseball. My father introduced me to football players like Tuffy Leemans, Ward Cuff, and Mel Hein. My father never got blasé about ballplayers. He thought they were special.

Once my dad and I sat on a trunk in the Yankee locker room with Tommy Henrich. Tommy had his arm around me and asked did I hit lefty or righty. My father was happy. He was beaming.

"Joe," said Henrich, as Joe DiMaggio walked by, "I'd like you to meet my friend Bobby."

Joe's hand shot out and he said gravely: "Glad to meet you, Bobby," and kept walking.

My heart nearly stopped. DiMaggio was so big, so grave, so dignified.

"Boy, daddy," I said later, "that Joe DiMaggio is some nice guy."

My father was so pleased.

My father always said DiMaggio had class. Ted Williams, too. At home in his den in later years there were framed photos of my father with DiMaggio, Williams, Marciano, Arnold Palmer, and many more. My father always thought the important figure in the photo was the athlete, but as I got older I came to see it differently. My father never thought of himself as a big hitter but he was as big as any of them, and bigger than most.

He won a number of prizes. Most surprised him. When he got

the Pulitzer Prize for "Sports of *The Times*" in 1956 he was astonished. He had always imagined that Red Smith might get it, if any sportswriter did, or one of the others. My brother Kevin told him: "They didn't give it to the cleverest guy on the sports page, but to the man who day after day wrote the best column."

He never gloated over his Pulitzer. He always wrote to each of his children every Monday, when they were away, and that week's letter to me read only: "This will be short, but very, very sweet. I have just been awarded the Pulitzer Prize. Love, Dad."

Afterwards he never tried to parlay his prize into book or magazine contracts. He never even asked for a raise. He didn't see where the Pulitzer improved his writing. It was a relief to know that now *The Times* would not fire him. At least not right away.

President Kennedy once asked to meet him, and took him along in a motorcade, talking sports. Later Kennedy sent a photo inscribed "from an avid reader." My father found it incredible that the President of the United States liked to read Arthur Daley.

My father was the only man I ever knew who was better than he thought he was.

He began writing "Sports of *The Times*" more than thirty years ago. He was told to write it until further notice. Further notice came last Thursday when he died, on his way to *The Times* office, the next column moving about in his head, where it stayed.

He was a shy man. I don't think he thought he could do the column at first, though he had been a *Times* sportswriter sixteen years by then. I heard him and Mom talking about it.

"Of course you can do it, Arthur," she told him.

It was a lovely marriage, by the way. They were married in this cathedral when she was eighteen and he was twenty-four, and they really cared about each other for forty-five years.

At first my father wrote seven columns a week, long columns, no photos in those days. Thousands of letters came in. He answered them all himself, every one. He went to thousands of games.

He read all the other papers' sports sections every day. He read all the sports magazines and the *Sporting News*. He collected every new sports book published. There were no days off. He filed away every clipping that interested him, four of five filing cabinets full now, the finest sports morgue in the country or world, no doubt. Everybody who has ever been anybody in sports is in there, from 1941 until last week. When I went through his papers I noted clips already marked and dated on his desk, waiting to be filed, and I could not throw them away just yet, because they were so important to him.

After many years he was told he could have Saturdays off. He would only have to write six columns a week. He took this to mean *The Times* executives were displeased with him. All the other *Times* columnists were writing only three columns a week, a status my father at last reached only recently.

He had no other life outside of sports and *The New York Times*. It was agony to try to buy him a Christmas present. He did not drink. He smoked a pipe for a time, then gave that up. He played no games, though as a boy he had been athletic. As a young man he broke his right thumb playing baseball, and it healed stiff and smooth. No joint showed, and as little kids we used to sit in his lap and marvel at my father's thumb and try to make it bend.

He knew nothing about office politics, and little about money. He was ingenuous in many ways. He disapproved of bad language. If he came to dislike a sports figure, he simply never wrote about him again. My father badmouthed nobody in print.

He wrote over 10,000 "Sports of *The Times*" columns, and if a man's life is measured in the amount of pleasure he gave others, then he ranked very high.

His best friend was Jack Mara, who owned the Giants. When Jack died, my father wrote a column calling Jack the finest man he ever knew. But at Jack's funeral I couldn't take my eyes off my father, who was suffering so much, and whose own funeral I probably would attend next year, or the year after; so that I began to cry, weeping not so much for Jack as for my father, thinking: Jack Mara isn't the finest man I ever knew, you are.

Index